VOLUME 24   NUMBERS 2–3   2018

Queers Read This!
LGBTQ Literature Now

Edited by Ramzi Fawaz and Shanté Paradigm Smalls

QUEERS READ THIS!

LGBTQ Literature Now

Ramzi Fawaz and Shanté Paradigm Smalls

Introduction

*I*s there such a thing as LGBTQ literature anymore? Clearly, the Lambda Literary Foundation thinks so, since it recognizes and awards emergent and established LGBTQ authors annually. Even the prodigious scholarship of queer theorists is now celebrated by the organization at its yearly award ceremony, alongside work in fiction, poetry, autobiography, comics, and graphic novels. Yet, as the lesbian author and cultural critic Sarah Schulman (2012: 146–47) compellingly points out in *The Gentrification of the Mind*, the mainstream literary world rarely spotlights the work of out LGBTQ writers who develop substantive fiction, poetry, and drama about equally out and actively sexual characters. If in 1973 gay and straight Americans alike made a lesbian novel such as Rita Mae Brown's *Rubyfruit Jungle* a national best seller, and if James Baldwin could spend his entire career writing and speaking about the intersections between race, masculinity, and homosexuality throughout the second half of the twentieth century, in 2017 no book by an out LGBTQ writer can claim such widespread appeal outside a few recent notable exceptions like Alison Bechdel's *Fun Home* (2006) or now-canonical works such as Tony Kushner's play *Angels in America* (1991–93) and Alice Walker's novel *The Color Purple* (1982). In 1991, at the apogee of the AIDS epidemic, members of the emergent activist group Queer Nation could garner the attention of potential LGBTQ audiences with a searing polemic titled "QUEERS READ THIS!" This command was meant to hail politically radicalized or "militant" queers as well as the most woefully conformist or disengaged members of the LGBTQ community. The polemic's exclamatory title not only issued a directive at so-called queers to read the content of the manifesto but also evoked an affective hope that the very act of reading might incite a transformative encounter with queer rage against both

GLQ 24:2–3
DOI 10.1215/10642684-4324765
© 2018 by Duke University Press

heterosexism and widespread LGBT complacency in the face of homophobia, the AIDS epidemic, and rampant violence against sexual and gender dissidents. "How can I tell you," the manifesto opens, "How can I convince you, brother, sister that your life is in danger: That everyday you wake up alive, relatively happy, and a functioning human being, you are committing a rebellious act. You as an alive and functioning queer are a revolutionary." By bringing together a kaleidoscope of queer voices in its overlapping, polemical entries, the manifesto sought to "convince" its readers of the necessity of embracing a revolutionary view of queer existence; as its first lines underscore, such a view was not posed as a question or possibility but as a declaration of fact indelibly marked in print.

What does the injunction "Queers Read This!" refer to now, more than two decades later? Would Gloria Anzaldúa's and Cherríe Moraga's foundational women of color anthology, *This Bridge Called My Back* (1981)—a transformational text for many queers and feminists of color, as well as white queers and feminists—have been published and read in today's market? Would a distinctly queer of color or trans-inspired version of "The Queer Nation Manifesto" carry equal force and political currency? What exactly *should* queers read now? How are we reading and writing queer texts? This special issue of *GLQ* seeks to animate a dialogue about the place, function, form, and intellectual and political possibilities of LGBTQ literature now. The "now" we invoke is an incitement or imperative to our contributors to think about how the history of queer literary production must necessarily be rewritten, reconsidered, and returned to in light of the dramatic historical and scholarly transformations that have shaped queer public and private life since the late 1980s.

At that key historical moment, queer literary production was under severe pressure from the violent and life-negating experience of HIV/AIDS. Perhaps counterintuitively, the mass deaths and subsequent cultural erasure of queer men's lives that took place as a result of the epidemic also created the conditions for an intellectual and creative counterassault in the form of AIDS cultural theory, the frantic yet impassioned outpouring of art, fiction, poetry, film, and performance by AIDS activists and artists, and the institutional emergence of queer theory as a field of knowledge focused intently on reading and interpreting the world from the position of sexual and gender dissidents. From one perspective, HIV/AIDS could be seen as the flashpoint that both consolidated and dispersed queer reading and writing into activism and the academy, and inadvertently away from the mainstream of popular reading, writing, and publishing. Since then, queer lifeways, politics, and culture have been dramatically shaken by innumerable historical transformations that overdetermine any attempt to map LGBTQ literature by the traditional coordinates of gay shame, the closet, and narratives of gay liberation, along with HIV/AIDS. LGBTQ literary production and history have been undoubtedly shaped, revised, and reorganized by each of these crucial historical frames, but also by 9/11, the advent of the digital era, mass incarceration, prison privatization, a more intimate relation with state power through the push for hate crimes legislation, the protracted struggle over gay marriage, gays in the military, and the ascendancy of transgender identity and rights in queer politics. We name these historical markers to indicate the new conditions under which queer literary production, and queer reading, takes place today.

Few terms carry as much weight and meaning in queer culture than that of *reading*. Far from a simple reference to textual literacy, for queers, the phrase *to read* (or better yet, *to do a reading*) indexes a range of creative and intellectual capacities, including but not limited to the ability to deconstruct the gendered and sexual performances of one's peers; to formulate an interpretation of, or wring queer meaning from, a cultural phenomenon with no explicit reference to same-sex or alternative sexualities; to negotiate, or "read," a situation of danger for those who do not comport with heterosexual norms; to note, notice, or "clock" queer and trans figures in the first place by "reading" another person through "gaydar"; or to call out, poke fun, challenge, "shade," or performatively "slay" a fellow queer. As has been well documented, when queers read—whether their sights are set on a traditional literary text, a particular performance, or an entire cultural scene—they do so as a form of survival just as much as a way to gain pleasure, develop knowledge and skill, and make a mark on the world. It would not be an understatement to suggest that the question of reading—how, why, when, who, and in what manner queers and all kinds of sexual and gender dissidents read—has been one of the longest-running concerns motivating the production of queer theory. After all, queer theory itself is an extended scholarly project to read what queers write, say, and do, both in the most literal sense of simply taking time to engage and comprehend the writing and cultural production of LGBTQ people and in the conceptual sense of interpreting or making meaning out of that production. Yet queer theory is also one of the most potent and sustained projects in reading or interpreting the world from *the perspective of sexual and gender dissidents*; one of the field's most ambitious projects has been to reveal the distinct perspective of LGBTQ subjectivity as potentially relevant for making sense of all forms of cultural production, even those texts, objects, and performances that do not appear to have any immediate relation to nonnormative sexuality or desire. This tension between the actual attention we pay to the specificity of LGBTQ writing and culture and the production of a more capacious queer theory capable of identifying the sexual and gendered logics of a vast range of institutions, performances, and cultural productions provides one of the originating conditions of queer literary studies.

In 1996 Eve Kosofsky Sedgwick edited a groundbreaking issue of the journal *Studies in the Novel* titled "Queerer Than Fiction" that laid the foundation for a generation of queer literary interpretation. Arguably one of the first of its kind, this issue identified literature as one powerful site where reparative reading practices take shape. She and others in the volume argued that the act of interpretation itself was a practice through which readers do something ameliorative with texts, making them functional for the flourishing of queer life. In her introduction, Sedgwick (1996: 279) movingly wrote, "The desire of a reparative impulse . . . is additive and accretive. Its fear, a realistic one, is that the culture surrounding it is inadequate or inimical to its nurture; it wants to assemble and confer plenitude on an object that will then have resources to offer to an inchoate self." This additive or accretive impulse, Sedgwick suggested, was modeled by the writers in her edited volume through a form of queer reading or interpretive practice that sought to tease out the presence of queer desire, pleasure, possibility, and sociality even in literary objects that seemed to wholly obscure them. While the many contributors to Sedgwick's edited collection conducted exceptionally fine-grained readings of both classic literary texts from Henry James to Toni Morrison and less canonical writing like that of Piri Thomas and William Gibson, all aspired to work through texts from a queer lens in the interest of expanding the scope and explanatory power of queer theory for *all* culture. This was the case even as they practiced a "reparative impulse" oriented toward nurturing LGBTQ writers, readers, and critics. After all, to annex literature and literary studies, a highly disciplinary field formation often dedicated to policing canons and defending the primacy of close reading, was a move of extraordinary ambition that sought to firmly ensconce queer sexuality, desire, pleasure, and lifeways at the center of humanistic inquiry. In her introduction, Sedgwick (ibid.: 278) claimed that a focus on modes of reparative reading could bring greater attention to the specificity of queer reading practices, consequently expanding what we can know and understand about the ways LGBTQ people engage with, take up, and do something with texts; as Marilee Lindemann (2000: 763) has pointed out, however, this focus on the specificity of LGBT reading practices was often downplayed or lost in the more ambitious desire to expand the coordinates of "queer," to make any book, any cultural text or phenomenon, subject to queer analytics. Despite its seeming novelty, "Queerer Than Fiction" can be understood as only one critical node in a much larger network of queer literary touchstones in the late twentieth century.

Directly preceding Sedgwick and other theorists of the 1990s queer theory academic boom were foundational queer and straight black feminist and women of color texts that dealt with the lives, deaths, and intersectional realities of people of color and racialized minorities in the United States and beyond. Writers such as Audre Lorde, Barbara Smith, Cheryl Clarke, Anzaldúa, Moraga, and others influenced an entire generation of queer writers and writing, yet they are not often afforded the nomenclature "theorist" and are certainly not centered as "queer theorists" even as their writing in the 1970s, 1980s, and 1990s radically engaged race, gender, sex, sexuality, and politics. Thirteen years before Kimberlé Crenshaw (1989, 1991) teased out the clarifying language of intersectionality, the Combahee River Collective enunciated the significance and reality of the need for black feminist—and by extension black queer feminist—politics. In its famous 1977 statement, the collective made these connections apparent:

> The most general statement of our politics at the present time would be that we are actively committed to struggling against racial, sexual, heterosexual, and class oppression, and see as our particular task the development of integrated analysis and practice based upon the fact that the major systems of oppression are interlocking. . . . As Black women we see Black feminism as the logical political movement to combat the manifold and simultaneous oppressions that all women of color face. (Combahee River Collective 1977: 1)

Sidestepping a critical theoretical debate on what work "paranoid" or "reparative" readings do, these black feminist writers—novelists, essayists, theorists, polemicists—centralized the realities of their life experiences and their social position as black women as their critical and creative lens. Their ability to "read" the material and historical realities that worked to dominate and kill made it possible for them to see and thoroughly theorize as queer not only the condition of the queer but the conditions and possibilities of the black, woman, queer, feminist working class. The violences they faced were not simply a cause for depression but a facilitation of an explosion of organizing, writing, community-building, and world making. As subjects who are often left behind or overlooked inside canonical queer theory and queer literary history, we take the time to note how these writings function inside white mainstream queer and academic circles as adjacent or additives, but are actually central theoretical modalities.

In his field-defining book *Aberrations in Black: Toward a Queer of Color Critique*, Roderick Ferguson (2003: 4) reminds us of the genealogy and indebtedness that queer of color critique owes to women of color feminism, arguing that "women of color feminism names a crucial component of [queer of color critique's] genealogy as women of color theorists have historically theorized intersections as the basis of social formation. Queer of color analysis extends women of color feminism by investigating how intersecting racial, gender, and sexual practices antagonize and/or conspire with the normative investments of nation-states and capital." Ferguson's interdisciplinary queer of color critique text weaves together the history of American sociology, canonical African American literary texts like *Native Son* (1940), *Invisible Man* (1952), and *Sula* (1973), and queer (of color) theory, to make plain the *longue durée* of simultaneous pathology and erasure placed on black sexual and gender expressions. That is to say, we understand the whiteness of queer theory and queer studies and seek not to reproduce its normativity by turning a blind eye toward it or reifying the bonds between "white" and "theorist." Rather, we point out how queer theory, in part, is informed by, and developed on the backs of, black bodies whose existence and behavior have historically stood for deviancy. Ferguson's work, like Siobhan Somerville's *Queering the Color Line: Race and the Invention of Homosexuality in American Culture* (2000), Anzaldúa and Moraga's *This Bridge Called My Back*, and José Esteban Muñoz's *Disidentifications: Queers of Color and the Performance of Politics* (1999), builds on authors like Smith, Alexis De Veaux, and Cheryl Clarke, as well as Cathy Cohen's foundational queer black intersectional essay, "Punks, Bulldaggers, and Welfare Queens: The Radical Potential of Queer Politics?" (1997). These texts aid us in connecting the relationship between cultural history, queer theory, gender, LGBTQ literature, and the racial politics of the United States. These present texts (and many absent ones) are here to remind us of the heterogeneity of queer and trans literary writings, readings, and genealogies. As Matt Richardson (2013: 6–7) reminds us when discussing the invisibility of black lesbian and black trans documentation in academe, black lesbian "renarration of the past explores . . . the realities of queer experience that are central to Black cultural life. . . . These tensions are worked out through queer vernacular epistemologies, or forms of expression, that comment on and resist the oppression of queer sexualities and genders, as well as create queer kinship networks, communities, and alternatives to diasporic displacement." Richardson's keen and much-needed work centering black lesbian and trans literature reminds us of the vital work that black sexualities and genders and their literatures do to illuminate and elucidate the truism that "epistemology is a politically relevant practice" and that "Black queer literature represents . . . a shift in knowledge" (ibid.: 15). The ways we read, who we read, and how *we* are read are a part of our wider queer collective practices, but even so, we recognize how the queer practices of any place are steeped in the hegemony of that very same locale.

Since the introduction of Sedgwick's model of paranoid and reparative interpretation in the mid-1990s, one initially grounded in the seeming local, intimate act of reading, the methodological ambitions of queer studies have expanded to include the vast institutional structures of neoliberal capital, the war on terror, the carceral system, American racial formation, global diaspora, and more. Even as literary and cultural texts remain central to much of queer theory, providing invaluable case studies that anchor the claims of a given author, the actual close analysis of those objects has often (though not always) become an alibi for forwarding a much wider claim about the operating logics of large-scale social and political phenomenon. It would appear, then, that analyzing the specificities of a work of literature, what it demands from a reader, who is reading it and why, and how it produces particular affects often appears simply too local, specific, or lacking in scale to seem adequate to the aims of a queer critique that wants to address the contemporary geopolitical world order.[1]

The contributors to this volume think otherwise, and they carefully consider how a return to actual LGBTQ literary and cultural texts (and to a focus on the specificities of distinct experiences among all who live within or claim those categories) allows us to capture the lived heterogeneity of queer existence at a time of extraordinary danger *and* expanded possibility for gender and sexual outlaws of all stripes. This special issue asked potential contributors to reconsider the place of reading, and literary production more broadly, in queer studies now. If the urgency of the AIDS epidemic in the 1980s and 1990s, for instance, demanded the rapid-fire production of new forms of writing, both creative and theoretical, to account for the extraordinary cultural impact of the disease, as well as the invention of innovative ways to read and interpret that same impact, we asked writers to consider how the many historical transformations of the immediate period surrounding the millennium have similarly required novel approaches to comprehending LGBTQ literary and cultural production. Some of the impetus for pursuing what might seem like an outdated, traditional, or "old school" return to literary production emerged out of our professional trajectories: both of us are interdisciplinary scholars (one holding a PhD in performance studies and the other American studies) who work on nontraditional cultural objects (hip-hop cultural production, media studies, and black critical theory, on the one hand, and comics, queer visual culture, and fantasy literature, on the other). Yet both of us work in English departments where classical literature and literary production remains highly valued alongside an expanding range of cultural products, as well as theories and practices of rhetoric and composition. In these environments, we often work closely with queer-identified students, students of color, and gender-nonconforming students. In our classroom practices, we have found that the mere introduction of LGBTQ literary texts to our students—from Lorde's *Zami: A New Spelling of My Name* (1982) to Leslie Feinberg's *Stone Butch Blues* (1993), from Armistead Maupin's *Tales of the City* (1978) to Janet Mock's *Redefining Realness: My Path to Womanhood, Identity, Love, and So Much More* (2014)—has an extraordinary impact on their sense of the possibilities for queer flourishing. Even as our students have access to countless queer cultural products through digital media, film, television, and music, the traditional literary text still holds a powerful place in their imagination as the location where queers are still simply *not represented*. Or when presented, queers and trans figures are rendered as incomplete, depleted, or destined for death and misery. When they see LGBTQ people writing and written about, living lives worth reading, in classroom spaces designated for the study of "Literature," they are seemingly constantly awestruck and inspired. Further, students express a desire to understand genealogies and trajectories of queer and trans belonging that are not simply "new" but also historically significant. For instance, historical figures they may know such as Carson McCullers, Lorraine Hansberry, Baldwin, and others have been straight-washed in their precollege educations. We have found that teaching such authors in the specific context of LGBTQ history and culture, not merely queer reading practices but actual texts by self-avowed or explicitly LGBTQ people, has a visceral impact on students that seems to override wide-reaching feelings of cynicism, political despair, and catastrophe, even if only for the duration of a class session.

Invariably when we do teach these texts, our students ask us, "What other LGBTQ books should we read?" Despite our own deep commitments to an expansive understanding of queerness as exceeding the limits of a specific sexual identity, then, our everyday pedagogical experiences have underscored the value of specificity, of the representational visibility of particular kinds of LGBTQ lives, and of knowing where to look for such stories. In a sense, we have seen in our students another expression of the plea that Smith (1978: 27) once dazzlingly articulated at the conclusion of her groundbreaking essay "Toward a Black Feminist Criticism": "I finally want to express how much easier both my waking and my sleeping hours would be if there were one book in existence that would tell me something specific about my life. One book based in Black feminist and Black lesbian experience, fiction or nonfiction, just one work to reflect the reality that I and the Black women whom I love are trying to create. When such a book exists then each of us will not only know better how to live, but how to dream." Far from diminishing or undermining queerness, introducing our students to books that index the *specificity* of varied experiences of LGBTQ life appears to give texture to, foment debate about, and encourage generous exchanges about what constitutes community, collectivity, and alliance among LGBTQ people variously construed. Of course, in our own everyday lives, circulating something "radically" queer to read between our friends, colleagues, and family, through social media posts, blogs, and links, and in photocopies, e-mail attachments, and yes, often actual printed books, is our daily life-blood. In our current political moment, the coeditors of this special issue intuitively sense how necessary reading and circulating queer texts is to the sustenance of LGBTQ life, hope, and resistance. We read for many reasons: to cope, to figure out what to do next, to distract ourselves, to become informed, to develop our own voice, to gain a deeper understanding of the world in which we live or in which we aspire to live. We do it so frequently it becomes easily forgotten that despite all the ways we have traveled far afield from the so-called literary object as the common coordinate of textual analysis, we queers still read, frantically, vitally, critically, lovingly. We solicited these essays in hopes of learning more about how to teach this generation of students, how better to scale the distance between the specificity of LGBTQ living and reading and aspirations for a culturally queer world, and perhaps simply find out what else *we* should be reading, but have not quite yet. In doing so, our aim has been to offer signposts, trajectories, and mappings of unexpected or lesser-recognized LGBTQ literary histories and contemporary queer theory as they overlap and inform one another.[2]

The essays in this volume range widely in terms of periodization, objects of analysis, method, and theoretical influences; they move between the eighteenth and twenty-first centuries, across poetry, novels, short stories, comics, autobiography, and film, and through contemporary interventions in affect theory, disability studies, queer of color critique, feminist theory, and queer Marxism. Taken together, the essays do not constitute a coherent or singular queer literary history, though they all address themselves to both the particular exigencies of LGBTQ writing and publishing, and deeply contextualize their chosen texts in LGBTQ culture and history; they also do not claim to offer a comprehensive mapping of the vast range of identities, embodiments, orientations, affects, and desires that constitute an ever-expanding queer and trans culture (whether in North America or globally). In fact, we concede that there are both representational and conceptual gaps that follow an academic call for papers. We selected the very best of the submissions and realize that no one volume can sufficiently do the work of reading queer literature. We invite responses, more volumes, criticism, and of course, more writing and reading both on what we present here in this volume and on explorations of the digital in circulating queer writing, LGBTQ fan communities and ethnographies of queer reading practices, trans literary production, popular gay writing and self-help literature, and queer publishing and writing from the global South, among many other key areas of inquiry. Collectively, however, the essays organized here accomplish four important conceptual projects that we believe might offer critical starting points for a queer literary study that can respond to the urgencies of our present moment.

First, each essay concerns itself with the question of *repair*, or how queer literary texts do the work of caring for and attending to the wounds inflicted on queer subjects by homo-antagonism, trans-antagonism, racism, ableism, and patriarchy. These essays conceive of repair not as one pole of a binary between "paranoid" and "reparative" interpretative practices but as an orientation the literary text itself takes that seeks to recognize the lived pain and struggle of its potential readers. This approach also offers tools for sitting with, exploring, reorganizing, or making use of that pain in idiosyncratic yet generative ways. For our authors, repair is a multifaceted project, taken up in a vast range of ways by distinct literary and cultural objects, and producing unpredictable affective, social, and political consequences. The essays are highly self-aware of their own production and circulation during a period of intensified fear, anxiety, and suffering for queer people under the crushing weight of global right-wing and white supremacist movements; consequently, each of our authors conceives of the return to the literary text, and its capacity for repair, not as a solipsistic or insular movement back toward an object of individual pleasure or aesthetic purity but as a way to generate another kind of social relation that queers have with the world through their engagement with material texts and objects. Second, these essays are centrally concerned with identifying, unpacking, and doing justice to a far wider range of queer reading affects, contexts, modalities, and approaches than have previously been described by existing models of queer literary studies. Our writers seek to make good on Sedgwick's (1996: 278) demand that queer theorists account for "ways of reading . . . that are actually being practiced," but not within her original terms or according to models of literary analysis now entrenched in queer studies. These writers invent new concepts, use heterogeneous sources and forms of historical or textual evidence, and ask different questions than the frameworks of paranoid or reparative reading, identity politics, antinormativity, or anti-antinormativity allow for. While we, along with our contributors, are deeply informed by all these theoretical modalities, we seek to wrestle with queer textuality in ways that do not simply affirm long-standing allegiances. This is perhaps why so many of our contributors carefully engage with recent interventions in affect studies, disability studies, and queer Marxism: fields that have demanded an expansion of the kinds of evidence we use to make analytic claims about the production and reception of culture, which includes visceral or gut-level responses to the world, gesture and cognitive and physical capacity, and the variety of ways that desire becomes reified in neoliberal capital. Third, all our authors centralize the importance of literary *form* to the specificities of nonnormative or queer sexualities and genders. Rather than simply "queerly reading" literary texts, our authors view the actual formal composition of a given text as an indicator of varied material histories of sexuality; in other words, for our authors, *form*—whether understood as the syntactical structure of a specific sentence, techniques and devices used to give shape to narratives, or the actual visual organization of words on a page—can be understood as a kind of evidence of how queerness is being lived and inhabited by different kinds of LGBTQ people at distinct historical moments. Finally, these essays collectively embrace the personal, political, and cultural power that ordinary or quotidian reading practices and objects can have even when they do not aspire to, or appear to, offer an imminent critique of institutional power structures. Without ever ignoring or turning away from the realities of such structures, our authors aim to take seriously the fact that many queer people negotiate or respond to the complexities of our contemporary world through micro-level engagements with literary texts whose effects can be monumental for any single given life. In so doing, they attend to queer literature and culture as everyday equipment for living.

In "Bad Reading: The Affective Relations of Queer Experimental Literature after AIDS," Tyler Bradway identifies queer experimental literature as a key site where writers innovate unexpected narrative or literary techniques that might respond to the immediate affective needs of LGBTQ readers at distinct historical moments. Bradway compellingly argues that more traditionally academic modes of queer literary interpretation, including Sedgwick's now tacitly embraced framework of paranoid and reparative reading, often unintentionally obscure the vast range of sensory responses that LGBTQ readers have to literary texts by trying to codify reading experiences within a limited range of concepts or terms. Turning to Samuel Delany's AIDS writing, particularly his experimental "pornotopic" novel *The Mad Man* (1994), Bradway explores how Delany attempted to counter the homophobic logics of the epidemic by developing narrative techniques that actively shift what readers could think and feel about queer eroticism (especially in its gay male expressions). For instance, by producing a novel in which every written sentence—not merely the content but also the syntactical and narrative structure of the words on each page—invokes the intimacy, intensity, and viscerality of gay male sexual cultures, Delany captured the genuine fear and anxiety that attended the loss of that culture in the face of HIV/AIDS while also drawing his readers into the pleasures of queer eroticism at a moment when such pleasures were exceptionally stigmatized. Neither the fear and anxiety Delany acknowledges nor the broad range of pleasures he activates can be easily accounted for within a binary model of paranoid and reparative interpretation. In one sense, then, Bradway seeks to dethrone the queer theorist or literary critic as the central arbiter of interpretation, who applies academic concepts to literary texts in order to confer meaning on them; rather, he demands that the queer theorist pay attention to the "wider social fields from which [queer hermeneutic practices] emerge," including the variety of ways that a given writer uses experimental forms to activate new sensations and affects within a reader while honoring those that are present as a lived response to the material conditions of LGBTQ life.

In "Witches, Terrorists, and the Biopolitics of Camp," Cynthia Barounis develops a new and timely approach to one of the most potent, long-standing, and contentious modes of queer reading in existence: camp. Barounis begins by citing the recent election of Donald Trump (and the catastrophic consequences of his ascendancy to power for LGBTQ people and their allies) as an event that requires us to reevaluate what camp can do for queers now as a mode of interpretation that bites back against the dominant social order through fabulous performances of queer exuberance. What are the uses of camp, Barounis queries, at a moment when all our attempts to laugh off or performatively poke fun at the horrors of this political moment fail? What happens, in other words, when our queer exuberance cannot cut through our genuine despair, despondency, and devastation in the face of genuine homophobia, transphobia, patriarchy, and racism? Barounis argues for a return to camp that downshifts its use as a form of masquerade or performance, and recenters its function as a coping mechanism in the face of intense rejection and denigration that values and embraces all that is thrown away and diminished by normative culture. To do so, Barounis argues for an approach to camp that acknowledges the biopolitical and crip possibilities inherent within this long-standing queer sensibility, namely, its tendency to attribute life and vitality to objects commonly deemed worthless or disposable, or else associated with lack of capacity or immaturity. Barounis performs this very logic through her choice of texts, focusing on cultural objects like *Hothead Paisan* (1999), Diane DiMassa's apocalyptic radical lesbian feminist comic strip, and *The Witch* (2016), the director Robert Eggers's contemporary Puritan horror thriller, both of which explore the affective experiences of putatively "crazed" or "psychotic" queer women. Barounis argues that these texts honestly register the pain, confusion, anxiety, and depression that attends the experience of late twentieth-century queer femininity, but do so in such hyperbolic ways that they invoke the "psychotic lesbian" or "witch" as an object to be embraced, taken seriously, and engaged. According to Barounis, texts like these train us to read, and value, our own painful affective and psychic responses to a horrifying world, thereby providing a reparative reading of our most paranoid, and perhaps accurate, visceral responses to our conditions of existence.

Samuel Solomon's "Offsetting Queer Literary Labor" unpacks the dense relationship between three key elements of late twentieth-century queer literary history: the shifting conditions of US print technology in the 1960s and 1970s, the emergence of an increasingly feminized and racialized typesetting workforce, and the rise of small presses dedicated to publishing work by LGBTQ writers and writers of color. Solomon explores these interlocking histories through a potent contextualized reading of the poetry of Karen Brodine. Brodine was a white lesbian feminist typesetter, writer, and labor activist who, beginning in the 1960s, produced a rich body of poetic work that explicitly addressed the labor conditions of contemporary typesetting factories; the erotic, social, and political intimacies developed between women in these spaces; and the conflicts over fair labor practices and racism in the printing and publishing industries. Rather than provide a traditional "queer reading" of Brodine's work—that is, to unpack how her poetry indexes same-sex desire or thwarts heterosexual norms—Solomon approaches her poetry as a textual index of the material conditions under which contemporary LGBTQ literature was forged. Solomon places Brodine's poetry within a vast network of archival materials, including her nonfiction prose, her rich biography as a queer and communist labor activist and typesetter, legal documentation of her many political activities, and oral histories of feminist, queer, and antiracist publishing houses. Solomon's approach reveals that literary texts like Brodine's poetry do not simply register resistance to oppressive structures of power, whether industrial capitalism, heteropatriarchy, or racism; they can also provide a map of how LGBTQ intimacy and desire have been forged and negotiated in and through the material conditions of late capital. As Solomon deftly shows, Brodine's understanding of her identity as a white, working-class lesbian within an increasingly racialized workforce, as well as her erotic and political commitments to other women, took place within the compromised conditions of contemporary typesetting factories—these were spaces of both constraint and possibility for countless women across sexual and racial lines, and Solomon shows how both aspects are registered in Brodine's meticulous organization of poetic lines on the printed page.

In "Beside Women: Charles Dickens, Algernon Charles Swinburne, and Reparative Lesbian Literary History," Natalie Prizel thinks through one hundred years of lesbian erotics and writing practices traced from the Victorian writers Dickens and Swinburne to Patricia Highsmith and Elizabeth Bishop, to argue for the usefulness of queer—lesbian, specifically—repair. Following Sedgwick's reparative reading and Muñoz's utopian futurity, Prizel puts Victorian authors to work "to think about how the period queered itself, offering what I am calling a reparative lesbian literary tradition." Prizel's return to lesbianism hinges on the "woman-centeredness" of the term, as she eschews the lack of specificity that *queer* often engenders, and the way *queer* cannot always read lesbian textual norms, even if the term works to instantiate forms of coalitional politics. The author implicitly notes the danger of insisting on a queerness without homosexuality, as this too can erase forms of love between women that may be considered too identity based for some queer readings. In this essay, Prizel takes on textual and social structures often associated with loss and sexlessness such as "lesbian bed death," "the urge to merge," and "possession." Prizel suggests that these structures, which appear across Swinburne's Sapphic erotics in *Poems and Ballads, First Series* (1866) and Dickens's work on women's romantic friendships in *Bleak House* (1853), as well as in Bishop's writing and Highsmith's *Price of Salt* (1952), afford readers the opportunity to reevaluate the risks and rewards of lesbian enmeshment, as that formation offers insight into the ethics of lesbian reparative reading practices. This transhistorical reading of lesbian repair does not seek a linear emergence of lesbian literary history but works to note the nodal points of literary "lesbian" desire grounded in the Victorian era and surging forward into the future.

Jenny James is also concerned with historical lesbianism in her essay, "Maternal Failures, Queer Futures: Reading *The Price of Salt* (1952) and *Carol* (2015) against Their Grain," in which she looks to Highsmith's midcentury novel and Todd Haynes's recent cinematic adaptation. In reading these texts alongside and through each other, James "argue[s] against a critical approach to queer parenthood that understands it as metonymic of class assimilation and neoliberal ascendancy for a twenty-first-century white queer elite, asking the question, how might stories of queer maternity work to resist, rather than reconfirm, the forces of white privilege that currently define queer family and community within homonormative, exclusionary frames?" James's essay pressures notions of white queer families by first regarding the seeming incommensurability of lesbian motherhood and lesbian desire in pre-Stonewall representations. James focuses on how the mother-daughter relationship is eroticized and allegorized in *The Price of Salt* and *Carol*. While Highsmith's rendition satirizes (and dismisses) the mother-daughter erotics, James argues Haynes's adaptation invites audiences to wrestle with the complexities of Carol as a mother to her own daughter, the tension of the eroticized relation to her younger lover, and the emotional palimpsest between mother, daughter, and lover in 1950s suburban New Jersey. Fundamentally, this essay argues for an against-the-grain reading that sees LGBTQ families as potential sites of radicalism, queer kinship formation, and powerful family bonds, rather than only an acquiescence to neoliberal, conservative, and regressive sociopolitical ideas of familial relationality.

Martin Joseph Ponce picks up on the critical considerations of race, gender, queer literary history, and memory in "Queers Read What Now?" In a seemingly direct response to our call for papers, Ponce's "essay reflects critically on commonsense reading practices in order to clear intellectual and institutional space for a comparative queer of color studies that renders racial and colonial domination and subordination constitutive of queer literary and social history." With Lorde's *Zami: A New Spelling of My Name* (1982), Craig Womack's (Muscogee-Creek and Cherokee) novel *Drowning in Fire* (2001), and Mock's memoir *Redefining Realness*, he works through both the institutional and other types of erasure queer and trans authors face, as well as the possibilities and limits of comparative queer and trans of color literary histories. Ponce points to reading practices as important for the formation of gay and lesbian identities, yet notes how the lesbian and gay (bisexual and transgender) reading canon cannot account for racial and literary genealogical differences. Simultaneously, Ponce worries that the intense self-identification of queer racial texts may preclude fertile work on comparative racialization. Using *Zami*, queer of color critique, and contemporary theories of comparative racialization, Ponce argues that Lorde's black feminist ethics of vulnerability and self-transformation can serve as a theoretical template for building a robust comparative queer and trans of color literary history.

Finally, in "The Black Ecstatic" Aliyyah Abdur-Rahman develops a new aesthetic and affective concept for describing exuberant, life-affirming, and vital responses to the catastrophic conditions of queer black life in the post–civil rights era, what she calls "the black ecstatic." Abdur-Rahman begins by questioning the tendency of African American literary theory and political thought to seek solace in "the heroism of black pasts *and* the promise of liberated black futures" as a response to the failure of the full realization of civil rights–era goals. She asks instead how black cultural producers of the post–civil rights period have alternatively developed a mode of expression that revels in the epic failures of the American democratic promise for black people, consequently dramatizing and magnifying the immediate embodied pleasures black Americans can wrest from the present. For Abdur-Rahman, "the black ecstatic is an aesthetic performance of embrace, the sanctuary of the unuttered and unutterable, and a mode of pleasurable reckoning with everyday ruin in contemporary black lives under the strain of perpetual chaos and continued diminishment." Abdur-Rahman suggests that the black ecstatic functions as an abstract aesthetic, one that is interested less in so-called realistic, or historically accurate, accounts of contemporary black life (ones that are necessary but often merely remind us of the social and political plight of black populations) than in conceptually, visually, and affectively focusing on moments of deep pleasure, reverie, and joy experienced through black communal practices. In a magisterial reading of the recent black queer cinematic triumph *Moonlight* (2016), Abdur-Rahman shows how the film maps the life trajectory of a young black boy named Chiron against the violent histories of black incarceration, drug addiction, and poverty without either reducing his life to those histories or promising a narrative of uplift and social reform. Rather, the film visually revels in moments when Chiron experiences intense embodied pleasures, including his first swim, his first erotic experience with another man, and his intimately charged reunion with his boyhood friend. Abdur-Rahman places *Moonlight* within a longer genealogy of texts that model the black ecstatic by unpacking the long-form poem "Heavy Breathing" by Essex Hemphill, a text that responds to the particular catastrophe of AIDS for black gay men in the late 1980s by textually invoking the erotic and carnal pleasures shared between them as a form of communion that transcends even material death. In the concept of the black ecstatic, Abdur-Rahman joins many of the writers in this collection by helping expand the range of affects, reading and interpretative practices, and approaches to LGBTQ literature that can be conceived, studied, and taken up now.

A final note: our cover features a vivid image of the gender nonbinary sorcerer Gaylord Phoenix, the lead character of Edie Fake's eponymously titled, award-winning 2009 graphic novel. *Gaylord Phoenix* visually narrates the psychic, erotic, and embodied adventures of its title character, a creature with extraordinary powers of transformation. Early in the narrative, Gaylord is attacked and wounded by a mystical creature named "Crystal Claw," who seems to infect Gaylord with overwhelming desires, lusts, and attachments (the hallmarks of sexuality itself). The story chronicles Gaylord's epic journey of self-discovery as they grapple with their burgeoning desires; develop, betray, and repair a range of erotic relationships; and mutate into a variety of bodily forms. In the scene we selected to adorn the cover of this issue, Gaylord uses a knife provided by a lover to reopen a wound associated with their earliest trauma, the scar left over from Crystal Claw's attack. Rather than irrevocably damaging themselves or merely reliving past suffering, Gaylord's willful cut releases unexpected, magical energies into the world that appear as a cloud of imaginative figures, shapes, and forms hovering above them like a thought bubble. In the following pages, this cloud becomes an extraordinary tidal wave, an ocean of personified shapes bearing eyes and mouths that envelop Gaylord and transport them to a wholly new realm. Echoing the iconic image of a child reading under a tree (perhaps most vividly associated with *The Giving Tree* [1964], Shel Silverstein's melancholic children's tale), this drawing evokes how queer pain, trauma, and violation can also be the source of our greatest imaginings. Even as the stump Gaylord sits on tells of a once-thriving tree cut in its prime, and even as their own body registers the pain of prior woundedness (as well as the difficulty associated with seemingly endless bodily transformation), such "cuts" open out into seemingly endless possibility in a text that attempts to represent the many forms of transgender, or gender-nonbinary, existence. In many ways, this image captures the imaginative work of queer reading and writing itself as a project of giving shape or form to lives that exceed the limits and constraints of heterosexual norms; moreover, it appears in a work of queer and trans* graphic storytelling, one of the recent sites where queer forms of embodiment and existence are being most richly rendered in contemporary LGBTQ literature. Like Gaylord Phoenix, the essays in our collection (and the texts they explore) reopen some of LGBTQ culture's most painful wounds to illuminate how those struggles provide us with ways to expand what we can feel, imagine, and hope for as we aspire to a world that supports queer flourishing.

Notes

1. We make this claim more as an overarching observation of general trends in queer theory rather than a critical judgment or categorical statement about the field's current foci. Works that centralize large-scale or geopolitical concerns as the object of queer theoretical analysis might include Jack Halberstam's *In a Queer Time and Place: Transgender Bodies, Subcultural Lives* (2005), Jasbir Puar's *Terrorist Assemblages: Homonationalism in Queer Times* (2007), and David Eng's *The Feeling of Kinship: Queer Liberalism and the Racialization of Intimacy* (2010). While these authors are all exceptional close readers of literary and media texts, their monographs focus on the capacity of queer theory to illuminate something about the operating logics of globe-spanning phenomena like neoliberal capital, counterterrorism, the liberal state, and even the very meaning of concepts like time and space. These texts and others like them might be understood to begin with the primacy of larger institutional or geopolitical structures, turning to literary and media texts to underscore the cultural, political, and social work of such structures as they manifest in material production. Alternatively, books like Robert McRuer's *The Queer Renaissance: Contemporary American Literature and the Reinvention of Gay and Lesbian Identities* (1997),

Heather Love's *Feeling Backward: Loss and the Politics of Queer History* (2009), and Darieck Scott's *Extravagant Abjection: Blackness, Power, and Sexuality in the African American Literary Imagination* (2010) tend to focus on the literary itself as the primary site where questions of larger significance are worked out imaginatively through aesthetic innovation and textual production. These books begin with the formal intricacies of particular works of literature, turning toward larger questions of subjectivity, affect, abjection, racialization, and queer history to underscore how specific texts open us up to such queries. Undoubtedly both sets of texts, or potential lineages, named here address themselves to large-scale issues of institutional and even existential significance (from the global "war on terror" to the status of the human) *as well as* offering fine-grained readings of literary and media texts; however, we suggest that the difference between them might be framed as one of emphasis on either side of the equation. The essays in this volume tend to fall more toward the latter mode, focusing on the specificity of texts and the imaginative work they accomplish in articulating the affective experience of queer existence in its many forms.

2. We are thrilled at the final essays we chose. The daring, care, and intellectual depth was stunning and pleasurable to behold. Simultaneously, during our various discussions over the eighteen months or so it took us to produce this volume, we realized some of the critical and genealogical differences between the two editors. Rather than attempt to sugarcoat or obfuscate the fact, we engaged in the practice of scholarly disagreement. We hope some of that dialogue and its tensions are reflected here in this introductory essay. What was most compelling about our vigorous discussions and disagreements was the fact that we have very differing perceptions and experiences of queer studies, queer literary history, and queer theory. Specifically, we noted some of the ways queer theory or queer studies does not quite capture queer work being done specifically in relation to race, especially work that has emerged in the last twenty years. Cohen pointed us to the conundrum of queer theory's racial blind spots in "Punks, Bulldaggers, and Welfare Queens." Significantly, in the last few years, conferences, special issues, and symposia have been organized around not just Cohen and her work but other black feminist theorists such as Hortense Spillers, Sadiya Hartman, and Sylvia Wynter. Though these three are not "queer" theorists in any strict disciplinary sense, their work on the black body, trauma, theories of the human and of the flesh, and the concomitant relationship of white supremacy and theories of gender and sexuality have made them foundational for many black and other queer theorists. For some recent work that engages black critical thought in order to think about queer theory, blackly, see Omise'eke Natasha Tinsley's "Black Atlantic, Queer Atlantic: Queer Imaginings of the Middle Passage" (2008); Kalia Adia Story's "(Re)Presenting Shug Avery and Afrekete: The Search for Black, Queer, and Feminist Pleasure Praxis" (2015); Savannah Shange's "A King Named Nicki: Strategic Queerness and the Black Femcee" (2014); and Zakiyyah Iman Jackson's "Sense of Things" (2016).

References

Combahee River Collective. 1977. "The Combahee River Collective Statement." Reprinted in Verso Books Blog, https://www.versobooks.com/blogs/2866-the -combahee-river-collective-statement, October 5, 2016.

Ferguson, Roderick. 2003. *Aberrations in Black: Toward a Queer of Color Critique*. Minneapolis: University of Minnesota Press.

Lindemann, Marilee. 2000. "Who's Afraid of the Big Bad Witch? Queer Studies in American Literature." *American Literary History* 12, no. 4: 757–70.

Richardson, Matt. 2014. *The Queer Limit of Black Memory: Black Lesbian Literature and Irresolution*. Columbus: Ohio State University Press.

Schulman, Sarah. 2012. *The Gentrification of the Mind: Witness to a Lost Imagination*. Berkeley: University of California Press.

Sedgwick, Eve Kosofsky. 1996. "Introduction: Queerer than Fiction." *Studies in the Novel* 28, no. 3: 277–80.

Smith, Barbara. 1978. "Toward a Black Feminist Criticism." *Radical Teacher* 1, no. 7: 20–27.

BAD READING

The Affective Relations of Queer Experimental
Literature after AIDS

Tyler Bradway

$\mathcal{A}$t the 1994 OutWrite convention a moderator asked a panel of young LGBTQ authors, "What do you think of experimental writing for gay writers?" (Delany 2005: 226). Norman Wong, a fiction writer, responded with disdain. "No experimentation!" Wong declared. "Experimental writing is just bad writing. . . . It mutes and muddies your ideas, makes for dull reading, and loses you your audience. So don't do it" (ibid.). Another panelist criticized experimental writing as being "subjective gushing in the present tense . . . [or] a cascade of unrelated sentences and sentence fragments." The panelist concluded, "It seems to me that's the last thing that gay writers—or any writer with something to say—would want to get involved in" (ibid.). These statements capture the popular aesthetic critiques of experimental writing: it is boring, insular, and incoherent; it is bad writing that only elicits bad reading. Moreover, experimental writing has little to say on its own terms through its manipulations of form; its resistance to the conventions of mainstream fiction obstructs the messages of socially engaged gay writers, those with "something to say." The audience responded to the panel's assessment with enthusiastic applause, with a notable exception. Samuel Delany, also in attendance, was distressed. Delany noted that many of the attendees share "just the sense of crisis that, a decade and a half ago I had (when I decided to write [an experimental] novel about AIDS)" (ibid.).[1] However, "[they] no longer see experimental writing as a way to deal with it aesthetically" (ibid.). In his view, the panel and audience reveal more than a preference for narrative realism. Their reaction bespeaks an emergent "publishing mentality" among queer authors that prioritizes mainstream marketability over intellectual or formal concerns (ibid.). As such, they no longer look to experimental writing, a marginal paraliterary genre, to explore queer

GLQ 24:2–3
DOI 10.1215/10642684-4324777
© 2018 by Duke University Press

social concerns. Indeed, Wong does not address the crux of the question—namely, what are the possibilities of experimental writing for gay writers and their readers? Putting aside the vexed question of what defines a "gay writer," Wong's judgment obscures contexts in which experimental literature has been—and continues to be—a site for the development of a queer politics of reading, particularly in the ongoing aftermath of the AIDS crisis.[2]

The marginalization of queer experimental literature does not simply evince a desire for mainstream success but, more distressingly, the homonormative pressure on LGBTQ writers to assimilate to the established reading protocols of the public sphere. Indeed, the fear of experimental writing's "a-marketability" (Delany 2005: 225) must be contextualized alongside the aesthetic politics of homonormativity that shapes the conception of LGBTQ literature after AIDS. Sarah Schulman (2012: 14) analogizes homonormativity to gentrification because it produces a sanitized and homogeneous culture that displaces more radical traditions of queerness and destroys an active historical relationship to AIDS. Schulman locates the gentrification of LGBTQ literature in the marginalization of texts that invest too heavily in queer eroticism as well as in experimental works that break with conventional modes of representation (ibid.: 16). Indeed, these elisions go hand in hand. Note, for example, that queer experimental writers such as William S. Burroughs, Kathy Acker, Jeanette Winterson, and Chuck Palahniuk are more often codified as "postmodern" rather than "LGBTQ," despite their queer identifications and representations of dissident sexualities. Yet, as the OutWrite panel suggests, gentrification not only operates by exclusion but also requires the production of new hermeneutic criteria, which constrict the aesthetic politics of LGBTQ literature to what José Esteban Muñoz (2009: 19–32) calls "gay pragmatism." Recall that Wong labels experimentalism "bad writing" because it may lose a mass audience's gaze. Rhetorically, his conceit reads as common sense. But politically, it narrows the agency of queer aesthetics to the existing structure of the public sphere. The imagined reader, a disembodied mass subject, does not share the text's lifeworld. To be accepted by this abstract reader, queer texts must comport themselves to the affective norms that underpin the consumer culture of reading—not being too unduly dull or esoteric, too abjectly disgusting or perversely titillating. Upon attracting this reader's gaze, literature's political function is exhausted because it has been recognized by and thus included within the status quo.

This is why, despite its marginalization, writers turn to queer experimental literature. No single style unites authors like Delany, Acker, or Winterson, yet they all use experimental aesthetics to elicit what I call *bad reading*—affective relations that contest the corporeal norms that fuse readers into the heteronormative public sphere.[3] As Michael Warner (2002: 123) argues, the public sphere is delimited by a "hierarchy of faculties" that "elevates rational-critical reflection as the self-image of humanity."[4] This hierarchy restricts the affective range of reader relations and, by doing so, limits the modes of aesthetic agency and social imagination available to queer authors. Warner writes,

> All of the verbs for public agency are verbs for private reading, transposed upward to the aggregate of readers. Readers may scrutinize, ask, reject, opine, decide, judge, and so on. Publics can do exactly these things. And nothing else. Publics—unlike mobs or crowds—are incapable of any activity that cannot be expressed through such a verb. Activities of reading that do not fit the ideology of reading as silent, private, replicable decoding— curling up, mumbling, fantasizing, gesticulating, ventriloquizing, writing marginalia, and so on—also find no counterparts in public agency. (ibid.)

Affective modes of reading that fail to conform to the protocols of the rational-critical public sphere appear to strip readers of social agency. Much like queer experimental literature, they are marked as uncritical and apolitical, as too solipsistic to constitute a meaningful engagement with the social world. Thus the hierarchy of faculties not only disavows embodied reader relations and the social bodies that enact them—it obstructs a queerer idiom for the politics of reading, one that would locate agency *within* the forces of affect, eroticism, and fantasy. Yet by soliciting putatively "bad" reader relations—perverse titillation, masturbatory fantasy, uncritical anxiety, and exuberant sentimentality—queer experimental literature contests the social relations that underlie the heteronormative public sphere. The affective relations fostered through queer experimental literature are therefore *incipiently social*—pitched between the "merely" affective and the "properly" political. The social is viscerally incipient in these texts, not simply figured or represented, because they conjure new economies of relation through the forces of affect. At the same time, these texts lack an idiom to conceive of their affective relations as socially meaningful because of their intractable distance from the proper discourses of political collectivity. At every turn, then, queer experimental literature confronts the discursive and political obstructions to the flourishing of queer relationality beyond its textual encounters.

Crucially, academic discourse functions as one obstacle to a queer politics of reading. Reflecting on the aesthetic and political devaluation of experimental literature, Delany (2005: 226–27) worries that "the codification of it in textbooks on how to write experimental fiction and poetry and academic considerations, even such as this one, have something to do with that [marginalization], however indirectly." In his view the academic codification of experimental literature cuts against its affective immanence. For Delany (ibid.: 213, 234), experimental writing "retards readability" and forces readers to "virtually learn *how* to read" anew. Experimental writing provides Delany a literary mode to contest the practices of reading sanctioned within academic discourse, particularly as they circumscribe the agencies of affect in reader relations. Queer experimental literature thus exemplifies a tension between queer and academic cultures that has been paradoxically obscured by the partial legitimation of queer theory within the academy. Although explicitly engaged with institutionally produced academic knowledge, these works are not themselves legible as knowledge because they disrupt authorized genres of academic discourse and critical interpretation. Queer theory has long refuted strict distinctions between institutionally authorized and nonauthorized knowledge.[5] However, queer experimental literature does not simply produce different objects of knowledge. These texts labor to bring new affective and hermeneutic relations into being that are acutely responsive to the urgencies faced by queer publics.[6] In short, the struggle to define *reading*—what it can do, who practices it, and how it is practiced—underlies queer experimentations with literary form. Thus queer experimental literature not only suspends the question of what "counts" as knowledge; it draws a new circuit of belonging among texts, readers, and their social worlds. As Elizabeth Freeman (2010: xix) argues in an analysis of queer experimental aesthetics, "Hermeneutics, the property of art as well as criticism, indirectly feeds the making of new social forms across space and time." I agree that hermeneutics is a perversely common property of queer aesthetics and criticism; however, this essay stresses the tensions that pertain between them to illuminate how queer experimentation elicits hermeneutic modes that diverge from those canonized by certain genres of academic discourse, including queer theory. My purpose is to repatriate the concept of queer reading from its disciplinary lineages, relocating queer hermeneutic practices within the wider social fields from which they emerge.

This repatriation requires that we suspend the monolithic narrative of paranoid and reparative reading as exhausting the plurality of queer hermeneutics. To do so, I locate Delany's turn to queer experimental literature alongside his anxiety about crafting a queer politics of reading in the earliest days of the AIDS crisis, when its historical, political, and medical meanings could not be stabilized. Delany, like queer theory, turns to deconstruction to develop a queer hermeneutic. Yet in his revision of deconstruction, Delany does not seek a paranoid demystification of apparently stable signifiers; instead, he finds in deconstruction an affective relation to the fear wrought by the epidemic of signification that defines the AIDS crisis. Delany's experimental writing reveals that an array of queer hermeneutic relations evolved alongside the institutionalization of paranoid reading. Anticipating the recent postcritical turn, Delany moves from deconstruction toward a hermeneutic of eroticism, which he elaborates in his second AIDS novel, *The Mad Man* (1994a).[7] *The Mad Man* recuperates the radicalism of queer eroticism disavowed by mainstream gay literature and safe sex discourses alike, and through its erotic provocations, it redefines the relationship between experimental aesthetics and affect. Contesting the conceit that experimental literature is politically solipsistic and affectively unpleasant, *The Mad Man* invites readers to encounter the incipiently social relations of queer eroticism. Thus queer experimental literature does not primarily equate queer reading with the deconstruction of meaning or the denaturalization of identity. Rather, in these texts, queer reading entails feeling our way toward more radical modes of erotic and social belonging in historical moments when these possibilities are increasingly foreclosed, stigmatized, and forgotten.

Beside Paranoid Reading

Critics have long recognized that AIDS elicited a crisis of reading. In Paula Treichler's (1987: 263) words, AIDS wrought an "epidemic of signification," which demanded constant interpretative attention to the discourses of the crisis.[8] These discourses included the moralizing rhetoric of religious and political figures, the framing of AIDS in militaristic terms, and the rarefied languages of public health. Despite their apparent objectivity, activists had to, in Michael Warner's (1993: xii) words, "insist over and over on the cultural construction of the discourses about AIDS." Warner does not indicate the multifarious idioms in which this insistence took place, nor does he elaborate whether terms such as "cultural construction" and "discourse" meant the same thing for nonacademics as they do for academics. Rather, he posits a homology between queer and academic cultures, insisting that "queers do a kind of practical social reflection just in finding ways of being queer" (ibid.: xiii). This homology grants desperately needed legitimacy to queer practices of knowledge, especially in 1993 when Warner published *Fear of a Queer Planet*, one of the foundational anthologies to establish the relevance of queer theory to social thought. Yet the equivalence fails to qualify the singularity of the "practical social reflection" conducted by nonacademic queer readers; it does not capture how their hermeneutic practices respond to or break with those legitimated by the academy.

The legacy of this blind spot is evident in Eve Sedgwick's (2002) paradigmatic essay on queer reading, which equates the hermeneutics of suspicion with nonacademic and activist responses to AIDS. The hermeneutics of suspicion, or what Sedgwick calls "paranoid reading," encompasses both academic and nonacademic interpretative relations to AIDS because it demystifies signs, exposes hidden causes, identifies conspiratorial connections, and dispels false consciousness. After all, as Sedgwick recalls, "This was at a time when speculation was ubiquitous about whether the virus had been deliberately engineered or spread, whether HIV represented a plot or experiment by the U.S. military that had gotten out of control, or perhaps that was behaving exactly as it was meant to" (ibid.: 123). By privileging paranoia as the primary affective relation of queer hermeneutics, Sedgwick obscures other interpretative modes, equally engaged with the politics of the crisis, that do not share the drive to demystify. Implicitly, Sedgwick acknowledges this alternative affective history.[9] Her essay begins with an anecdote about Cindy Patton, the "activist scholar" who questioned conspiratorial narratives, wondering "what would we know then [about the crisis] that we don't already know?" (ibid.: 123). Patton's skepticism of paranoid reading signifies, for Sedgwick, an alternative affective and epistemic relation for queer reading. Yet she positions Patton as a proleptic critic of contemporary queer theory, missing an opportunity to identify hermeneutic relations that were elaborated *concurrently* with the AIDS crisis and positioned ambivalently beside paranoid reading.[10]

While I draw inspiration from Sedgwick's locating the affective relations of queer reading within their social contexts, I want to step beside her dichotomy of paranoid and reparative reading. I do not reject paranoia and reparation so much as see them as two affective modes of queer reading among many more that have yet to be narrated within literary criticism. To affirm that a plurality of affective modes emerge *beside* paranoid reading does not presume a truer "origin and telos" (ibid.: 8) for queer reading. As Sedgwick notes, the preposition "beside" affords queer theory a "spacious agnosticism about several of the linear logics that enforce dualistic thinking" (ibid.). By looking beside paranoid reading, we discover experiments in reading that disrupt the dualistic genealogies coalescing around the turn from critical to postcritical reading. For example, Sharon Marcus and Stephen Best (2009) narrate this turn as a narrowly disciplinary affair. In "Surface Reading: An Introduction," they contend that symptomatic reading enabled "exchanges between [academic] disciplines" and was formative for "a relatively homogeneous group of scholars who received doctoral degrees in either English or comparative literature after 1983" (ibid.: 1). Focusing solely on the disciplinary context of literary studies misses a heterogeneity of aesthetic experimentations with critical and uncritical reading alike, which developed alongside academic discourses of reading. We miss these experimentations because, as François Cusset (2008: 338) argues, academic culture brings "harsh judgment to bear on any strange or foreign readings" of critical discourse. To preserve our authority over "legitimate interpretations," we ignore "felicitous misreading[s]" and "creative, even performative misprision[s]" that constitute a "vast zone in which both political *and* cultural virtues can be discovered" (ibid.: 338, 337). The "felicitous" zones of bad reading in queer experimental literature are acutely responsive to their social contexts, redrawing the parameters of what counts as an efficacious politics of reading in the public sphere.

For this reason, we must resist narrating queer reading primarily through the critic's affective relation to the text. Indeed, Sedgwick's dichotomy inadvertently prioritizes the critic as the agent of reparative care and paranoid exposure. Instead, we might trace how queer literature solicits its own affective relations, which do not presume the literary critic as the hero in the dramatic scene of reading. While other literary traditions may participate in this project, queer experimental literature makes its affective agencies distinctly visible by drawing attention to literary form's capacity to work on and through the bodies of readers, immanently restructuring their felt relations to the aesthetic object. Rather than impose an affect theory from above, then, I share Adam Frank's (2015) understanding of aesthetic objects as composing their own affective poetics. Such an approach enables us to see that relays of affective and aesthetic "contact can take many forms" (ibid.: 3); it draws us into many different scenes of contact, learning new modes of affective reading from the aesthetic object itself. This method requires, as Rita Felski (2015: 12) argues, that we "place ourselves in front of the text, reflecting on what it unfurls, calls forth, makes possible."[11] Such an approach necessarily suspends a foundational question of queer literary criticism: *How can we "queer" a text by reading it aslant of its manifest content?* Yet a new question becomes salient: *How do the affective relations unfurled by a text "queer" its readers and the social relations of reading itself?* Undoubtedly, the turn to affective reading has been critiqued for its emphasis on the presubjective forces of affect; for some, such an emphasis appears to forsake the social mediation of affect and the agency of critique.[12] For queer experimental literature, however, affective reading preexists this recent institutional turn and should not be conflated with its disciplinary formation. More important, the turns to affective reading by queer writers derive from a concern about what the literary object can *do* for queer publics— what it can foment through its own forces of language, narrative, and form. In short, their investment in affective reading is intimately bound up with the aesthetic and political agencies of queer literature. As I show, these agencies contest the abstractions of "queer reading" and the "queer reader," marking them as irreducibly social relations stratified by race, sexuality, gender, and class. Rather than oppose politics to aesthetics, or critical to postcritical, then, we glimpse their imbrication *within* the affective relations of queer experimental literature.

Of course, the question of what queer literature can do is fundamentally shaped by the event of AIDS. Indeed, the crisis provokes Delany's turn to experimental writing to compose "The Tale of Plagues and Carnivals" (1985), among the first published novels to address AIDS. Using experimental form, Delany (1994b: 157) asks: How can any novel refer to reality when "reality is constantly and catastrophically—with the death of thousands as both result and cause—changing?" Through a dizzying mixture of minor literary modes—the novel blends speculative fantasy, postmodern metafiction, memoir, and an intertextual commentary on the works of Walter Benjamin and Mikhail Bakhtin—Delany rejects the conceit that literature can stably document the crisis. Thus, while "The Tale of Plagues and Carnivals" searches for historical and literary analogues to AIDS, Delany perpetually deconstructs any figurative mediation of the crisis. The goal, he hopes, is to find a "*better* metaphor," one that can "stabilize those thoughts, images, or patterns that, *in the long run*, are useful—useful to those with the disease, to those who care for them, or even to those who only know about them" (Delany 1985: 179). Yet Delany concludes the novel in defeat:

> By now, I'm willing to admit that perhaps narrative fiction, in neither its literary nor its paraliterary mode, can propose the *radically* successful metaphor. At best, what both modes can do is break up, analyze, dialogize the conservative, the historically sedimented, letting the fragments argue with one another, letting each display its own obsolescence, suggesting (not stating) where still another retains the possibility of vivid, radical development. But responding to those suggestions is, of course, the job of the radical reader. (ibid.: 339)

Delany retains his belief in the potential efficacy of the aesthetic object, yet he displaces that potentiality from the radical signifier to the radical reader. Both conventional and paraliterary fiction can free signs from historical sedimentation. Yet their dialogic forms can only "*invite* a certain richness of reading. . . . they cannot *assure* such a reading. That is something that can only be supplied by the radical reader" (Delany 1999: 126). The queer text cannot make promises about its effects in the world. If any effects are to be successful, they will emerge from a reading that cannot be expected or guaranteed, only invited by the text.

This is an aching conclusion for a writer to make, particularly a writer seeking to articulate a *useful* response to queer trauma from within the realm of the aesthetic. What else can literature do if not construct metaphors? As we will see, Delany turns again to experimental aesthetics to invite affective relations that may recuperate the usefulness of queer literature in the wake of the crisis. Before heeding this invitation, however, we must attend to Delany's theorization of "radical reading" and his critique of academic discourses of deconstruction. Delany reframes deconstruction as an affective relation, shaped by a frightening relationship to language, power, and the body; thus, he forces its theorists to understand the instability of signifiers as a politically constituted violence for queer publics. Delany's revision of deconstruction underlines that even queer hermeneutics that draw on academic discourse are not necessarily equivalent to the hermeneutics of suspicion as we have understood them. In Delany's hands, deconstruction does not solely demystify signifiers; it affords an openness to AIDS as a *felt* crisis for queer publics, marked by a desperate lack of epistemic mastery. By tracing these affective relations in Delany's theory of reading, we see the necessity for broadening the history of queer hermeneutics beyond the disciplinary itinerary of critical reading.

The Affective Relations of Queer Reading

Deconstruction is often aligned with the hermeneutics of suspicion and seen as an exemplary mode of queer reading. Yet Delany finds inspiration in deconstruction for his theorization of queer hermeneutics precisely because, on his reading, deconstruction undermines an omnipotent position over the textual object and language itself. Delany (1994b: 4, 7) looks to deconstruction to challenge the figure of the "idealized and ultimately nonextant and masterful reader," who arrives at truth in a "transcendental experience of understanding." "The fine points of reading," Delany insists, "lie in the margins of a mastery never ours" (ibid.: 16). These are not points of insight but the ways in which insight fails to be complete. Reading is "always a tangle of glitches, inattentions, momentary snags, occasional snoozes, chance oversights, and habitual snarls" (ibid.: 7). While deconstruction is not a phenomenological method, Delany foregrounds the affective relations of deconstructive reading—the body's experience of finding itself snoozing or snarling, snagged or tangled, becoming aware of its lack of mastery over the text through an affective relation to semiotic excess. When describing experimental writing's capacity to produce undecidability, he similarly characterizes the experience as an "undecidability [that] registers as an uncertainty *in the body*" (Delany 2005: 243, my emphasis). At stake in Delany's engagement with deconstruction, then, is a revisionary account of queer hermeneutics, attending to AIDS as an embodied event of undecidability while supplementing deconstruction with an attentiveness to the affective relations of its own historical location.

In place of the masterful reader, Delany substitutes the "vigilant" reader. "Even if blindness is inevitable," he writes, "it is readerly vigilance that frees us" (Delany 1994b: 6). Vigilance seems to evoke the hermeneutics of suspicion and its subject—the ever-attentive reader who holds a lookout over the battlements of discourse. Yet vigilance condenses an attentiveness to one's proximate relation to the text: "Only through the vigilance needed to keep close to the text can the careful reader know just how distant (and idiosyncratic that distance is for each one) they are, text and reader, one from the other" (ibid.). This paradoxical sentence points out how radically Delany's hermeneutics complicates the figures of "close" or "distant" reading. Delany displaces any transcendental reference point for closeness or distance, implying that textual relations are relative and subject to immanent redefinition. This move undoes idealist definitions of hermeneutics as "close reading," rendering that phrase radically undecidable as closeness and distance fold into each other. Delany's vigilance also implies that all readerly relations, insofar as they are relations of proximity, are idiosyncratic. Yet idiosyncrasy is not only an effect of readerly subjectivity; it also derives from the text's use of form to slant and undo the codified protocols of reading that a reader brings to the text. In short, the vigilant reader does not recuperate mastery over the text but, instead, becomes open to the ever-shifting affective torsions that emerge in the textual encounter, experiencing those relations as vital and immanent. In Delany's hands, deconstructive reading attends not only to the slippages of meaning but also to the body's implication in and response to them.

Clearly, Delany's interpretation of deconstruction as a theory of *reading* (as opposed to *writing*) is influenced by its reception in the United States.[13] Yet Delany speaks back to the critics that inspire his appropriation of deconstruction, urging them to reflect on the consequences of deconstruction's structure of feeling for those grappling with the AIDS crisis. For example, Delany places an epigraph from Michael Ryan's *Marxism and Deconstruction* (1982) at the outset of *Flight from Nevèrÿon*, the collection that includes "The Tale of Plagues and Carnivals." Ryan states, "There is no such thing as an absolutely proper meaning of a word, which is not made possible by the very impropriety of metaphorical displacement it seeks to exclude" (quoted in Delany 1985). We have already noted Delany's ambivalence about the impropriety of metaphors associated with AIDS. Even if Delany agrees that signs are inherently iterable, he expresses uncertainty about Ryan's political corollary to this linguistic condition. Ryan (1982: 8) contends that the "impropriety of displaceability of meaning and of infinite openness of syntactic reference" engenders "the continuous revolutionary displacement of power toward radical egalitarianism and the plural defusion [*sic*] of all forms of macro- and microdomination." In other words, the instability of signification is not merely a metaphor for political revolution; it *is* a revolutionary force that outstrips sovereign power.

By contrast, Delany hesitates about the affective and political implications of language's impropriety. He considers Ryan's epigraph in the second appendix to *Flight from Nevèrÿon*:

> *Do* I believe, then, Michael Ryan's assertion with which I opened this volume, i.e., that the impossibility of individuating meanings at the level of the word . . . is a *material* force?
>
> Frankly, I don't know.
>
> But I think the possibility must be seriously considered by anyone interested in either language or power, not to mention their frighteningly elusive, always allusive, and often illusive relations. (Delany 1985: 360)

Delany tables the question of belief regarding the politics of deconstruction, although he calls for a future hearing of its validity. But in a seemingly minor descriptive caveat, Delany emphasizes the *frightening* nature of the "elusive" relations between language and power. Even if iterability provides opportunities for subversion, Delany underlines the concomitant anxiety it stimulates. Of course, *différance* cannot be "experienced," but its effects can be registered in feeling, however retrospectively, and Delany does not figure AIDS's "impropriety of displaceability" as an inherently egalitarian revolution. If the ethos of American deconstruction lauds iterability in abstract terms, Delany offers a queer rejoinder. Not only does the affective suffering wrought by displaceability matter, it must be part of the analysis of the politically constituted relationship between language and power.

Delany's revision of deconstruction responds to critics that identify decontextualized anxiety or ecstasy as the sole affective responses to the instability of language.[14] Paul de Man (1979: 19) claims the "resulting pathos" that one feels in the "suspended ignorance" of deconstruction is either "an anxiety (or bliss, depending on one's momentary mood or individual temperament)." As much as Delany finds inspiration in deconstruction's suspension of hermeneutic mastery, he understands that condition as traumatically implicated in—and intensified by—AIDS. As Delany (1985: 352) notes, "What is *known* about AIDS . . . has been changing month to month for more than a year and will no doubt continue to change until after a vaccine is developed." While "The Tale of Plagues and Carnivals" strives to be a historical document, Delany concedes that "largely what it documents is *misinformation, rumor*, and *wholly untested guesses* at play through a limited social section of New York City during 1982 and 1983, mostly before the April 23, 1984 announcement of the discovery of a virus (human t-cell lymphotropic virus [HTLV-3]) as the overwhelmingly probable cause of AIDS" (ibid.: 351).

Here Delany imprints de Man's "suspended ignorance" with historical markers and links it directly to the social experience of queers. Yet this experience is itself undecidable because of the uncertainty of the cause of AIDS. Rumor spreads in the absence of certainty, making the experience of language untrustworthy and wrought with anxiety. "The Tale of Plagues and Carnivals" attempts to communicate this affective history through its reader relations; indeed, it is through a hermeneutic relation to anxious uncertainty that Delany is able to "figure" the affective relations of the crisis. As he suggests, "History begins only when we do not know what happened—when there is disagreement over what happened. When everyone 'knows' what happened. . . . there is only mythology. And nothing is forgotten faster" (Delany 1994b: 147). Foregrounding the affective relations of a historically constituted queer ignorance, Delany resists the forgetting perpetuated by narratives predicated on the myth of objectivity. Paradoxically, the reader's relation to uncertainty preserves the possibility for dialogic history and social agency to emerge through the literary object. Thus Delany (1985: 333) turns to queer experimental literature not "to allegorize a political situation" but to "allegorize a feeling" that structures the queer relation to AIDS—namely, a radical displacement from one's words, body, and social belonging.

By revising the precepts of academic discourse, queer experimental literature faces a unique concern about whether it can be read on its own terms. Will academic readers reject the "uncritical" reconfiguration of their discourse? Will nonacademic readers work with the text if they do not recognize its critical idioms? In Delany's AIDS writing, the stakes for these questions are high. These texts yearn to be *useful* for their publics. But if paraliterary marginality is a locus of incipiently social usefulness, it is also a potential barrier to reception. Delany (1996: 87–118) reflects on this problem in his engagement with Donna Haraway's "Cyborg Manifesto" (1991), which looks to Delany's fiction for an example of radical cyborg figuration. By responding to Haraway's response to his fiction, Delany reverses the power relations of criticism, where the fictional text often serves as (mute) example for the writer's claims. Yet Delany (1996: 118) wonders whether his reading of Haraway, which he calls "a simulation of an interpretation," is merely a "simulation of a passage": "By reading, do we halt it? By reading, do we move it along? Do we move along it?" These questions exemplify the experimental writer's anxiety about what passage can possibly occur across the idioms of academic and non- (or not-enough) academic reading. Is Delany's "reading" of Haraway a reading or merely a "simulation of an interpretation"? (ibid.). Who is the "we" that reads, and will their hermeneutic relations enable the text's passage? Delany crystallizes this uncertainty about reception in his conclusion: "But, now, we'd best let Helva have back her screw and get on with her work. Pace, and good luck, Ms. Haraway, with yours" (ibid.).[15] *Pace* signifies respectful disagreement and, in its archaic usage, passage. If critique and passage are mutually constitutive, these lines express hope for reading(s) that move across discordant idioms and their attendant relations of power. By inviting future readings, the essay builds a bridge for a queer collectivity of readers to emerge through that interpretative labor. Yet the image of Helva getting "on with her work" is also ambivalent. It may signify the parting of ways between Haraway and Delany and their respective publics, back to the codified boundaries of critical theory and literature, respectively.

The passage between theory and literature is therefore key to Delany's aesthetic invitation of radical reading—his attempt to elicit a queer hermeneutic that moves deftly among academic and nonacademic publics. Notably, in the ongoing aftermath of AIDS, Delany positions queer eroticism as the means of passage between these publics. This is because queer eroticism expands the affective relations of queer reading beyond deconstructive uncertainty, which increasingly converges with a reactionary discourse about the disease. Reflecting on "The Tale of Plagues and Carnivals" over a decade later, Delany (1999: 137) observes, "The *controlling* metaphoric structure for AIDS from the very beginning was: '*What* metaphor shall we use for it?' AIDS has been from the beginning a term-in-search-of-a-metaphor—and, in that sense . . . [my book] fall[s] right *into* the controlling, dominant metaphoric structure." Delany subsequently fuses queer eroticism to radical reading because he regrets his complicity with safe-sex discourses. In the postscript to "The Tale of Plagues and Carnivals," he advised, "Given the situation, total abstinence is a reasonable choice. Whatever adjustment one makes, one must bear in mind that the social path of the disease is difficult to trace" (Delany 1985: 352). If not ceasing to have sex altogether, Delany recommended sex within "known circles, closed if possible," particularly in "monogamous relationships" (ibid.). Retrospectively, Delany (1994b: 160) sees this advice not as "responsible caution" but as complicit with "a discourse as murderous, pernicious, and irresponsible as the various antisemitic and racist pronouncements from Germany before and during World War II."

Thus Delany blends experimental writing with erotica to elicit a queer hermeneutic that embraces the incipiently social economies that can emerge through queer eroticism. To understand the significance of Delany's experimental aesthetic, we must suspend the predominant affective narrative about experimental writing—namely, that its "difficulty" works to alienate readers. For example, Kathryn Hume (2012) characterizes experimental writing as "aggressive fiction" that breaks the "author-reader contract," which promises pleasurable edification as the motive for reading. For Hume, these texts disturb and disgust, and readers do "not like the feeling of being unable to follow the text and hence of having lost control of it" (ibid.: 9). When Hume speculates about readers who *do* enjoy experimental writing, she imagines a coterie of professional critics who master the text via external interpretative codes. Notably, Hume does not conceive of coteries as subcultures or counterpublics. Rather, she reads the text's "unfriendliness towards readers" (ibid.: xii) as a problem to be overcome by the critical reader rather than an alternative configuration for the author-reader contract itself. Hume's narrative cannot account for *becoming*—for the text's conjuring of readerly and social relations that outstrip the existing landscape of its reception. These relations are incipient in Delany's texts; they do not exist outside the diegesis as a sovereign hermeneutic. But more important, Delany does not forsake pleasure; he actively solicits it as the way to resist the gentrification of queer culture. To glimpse the incipiently social possibilities of his queer hermeneutics of eroticism, let us now turn to *The Mad Man*.

The Hermeneutics of Eroticism

The Mad Man is a five-hundred-page historical pornographic novel that cross-pollinates gay erotica (which Delany calls "pornotopic fantasy"), magical realism, academic novel, mystery fiction, and Greek and Romantic philosophy. Delany underlines the significance of his promiscuous and experimental folding of divergent idioms by beginning the book with a disclaimer and concluding with the most recent academic study of risk factors in HIV seroconversion. For Delany (1994a: xiii–xiv), the fact that the study was published in 1987, while his novel was published in 1994, is an "appalling, horrifying, and ultimately criminal" testament to the continuing dearth of research on AIDS. In this context, Delany insists that *The Mad Man* is "about various sexual acts whose status as vectors of HIV contagion we have no hard-edged knowledge of because the monitored studies that would give statistical portraits between such acts and Seroconversion (from HIV- to HIV+) have not been done" (ibid.: xiii). Delany continues to frame AIDS within a narrative of uncertainty. But here uncertainty is produced by the ongoing lack of scientific research, which is a consequence of the willed cultural ignorance about the relationship between HIV transmission and a diversity of queer sexual acts. *The Mad Man*'s innovation of pornotopic fantasy strikes at the heart of that cultural repression. As Delany (1999: 133) explains, pornotopia does not indicate "the 'good sexual place.' (That would be 'Upornotopia' or 'Eupornotopia.')" It's simply *the* 'sexual place'—the place where all can become (apocalyptically) sexual." Indeed, the novel narrates—in intensely specific and erotic detail—sexual acts that fall outside heteronormativity's gaze and have an ambiguous relationship to HIV in the moment of Delany's writing *and* in the historical moment that the novel depicts.[16] These acts primarily include oral sex, piss drinking, and shit eating. (Notably, the novel never represents anal sex.) *The Mad Man* places these pleasures at the core of its plot, which traces the protagonist John Marr's experimentations with sex publics in New York City from 1980 to 1994, largely among black homeless men. Delany recalls that "*any* suggestion at all [in 1984] that one mode of bodily sexual behavior was safer than another was considered totally irresponsible" (ibid.: 50). The novel challenges this discursive prohibition simply by figuring a panoply of queer eroticisms. Yet pornography also titillates; it stimulates the reader's hermeneutic curiosity about sex. In Darieck Scott's (2010: 30) words, *The Mad Man* "attempts to achieve for readers what it represents for John Marr through a sexual or erotic practice—in this case, primarily, an erotic and sexual *reading* practice—of Marcusian exuberance." By eroticizing acts barely considered sexual, let alone pleasurable, *The Mad Man* elicits a queer hermeneutic of eroticism: it challenges the constriction of sexuality in safe-sex discourses and condenses an interpretative relation to an unwritten affective history of queer eroticism, which is irreducibly marked by uncertainty about its own implication in the transmission of HIV.[17]

The Mad Man strives to figure structures of feeling that dominate during the crisis. Yet, unlike Delany's earlier AIDS writing, *The Mad Man*'s interpretative dilemma does not center on the epidemic of signification. Rather, the stakes for *The Mad Man* lie in developing a hermeneutic relationship to queer eroticism that charts its changing historical meaning and social value among queer communities. The novel maps these changes through the first-person narrative of Marr, an African American philosophy graduate student. Marr's doctoral research focuses on Timothy Hasler, a brilliant young Korean American philosopher of semiotics who was mysteriously murdered in 1973 before receiving his doctorate. As Marr discovers, Hasler was gay, and much like Marr, enjoyed a number of queer fetishes, including public sex. Despite the similarities between them, Marr insists that an "incredible historical, fundamental abyss" exists between Hasler and himself (Delany 1994a: 177). For Marr, that abyss cannot be encapsulated by a reductive "homily like 'Hasler was a gay man before the age of AIDS'" (ibid.). It lies in the excruciating affective "experience" Marr has when he discovers that sex in the midst of the crisis means "gambling, and gambling on one's own—rather than seeking some possible certain knowledge" (ibid.: 176). Indeed, Marr insists the disease must be "reinscribe[d] over" all the "inner drama" of the sexual experiences he narrates (ibid.: 172). He admits, "I thought about AIDS constantly and intently and obsessively. . . . we [gay men] move through life fully and continually oppressed by the suspicion that we must already have it!" (ibid.: 172–74).

Delany underlines the collective—yet individualizing and isolating—anguish of gay men who risk queer eroticism in the midst of so much uncertainty about the consequences of their sexual acts. Yet he marks the hermeneutics of suspicion as an *oppressive* affective relation that, if given free rein, drains away the incipiently social relationality enabled through queer eroticism. The abyss between Marr and Hasler thus stands in for the discontinuity between reading queer eroticism before and after the emergence of AIDS. At the same time, Delany critiques a hermeneutic understanding of queerness as a secret waiting to be revealed to the gaze of a heteronormative public. This is made evident in the eighty-page letter that Marr writes to his white heterosexual friend, Sam, who asks Marr to explain gay sexuality in the midst of AIDS. In his letter, Marr offers narrative snapshots of his erotic adventures in loving detail; notably, his narration to Sam is not distinguished from the rest of the novel's pornotopic style. This is because, in Marr's view, "I don't think anyone *can* really understand what AIDS means in the gay community until she or he has some understanding of the field and function—the range, the mechanics—of the sexual landscape AIDS has entered into" (ibid.: 179). Hence the novel's stylistic and narrative experimentalism mirrors Marr's sexual experimentation. Undoubtedly, Marr sneers at Sam's notion of a representative "gay experience," emphasizing the exclusions that render his narrative singular and fragmentary. Yet Marr implies that *some* understanding is possible, if Sam can read the richness of queer eroticism itself—how it operates within an economy of pleasure, fear, vulnerability, attachment, and anonymity. To do so, Sam must dispense with her presumption that "the secret self resides within the private self, which resides within the clearly public self. Such a model holds that to delve through to the private or to the secret is to explain and obviate the public area we've just passed through to reach them" (ibid.: 182). Marr concludes: "Sam, I hope this hasn't been too demanding" (ibid.: 183). Yet his letter, like *The Mad Man*, demands queerer relations to reading, subjectivity, and sex. After all, their norms of privacy are underwritten by the same hierarchy of faculties. *The Mad Man* denies the disinterested distance of the unmarked liberal subject, refusing her conception that the secret of queerness can be voyeuristically revealed and assimilated to an extant understanding of sociality. Instead, through her reading, Sam must immerse herself in the affective economies of queer eroticism, which fundamentally redraw the relations of privacy and publicness alike.

Contrary to Hume, queer experimental literature elicits a rigorous engagement with pleasure, provoking readers to imagine a public that does not require the repression of putatively uncritical affects as the precondition for social agency. Yet, exemplifying its aesthetic marginality, the novel positions academic characters as the indexes of heteronormativity and white supremacy, which discount the agencies of queer eroticism. Marr's dissertation adviser, Irving Mossman, intends to write a biography of Hasler but abandons the project when he discovers that Hasler enjoyed "the most degrading—and depressing—sexual 'experiments'" (ibid.: 22). "Rather than try to separate the sexual practices from the thinking," Mossman concludes with racist and homophobic disgust that Hasler was "an obnoxious little chink with an unbelievably nasty sex life" (ibid.: 46–47). Mossman refuses to read Hasler's journals because they include lengthy entries devoted to foot fetishism and bestiality fantasies. By contrast, Marr refuses to "separate the sexual practices from the thinking" (ibid.: 46). Indeed, Marr relates Hasler's sexual experimentations to his writing on semiotics, reading Hasler's fantasies *as fantasies*—not literal transcriptions of experience but aesthetic transfigurations of erotic desire. Concomitantly, Marr refuses to segregate Hasler's philosophical and science fictional writing. Because of its own academic liminality, Marr's research can be published only in such venues as science fiction collections and *Umbilicus*, a "Canadian magazine of radical sexual politics" (ibid.: 493). Marr's department chair believes that it is apt that Marr's writing "occup[ies] an identical position" to that of Hasler, who never received a doctorate and much of whose writing was "marginal to scholarly pursuits" (ibid.: 240). Yet *The Mad Man* suggests a queer hermeneutics emerges in these venues because they permit experimental bridges between "legitimate" scholarship and bad reading. These paraliterary and para-academic spaces embrace the analysis of degraded subjects and subject positions that philosophy marginalizes, specifically queer writers of color. To cleave space for these subjects and their unsanctioned idioms, queer experimental literature upends the hierarchy of faculties that segregates the intimacies of intellect and sex.

Unlike the hermeneutics of suspicion, then, the hermeneutics of eroticism invites readerly immersion within the affective economies from which queer writing emerges. Note that Delany (1999: 133) conceives "pornotopia" as an aesthetic mode "where *any relationship* can become sexualized in a moment, with the proper word or look—where *every relationship* is potentially sexualized even before it starts" (my emphasis). Queer aesthetics harbors a virtual eroticism that re-creates the relational boundaries of reading and sociality. In this respect, Delany counters queer theory's tendency to locate queer aesthetic agency in the disruption of representation.[18] For example, Kevin Ohi (2011: 1) figures the queerness of style as a "radical antisociality that seeks to unyoke sexuality from the communities and identities—gay or straight—that would tame it, a disruption that thwarts efforts to determine political goals according to a model of representation." Ohi characterizes this disruption as the "*corrosive* effect of queerness . . . on received forms of meaning, representation, and identity" (ibid., my emphasis). While Delany also resists identity politics, he intimates that antisocial *corrosion* may not be the only (or even the most radical) force of queer aesthetics. Queer experimental literature also affords an *adhesive* modality via the incipiently social relations of queer eroticism. Queer eroticism, as Freeman (2010: 13–14) argues, "traffics less in belief than in encounter, less in damaged wholes than intersections of body parts, less in loss than in novel possibility (will this part fit into that one? what's my gender if I do this or that to my body?)." Note the *experimental* nature of eroticism—it suspends the subject's grasping for meaning to engender corporeal contact and transformation. The body becomes a composition of bodies and body-parts whose connective possibilities can be curiously reimagined. Likewise, this assemblage of bodies is not subordinated to a dialectic of subject and object. The speculative dialectic gives way to a different mode of speculation—a playful fabulation of nonexclusive potentialities. As Freeman notes, "Artifice is part of the pleasure: the fetishistic belief in the lost object is less important than the titillation of 'but all the same . . .'" (ibid.: 14, ellipsis original). The aesthetic is enmeshed in the scene of queer eroticism—not only as an agency for figuring and coordinating eroticism but as a surface to be affectively encountered and drawn into adhesion with the assemblage of bodies. The titillation of "but all the same" registers the aesthetic's pull toward queer relationality—its solicitation of the body's potential to become differently stuck together with other bodies, body-parts, and body-politics.

If Freeman is right that scholars "know a lot less about how to do things with sex than we know about how to do things with words," then queer experimental literature invites readers to discover the incipient sociality of queer sex (ibid.: 172). As Delany attests, pornotopia forges relations across boundaries of race and class without subsuming difference into a reified "gay" identity. Concomitantly, its queer relationality contests gentrification. Delany's (1999: 123) writing transforms "an older, pre-AIDS discourse, which privileged sexual reticence, into a discourse that foregrounds detailed sexual honesty, imagination, and articulation. AIDS makes such a discursive adjustment imperative." Hence Delany calls for "all of us begin to put forward the monumental analytical effort, in whichever rhetorical mode we choose, needed not to interpret what we say, but to say what we *do* [sexually]" (ibid.: 56). *The Mad Man* does not offer a mode of confession that reveals the truth of queer eroticism to a mass gaze or a narrow appeal to an extant counterpublic. Rather, Delany's experimentalism expands the viable "rhetorical mode[s]" in which the "analytic effort" of sexual and social imagination can be articulated, demonstrating that, even if we suspend the pressure to "interpret what we say" about sex, the hermeneutic obstacles to reading with pleasure are still very much ours (ibid.).

Queer Hermeneutics as Affective Inheritance

Many critics have urged queer theory to keep alive a historical relationship to AIDS.[19] This is due in no small part to the gentrification of the radical politics of the AIDS era. Scholars such as Gregory Tomso (2010) argue that the crisis is by no means "over," as mainstream narratives suggest; indeed, he calls for the humanities to construct new methodologies of interpretation, informed by the social sciences, to contend with the enduring implications of AIDS. Rather than look beyond the humanities, we have looked back to queer literature, to the plurality of hermeneutic relations that emerged in response to AIDS's crisis of reading. My goal has been to broaden the prevailing equation of queer hermeneutics with paranoid and reparative reading. Moreover, I have stressed that queer reading does not solely emerge from what Brian Massumi (2002: 13) calls the "intemperate arrogance of debunking." Delany's queer hermeneutics illuminates the affective and social relations that are redrawn by the suspension of epistemological mastery engendered by the crisis. Thus the work of queer reading is not only to suspect or repair the text but, instead, to immerse itself in the text on its own terms. After all, Massumi notes that the choice between critique and affirmation must be approached as "a question of dosage," conditioned by "timing and proportion" (ibid.). Massumi's metaphor of dosage is more apt than he realizes. Queer reading emerges from an intersection of historical, political, and bodily economies, and—long before the postcritical turn—queer writers have experimented with complex affective compositions, mindful of the exigencies faced by their publics.

Despite its marginality, queer experimental literature illuminates why the affective and social agencies of queer reading became entwined with each other.

As Anthony Reed (2014: 1) argues, experimental writing creates a "hiatus of unrecognizability [that] can spur new thought and new imaginings, especially the (re)imagining of collectivities and intellectual practices." Queer experimental literature fuses this hiatus to the most degraded of affective relations. Hence these texts often appear insufficiently concerned with the social world. As John Marr discovers, flights into fantasy may read as solipsistic withdrawal. However, as Jennifer Doyle (2013: 72) argues, "the rhetorical deployment of the personal and the emotional should not be assumed to be a retreat into an ahistorical, apolitical self; such explicit turns to emotion may in fact signal the politicization, the historicization of that self and of the feelings through which that self takes shape in relation to others." At the moment when queer experimental literature appears to retreat from the legibility of critical subjectivity, its affective forces may be advancing outward, in a newly politicized threading together of affective and social relation. Queer experimental literature thus affords a privileged site to glimpse the creation of new modes of queer relationality, which emerge in a hiatus that suspends authorized reading practices.

Experimental literature enables Delany to move agonistically and passionately alongside modes of reading codified within academic discourse. Yet I want to stress that the larger stakes for his queer hermeneutics rest, finally, on perceiving reading itself as a fundamental layer of the "accreted historical meanings" that Heather Love (2009: 30) identifies as constitutive of queerness. My concern is that recent appeals to objective methods of reading, including Love's (2010) "descriptive reading," obscure the accretions of queer hermeneutics—those unsanctioned, degraded, and vital ways of reading that have developed among queer publics and been bequeathed to future generations as an unconscious cultural inheritance. The turn to objectivity overlooks how queer hermeneutic relations not only enable us to perceive affective history—*they are themselves affective history.* As Fredric Jameson (1981: 9) once argued, "We apprehend [texts] through the sedimented layers of previous interpretations, or—if the text is brand-new—through the sedimented reading habits and categories developed by those inherited interpretive traditions." Indeed, texts also (and simultaneously) solicit *new* interpretative relations that operate aslant of the ones that condition their reception. The dichotomy of "paranoid" and "reparative" reading is thus too narrow to identify the dynamic, plural, and noninstitutionalized relations solicited by and sedimented through queer experimental literature. Yet its conjunction of feeling with reading correctly understands queer hermeneutics as an *affective* sedimentation, a queer habitus inherited through the body and activated in modes of relationality. In this sense, AIDS is not only a historical event waiting to be read or an ongoing crisis requiring new hermeneutic paradigms. It is an irreducible event in the history of queer reading itself, a hermeneutic inheritance that cannot be transcended or effaced because it is imprinted in the affective relation between queer readers and their social worlds.

Notes

I want to thank Ramzi Fawaz and Shanté Paradigm Smalls for their editorial care and intellectual generosity and for their labor in organizing this important conversation on LGBTQ literature. I am also grateful to two anonymous readers for their incisive feedback and to the attendees of the 2016 MLA "Queers Read LGBT Literature" panel, who helped me think through the affective politics of queer experimental literature in the context of gentrification.

1. Delany reserves "experimental" to describe only a handful of his works, using "paraliterary" for his fiction more generally. At stake in this distinction is the specificity of experimentalism in Delany's development of a queer hermeneutics that is responsive to AIDS. More broadly, his distinction points to a genealogy of queer experimentalism that has been subsumed within the categories of paraliterary and postmodern fiction. Queer experimental literature shares the aesthetic marginality of the paraliterary, but these texts aggressively seek to transform the protocols of reading that condition their reception; queer experimentalism also uses postmodern stylistics—pastiche, narrative metalepsis, boundary-crossing intertextuality, and historiographical metafiction—but contests postmodernity's atrophied social imaginary, of which these styles are said to index, by provoking incipiently social modes of belonging through its putatively solipsistic and anarchic forms. On the tensions between queer experimentalism and postmodernism, see Bradway 2017, from which portions of this essay have been drawn and reproduced with the permission of Palgrave Macmillan.

2. On the concept of the gay writer, see Delany 1999: 111–14.

3. On bad readers and the public sphere, see Millner 2012 and Emre 2017, which appeared while this essay was in press.

4. On the "uncritical," see Warner 2004.

5. See, e.g., Warner and Berlant 1995 and Halberstam 2011. On queer experimental literature as exemplifying a "para-academic mode," see Bradway 2017.

6. For a different approach to queer hermeneutics influenced by Hans-Georg Gadamer, see Hall 2009.

7. Delany has published revised editions in 2002 and 2015. I do not address these editions here, as my argument hinges on Delany's historically specific return to experimental writing in 1994 to craft a literary response to AIDS.

8. On AIDS as a crisis of reading to which Delany's fiction responds, see Tucker 2004: 230–76.

9.   On the affective politics of AIDS, see Gould 2009 and Diedrich 2016.

10.   For a relevant approach to queer theory's affective history, see Amin 2016.

11.   Postcritical and reparative reading both foreground the text's affective agencies, but Sedgwick (2002: 149) tends to locate agency in the reparative reader who "wants to assemble and confer plenitude on an object that will then have resources to offer to an inchoate self." Here the object requires the reader's affect to nourish it in the face of a culture that is "inadequate or inimical to its nurture" (ibid.). By contrast, the present essay looks to the affects that the object confers on readers and how these affects nurture the emergence of more hospitably queer cultures on their own terms.

12.   See, e.g., Leys 2011.

13.   See Cusset 2008: 113.

14.   On affect in deconstruction, see Terada 2001: 128–51.

15.   Helva is the protagonist of Anne McCaffery's novel *The Ship Who Sang* (1985), which Haraway also cites.

16.   On Delany's erotics of abjection, see Foltz 2008 and Scott 2010.

17.   On the problem of interpreting pleasure as a historical referent, see chapter 2 of Bradway 2017. In the present context, I offer the "hermeneutics of eroticism" as a more encompassing mode for understanding Delany's resistance to gentrification.

18.   See, e.g., de Lauretis 2008 and Ohi 2011.

19.   See, e.g., Schulman 2012 and Warner 2002.

References

Amin, Kadji. 2016. "Haunted by the 1990s: Queer Theory's Affective Histories." *WSQ* 44, nos. 3–4: 173–89.

Bradway, Tyler. 2017. *Queer Experimental Literature: The Affective Politics of Bad Reading*. New York: Palgrave Macmillan.

Cusset, François. 2008. *French Theory: How Foucault, Derrida, Deleuze, & Co. Transformed the Intellectual Life of the United States*. Translated by Jeff Fort. Minneapolis: University of Minnesota Press.

Delany, Samuel R. 1985. "The Tale of Plagues and Carnivals." In *Flight from Nevèrÿon*, 173–353. Toronto: Bantam Books.

———. 1994a. *The Mad Man*. New York: Richard Kasak.

———. 1994b. *Silent Interviews: On Language, Race, Sex, Science Fiction, and Some Comics*. Hanover, NH: University Press of New England.

———. 1996. *Longer Views: Extended Essays*. Hanover, NH: University Press of New England.

———. 1999. *Shorter Views: Queer Thoughts and the Politics of the Paraliterary*. Hanover, NH: University Press of New England.

————. 2005. *About Writing: Seven Essays, Four Letters, and Five Interviews*. Middletown, CT: Wesleyan University Press.

De Lauretis, Teresa. 2008. *Freud's Drive: Psychoanalysis, Literature, and Film*. New York: Palgrave Macmillan.

De Man, Paul. 1979. *Allegories of Reading: Figural Language in Rousseau, Nietzsche, Rilke, and Proust*. New Haven, CT: Yale University Press.

Diedrich, Lisa. 2016. *Indirect Action: Schizophrenia, Epilepsy, AIDS, and the Course of Health Activism*. Minneapolis: University of Minnesota Press.

Doyle, Jennifer. 2013. *Hold It against Me: Difficulty and Emotion in Contemporary Art*. Durham, NC: Duke University Press.

Emre, Merve. 2017. *Paraliterary: The Making of Bad Readers in Postwar America*. Chicago: University of Chicago Press.

Felski, Rita. 2015. *The Limits of Critique*. Chicago: University of Chicago Press.

Foltz, Mary Catherine. 2008. "The Excremental Ethics of Samuel R. Delany." *SubStance* 37, no. 2: 41–55.

Frank, Adam. 2015. *Transferential Poetics, from Poe to Warhol*. New York: Fordham University Press.

Freeman, Elizabeth. 2010. *Time Binds: Queer Temporalities, Queer Histories*. Durham, NC: Duke University Press.

Gould, Deborah B. 2009. *Moving Politics: Emotion and ACT UP's Fight against AIDS*. Chicago: University of Chicago Press.

Halberstam, Judith. 2011. *The Queer Art of Failure*. Durham, NC: Duke University Press.

Hall, Donald E. 2009. *Reading Sexualities: Hermeneutic Theory and the Future of Queer Studies*. London: Routledge.

Haraway, Donna. 1991. "A Cyborg Manifesto: Science, Technology, and Socialist-Feminism in the Late Twentieth Century." In *Simians, Cyborgs, and Women: The Reinvention of Nature*, 149–82. New York: Routledge.

Hume, Kathryn. 2012. *Aggressive Fictions: Reading the Contemporary American Novel*. Ithaca, NY: Cornell University Press.

Jameson, Fredric. 1981. *The Political Unconscious: Narrative as a Socially Symbolic Act*. Ithaca, NY: Cornell University Press.

Leys, Ruth. 2011. "The Turn to Affect: A Critique." *Critical Inquiry* 37, no. 3: 434–72.

Love, Heather. 2009. *Feeling Backward: Loss and the Politics of Queer History*. Cambridge, MA: Harvard University Press.

————. 2010. "Close but Not Deep: Literary Ethics and the Descriptive Turn." *New Literary History* 41, no. 2: 371–91.

Marcus, Sharon, and Stephen Best. 2009. "Surface Reading: An Introduction." *Representations* 108, no. 1: 1–21.

Massumi, Brian. 2002. *Parables of the Virtual: Movement, Affect, Sensation.* Durham, NC: Duke University Press.

McCaffery, Anne. 1985. *The Ship Who Sang.* New York: Del Rey.

Millner, Michael. 2012. *Fever Reading: Affect and Reading Badly in the Early American Public Sphere.* Durham: University of New Hampshire Press.

Muñoz, José Esteban. 2009. *Cruising Utopia: The Then and There of Queer Futurity.* New York: New York University Press.

Ohi, Kevin. 2011. *Henry James and the Queerness of Style.* Minneapolis: University of Minnesota Press.

Reed, Anthony. 2014. *Freedom Time: The Poetics and Politics of Black Experimental Writing.* Baltimore, MD: Johns Hopkins University Press.

Ryan, Michael. 1982. *Marxism and Deconstruction.* Baltimore, MD: Johns Hopkins University Press.

Schulman, Sarah. 2012. *The Gentrification of the Mind: Witness to a Lost Imagination.* Berkeley: University of California Press.

Scott, Darieck. 2010. *Extravagant Abjection: Blackness, Power, and Sexuality in the African American Literary Imagination.* New York: New York University Press.

Sedgwick, Eve Kosofsky. 2002. *Touching Feeling: Affect, Pedagogy, Performativity.* Durham, NC: Duke University Press.

Terada, Rei. 2001. *Feeling in Theory: Emotion after the "Death of the Subject."* Cambridge, MA: Harvard University Press.

Tomso, Gregory. 2010. "The Humanities and HIV/AIDS: Where Do We Go from Here?" *PMLA* 125, no. 2: 443–53.

Treichler, Paula. 1987. "AIDS, Homophobia, and Biomedical Discourse: An Epidemic of Signification." *Cultural Studies* 1, no. 3: 263–305.

Tucker, Jeffrey Allen. 2004. *A Sense of Wonder: Samuel R. Delany, Race, Identity, and Difference.* Middletown, CT: Wesleyan University Press.

Warner, Michael. 1993. Introduction to *Fear of a Queer Planet: Queer Politics and Social Theory*, edited by Michael Warner, vii–xxxi. Minneapolis: University of Minnesota Press.

———. 2002. *Publics and Counterpublics.* New York: Zone Books.

———. 2004. "Uncritical Reading." In *Polemic: Critical or Uncritical*, edited by Jane Gallop, 13–38. New York: Taylor and Francis Books.

Warner, Michael, and Lauren Berlant. 1995. "What Does Queer Theory Teach Us about X." *PMLA* 110, no. 3: 343–49.

WITCHES, TERRORISTS, AND THE BIOPOLITICS OF CAMP

Cynthia Barounis

Camp humor is a system of laughing at one's incongruous position instead of crying. . . . I saw the reverse transformation—from
laughter to pathos—often enough, and it is axiomatic among the
impersonators that when the camp cannot laugh, he dissolves into a
maudlin bundle of self-pity. One of the most confounding aspects of
my interactions with the impersonators was their tendency to laugh at
situations that to me were horrifying or tragic.
—Esther Newton, *Mother Camp*

My heart has turned to stone. . . . And since Samuel disappeared,
I have such a sad weakness of faith, I cannot shake it. I cannot see
Christ's help as near. I pray and I pray but I cannot. I fear I cannot
ever feel that same measure of love again.
—Katherine in *The Witch: A New-England Folktale*, directed by
Robert Eggers

First she's funny for a few minutes. . . . Then bam! She loses her shit!!
—Chicken in *The Complete Hothead Paisan: Homicidal Lesbian
Terrorist*, by Diane DiMassa

*W*hat is the fate of camp in the Trump era? While the camp aesthetic initially
emerged as a powerful strategy for denaturalizing entrenched forms of institutional
power, queer poses of detachment no longer feel entirely adequate as tools for dis-
arming the political Right's ever-increasing arsenal of "alternative facts." Furthermore, if camp critique requires the ability to maintain an ironic distance from
what would otherwise make us cry, then what happens when the weight of our

GLQ 24:2–3
DOI 10.1215/10642684-4324789
© 2018 by Duke University Press

realities (both individual and collective) press too close? At these moments we may find that, like Katherine in *The Witch*, we "cannot laugh," "cannot shake it," and "cannot ever feel" the way we used to, or the way we want to, about our situation. Some incongruities threaten to swallow us whole, and in these instances, pathos may be the only possible response.

Indeed, when Kate McKinnon, costumed as Hillary Clinton, performed Leonard Cohen's "Hallelujah" on the *SNL* stage on November 12, 2016, following Trump's devastating victory, there was no trace of irony in her delivery and no attempt at comedy. Instead, we were presented with a melancholic *congruity* between Cohen's lyrics and Clinton's loss, as McKinnon longingly sang, "I did my best, it wasn't much / I couldn't feel, so I tried to touch / I've told the truth, I didn't come to fool you." These performances of "self-pity" may very well be "maudlin," but despite Esther Newton's observations in *Mother Camp*, they need not signal a dissolution of the self, nor are they necessarily incompatible with the camp aesthetic. From the perspective of crip theory and mad feminism, self-pity might simply be another way to name the necessary coping mechanisms we develop for our survival, evidence of a willingness to be honest with ourselves and others about where the damage is and what it looks like. It may mean allowing ourselves to cry about our incongruous situation instead of—or as well as—laughing.

I would like to begin by offering two related anecdotes. In March 2016, as the Republican primary narrowed to three candidates, I happened to visit an old friend in Janesville, Wisconsin, several days before Donald Trump was scheduled to make a campaign appearance there. Trump had not yet taken a definitive lead; many of us were only just beginning to wrap our heads around the unlikely possibility that he could become his party's nominee (that he could win the presidency was still unthinkable). We understood his campaign to be an elaborate joke, albeit a terrifying one, and we awaited the inevitable punch line. It was in this context that my friend and I discovered an unforgettable artifact. Spotted on the ground during a late afternoon stroll near the river, it appeared to be a discarded *Sesame Street* picture book. Called *Sleep Tight!*, its cover featured a smiling Elmo, nestled into a yellow crescent moon doubling as his bed. Tucked in and surrounded by clouds and stars, he clutches a small brown teddy bear. The title page, however, held a surprise. A sleepy Big Bird reclines in his nest and gazes contentedly into the distance. Emerging from his beak in blue ballpoint pen was a cartoon speech bubble containing three words: "Vote for Trump."

Further investigation revealed that each page in the picture book had been "annotated" with similar speech bubbles containing pro-Trump messages. For example, on one page the printed text reads: "On the way home from the park,

Elmo and his daddy see lots of other people on their way home, too. It's almost bedtime for little monsters."[1] In the accompanying image, a crossing guard halts traffic so that father and son can make it across the intersection safely. Speech bubbles have been added to this image: as they cross, Elmo's father asks, "Are you tired of fraud, waste, and abuse? Vote Trump." Elmo adds: "If you don't trust Hillary Clinton, Vote for Trump." Behind them, a bystander declares to no one in particular, "I love Trump." Even the crossing guard remarks that "America needs Trump."

The original bedtime story moves the reader through a bustling town scene, traversing multiple landscapes and encountering familiar Muppet characters. As a result, the rogue "cartoonist" was able to create an uncanny consensus among the Sesame Street population, who uniformly endorsed Trump as their candidate. "Sleepy twiddlebugs snuggle under their leaf blankets" while Ernie reassures them that America will "win at everything when Trump is in office." The Count counts sheep while also counting on Trump to "put America back on track." In the book's concluding image, a sleepy Elmo dozes off to the rumination that Trump's America is "a safe America." "Sleep tight, little Elmo," reads the original.

How is a queer to read these images? I will confess that these textual appropriations convey something different to me now than they did a year ago. Initially, I approached our odd little discovery with the glee of a camp connoisseur. Its ugliness provoked delight, what Susan Sontag ([1964] 1999: 54) might call a "good taste of bad taste." Pairing childhood nostalgia with dystopian futurity, sweet dreams with political nightmares, cooperative communitarianism with sexism, racism, and xenophobia, the familiar with the absurd, our defaced children's book felt novel in its endless campy incongruities. Mystery surrounding the object's origins deepened these pleasures. Was this the work of a zealous Trump supporter attempting to spread the word? A queer parody of small town America? A socialist critique of gentrification and its rhetorics of safety? The work of bored teenagers? How many books like this existed, or was ours unique? Was it intentionally placed or carelessly discarded? Ultimately, however, the answers to these questions did not matter—whether this was a piece of naive or calculated camp, it was easy to maintain a critical distance. It lent itself to laughter, irony, and anecdotal pleasure.

Returning to these images now, after the election and in the wake of everything that has passed since Trump took office, it is harder to find humor in its incongruities. On the morning of November 9, 2016, as I prepared to board a plane to Montreal for an academic conference, I began to experience an anxious paranoia that one might visualize in terms similar to the images I have just described. Sleep deprived and still processing my emotions from the night before when the electoral map turned red, I began to feel a wild suspicion of every bystander who passed me in the airport terminal. Who among us had cast their vote for this overblown caricature of rape culture? Who among us harbored uncritical disdain for queers, women, racial minorities, immigrants, and refugees? As I waded through the crowd, pro-Trump thought bubbles floated above everyone's heads as hazy warnings that the world was no longer safe (not that it had ever been). I needed to know which monsters had slept tight the night before.

A second anecdote. Prior to my trip to Janesville, my friend had alerted me that my visit would coincide with her sibling Dylan's fourteenth birthday, and that I would be included in the celebrations. She also shared with me that Dylan had recently begun to identify as both genderfluid and bisexual, and asked if I would be willing to act as a queer confidante, should Dylan desire one. She imagined that as a fourteen-year-old living in a small conservative town, Dylan might want support or guidance as they navigated their coming-out process. I accepted this potential new role with enthusiasm and immediately began to brainstorm reading suggestions. What books did I wish someone had dropped into my hands as a queer adolescent living in the suburbs of Chicago in the 1990s? Could those same books be relevant to a transmasculine teenager living in Wisconsin in 2016? What do queer kids need, read, or *need to read* now?

Drawing from my experience as a professor of queer studies, friends' recommendations, and the novels that aided my own queer coming-of-age, I developed a short list of carefully curated book recommendations that I thought might help Dylan make sense of their gender identity and sexuality. But as I listened to Dylan casually explain to me their identification as agender and their preference for they/them pronouns, it became clear that Dylan did not need my help. Born in 2002, they grew up in a world already transformed by queer visibility, and with access to social media platforms that interlinked with the queer and feminist blogosphere. As we chatted, I learned about the high percentage of out queer students at their high school, its robust gay-straight alliance, and the name of their current crush. While there is certainly much I could teach them about LGBT literature, history, theory, and politics, it was inaccurate to assume that they were experiencing isolation or lack of access to queer knowledge networks. I did recommend a couple of books. But mostly, we enjoyed each other's company, and the birthday celebration culminated with a family outing to see *The Witch* (2015), a Puritan horror film by Robert Eggers.

The convergence of these stories illustrates what is, perhaps, a simple point: it does not get better, it gets worse. Or perhaps more accurately, even as it gets better, it also gets worse. My friend and I had been locating trauma in the wrong place, measuring the imagined isolation of Dylan's queer adolescence against the queer socialities of a promised futurity. But ultimately, the defaced Sesame Street book we discovered on Dylan's birthday functioned less as a quaint artifact than as a portentous omen signaling the chain of calamities to come. To maintain a traditionally campy approach to its incongruous speech bubbles requires faith in a world where Trump could not have been elected president. In a world where such outcomes are not only possible but have come to pass, a more truthful affective response is horror. We should have been more frightened by Bert and Ernie's lockstep march into a horizonal fascist future. We should have anticipated the rumblings of a new (and also very old) American teleology in which "greatness" is continually and nostalgically inscribed as a site of eternal return. Hermeneutically, what is called for is paranoia. We should have, in short, been reading like Puritans.

In what follows I suggest that if camp is to remain relevant to queer life, we need to recall its status as a therapeutic gesture, evidence of the way we have had to learn, in Newton's ([1972] 1999: 106) words, to "laugh at [our] incongruous position instead of crying." As an aesthetic practice, camp has always, to some extent, urged us to take trauma and its aftermath seriously. Thus, despite my chosen archive of film and graphic narrative, this essay is less interested in what camp *looks* like than in what camp *feels* like. It seeks to develop a new crip application of the camp aesthetic that explores how some of camp's origin stories, as a coping mechanism and as an affective relation to and between objects, can resonate powerfully with disability studies' recent turn toward mad feminism, new materialism, and biopolitics.[2] The affective turn in queer theory asks us to trade, or at least supplement, our paranoid models with reparative ones. But as we collectively grieve the future that did not happen and grapple with the one that continues to unfold, our paranoia (expressed in our continued collective mantra that "this is not normal") may prove to be what sustains us. This essay thus explores what it might look like to read paranoid texts reparatively. It requests, in other words, that we remain open to the textures of paranoia, receptive to strong theories and anticipatory reflexes.

I begin by sketching a broad outline of the relationship between disability and camp. Here I propose a biopolitical approach to the camp object that is attuned to objects and affects. Using this approach to rethink representations of queer and feminist psychiatric disability, I argue for the renewed relevance of lesbian comic series like Diane DiMassa's controversial *Hothead Paisan: Homicidal Lesbian Terrorist* (1999). A self-avowed "psychotic" feminist who vents her rage against heterosexism through episodes of cartoonish violence against men, Hothead presents an unconventional camp revision of feminism's canonical "madwoman in the attic." Such a practice may risk extending critical traditions that appropriate disability as a fetishized symbol of subversion. I argue instead that DiMassa's reparative embrace of paranoia, depression, and rage presents a nuanced portrait of everyday trauma in ways that anticipate contemporary camp stagings of queer and feminist psychiatric disability. Positioning Robert Eggers's anxious Puritan period piece *The Witch* (2015) as emblematic of this newer queer-crip archive, I suggest that the film trains us to take paranoia and its causes seriously. While *The Witch* gestures toward a set of caricatured associations between queerness, feminism, madness, and witchcraft, it also, more powerfully, requires its audience to adopt a stance of radical faith and confidence about women's often-disqualified experiences of depression and anxiety.

These two texts may make an incongruous pairing, with DiMassa's cartoonish depictions of queer rage sitting uneasily alongside the realism of Eggers's brooding Puritan landscapes. The dialogue in *Hothead* is littered with excessive exclamation points and is unconcerned with grammar, while *The Witch*'s painstakingly accurate lines of seventeenth-century dialect are softly spoken and difficult to follow. But in addition to their shared preoccupation with the psychic lives of women, each of these texts stages a set of feminist, queer, and crip investments that ultimately chafe against each other. In these camp visions, feminist humorlessness sits uneasily with queer parody, and psychiatric disability confounds the swagger of feminist bravado. Championing humorlessness, and modeling a reparative approach to paranoid sensibilities, Eggers and DiMassa dramatize those incongruities that remain relentlessly and hysterically unfunny. In so doing, they recalibrate our assumptions about what camp's affects are or should be.

Broken Object Lessons

Contemporary discussions of camp tend to focus on theatricality and spectacle— those outlandish performances that expose (and threaten to undo) a range of social norms through parody, exaggeration, and irreverent wit. This approach to camp reflects, to some extent, the victory of what Moe Meyer (1994: 7) has called a "performance-centered methodology" that revised earlier understandings of camp as a property of and relation between objects. Against the "objectivist bias" of camp theorists like Sontag, scholars like Meyer asserted camp as a specifically queer mode of political critique and cultural production that stresses the "agency of knowledgeable performers" (ibid.: 7–8). As a historically gay sensibility, camp reveals the extent to which all sexualities are perverse, all gender is drag, and all bodily gestures enter the realm of stylized performance. It trains us to identify and celebrate those moments when heteronormative ambitions become too ambitious to take seriously, making themselves vulnerable to parody and appropriation. Many of camp's pleasures lie in the thrill of wading into forbidden territories of representation—laying hands on those rarefied cultural forms that do not belong to us and flaunting the dirty words (faggot, dyke, queer) that have marked us as other. A performance-centered methodology, in other words, allows us to recognize camp as queer.

It has also more recently allowed us to recognize camp as crip. Disabled performers and scholars have a rich history of using parody and appropriation, from *The Scary Lewis Yell-a-Thon* (2004) to Liz Carr's more recent *Assisted Suicide: The Musical* (2016), in which Carr uses show tunes to lampoon the flimsy rhetoric of "choice" that props up most defenses of right-to-die legislation. Indeed, the earliest academic delineations of crip theory, as distinct from some of the more identitarian commitments of disability studies, were explicitly inspired by queer vocabularies of camp and animated by its performance-centered methodologies. Focusing on the "wicked humor" (Sandahl 2003: 37) and fierce irony embedded in the work of several disabled performers, crip theorists including Carrie Sandahl, Robert McRuer, and Petra Kuppers have illuminated the oppositional force that camp can have in undermining compulsory able-bodiedness.[3] Elsewhere, I have used a performance-centered methodology to make a case for reading Christopher Nolan's Joker, in the *Dark Knight* (2008), as a subversive camp agent who uses his disfigured smile to enact an important form of disability drag—what Tobin Siebers (2004) has provocatively referred to as *disability masquerade*.[4]

Asserting the theatricality of the camp *subject* over the inertia of the camp *object*, we are in many respects better positioned to assume antinormative postures. But, in line with Robyn Wiegman's observations in *Object Lessons* (2012), I now want to speculate on what theoretical objects (both literal and figurative) might be obscured in queer and crip celebrations of antinormativity, expressed in this case through a celebration of camp's calculated ironies. If a performance-centered methodology privileges the visual and the spectacular, I consider what it would look like to fashion a crip approach to camp that privileges less visible disabilities, including psychiatric impairments. Further, against theatrical models of camp that celebrate the camp subject's knowing transgression norms, the biopolitical approach that I put forward in this essay necessitates a return to the seemingly passive site of the camp object.

In one of her less-remarked-on observations in *Touching Feeling: Affect, Pedagogy, Performativity*, Eve Sedgwick (2003: 149) suggests that camp "may be seriously misrecognized when it is viewed . . . through paranoid lenses" that align it with "the projects of parody, denaturalization, demystification, and mocking exposure." Emphasizing camp as a matter of intimacy, empathy, and care, she proposes instead that we understand camp through reparative practices that involve "passionate, often hilarious antiquarianism" and "the 'over' attachment to fragmentary, marginal, waste or leftover products" (ibid.: 150).[5] In her emphasis on "waste and leftover products," Sedgwick hints at the biopolitical stakes that have always been embedded in the camp sensibility. Biopolitics describes those institutional processes and practices through which we "make live and to let die"—or, in the case of disability, designate certain bodies as better off dead. Biopolitics determines which populations are folded into life and made to thrive and which are consigned to the sphere of neglect or abandonment, marking the difference between the dignity of humanized subject and the disposability of the "lifeless" object.

With this mind, we might return to Sontag's early description of camp in 1964 as the revitalization of what has been discarded or consigned to the sphere of neglect: "It was Wilde who formulated an important element of the Camp sensibility— the equivalence of all objects—when he announced his intention of 'living up' to his blue-and-white china, or declared that a doorknob could be as admirable as a painting. When he proclaimed the importance of the necktie, the boutonniere, the chair, Wilde was anticipating the democratic *esprit* of Camp" (ibid.: 63). Sontag's emphasis on the aesthetic elements of camp—as a question of taste and an attribute of objects—has been dismissed by queer scholars as elitist, apolitical, and out of touch with the queer uses of camp as tool of political protest. But if biopolitics is a system that determines which populations are folded into life or endowed with liveness, then Sontag's seemingly apolitical model may nonetheless provide a lens for addressing the precarity of populations understood to be "discardable," and for approaching the processes of objectification and dehumanization that haunt disability. By overturning scales of aesthetic worth, in other words, camp also has the potential to overturn scales of human worth as it recalibrates the frameworks through which we name certain bodies or populations as capitalism's unwanted debris. Against dominant narratives that understand disabled and debilitated lives as surplus, excess, or drain, there may be a crip value in thinking about camp as a salvage operation focused on "the rediscovery of history's waste" (Ross 1999: 320).[6]

To explore a biopolitics of camp, then, is to lend a crip edge to John Waters's "trash aesthetic," which, as Matthew Tinkcom (2002: 157) observes, "embraces all manner of marginal subjects" including the "eccentrics" and the "downright mad." A biopolitics of camp may, for example, open up new possibilities in Siebers's (2009: 203) observation that

[t]o be disabled in the cultural imaginary is to cease to function. Our high-ways are scattered with "disabled" vehicles—sad, static things of no use or importance. Lack of movement and autonomy equals lack of ability to act and to will. . . . "How many people," Nancy Mairs asks, "do you know who would willingly take home a television set that displayed only snow or a loaf of bread that had fallen from a shelf under the wheels of a shopping cart?" Broken or discarded objects are rejected as belongings; the disabled do not belong, and rare is the human being who finds them appealing. People with disabilities are cast as objects of mourning. The feeling of grief directed at them exposes the idea that they have somehow disappeared—that they have become nothing, that they are dead—even though they may insist that they are not dead yet.

Siebers's language here is richly evocative of the camp sensibility in ways that he may not have intended, but which gesture toward a shared ethos. Under the camp eye, "broken or discarded objects" are transformed into beloved "belongings." Their lack of "function," in many cases, is part of their appeal. "What if," Tink-com (2002: 9) asks, "certain commodities betrayed the knowledge that they were destined to become 'useless'?" While a "television set that displayed only snow" may not circulate well as a capitalist commodity, its avant-garde appeal makes it exactly like the type of object one might find in the home of one of the camp queens in Newton's ([1972] 1999: 103) study who, for example, "[grew] plants in the toilet tank."

It could be argued that such comparisons further the objectification of dis-ability or frame disabled bodies as passive, dependent, and in need of rescue. While this is a valid critique, it makes sense only if we are to understand objects, as Siebers does, to be "sad static things" that are always already "dead." But mate-rialist trends in disability studies and queer theory remind us of the way objects can carry a powerful agentic force as site of relationality.[7] Refusing to enshrine or exceptionalize the category of the human, these discussions blur the lines between human and nonhuman matter in ways that create space for considering a radi-cal democracy of objects or "queer inhumanisms" (Chen and Luciano 2015). As Mel Chen (2012) argues, taking objecthood seriously means challenging the "ani-macy hierarchies" that direct us to assign agency based on (racialized, gendered, and ableist) perceptions of liveness or vitality. And in his fascinating book *The Hoarders: Material Deviance in Modern American Culture* (2014), Scott Herring notes how the perceived excesses of pathologized collecting often owe to the radi-cal inclusivity represented in the hoarder's overflowing home. Making few distinctions between valuable objects and literal trash, hoarders' democratic approach to objects confounds the culturally assigned values of the market in ways that "disregard both affective and socioeconomic worth" (Herring 2014: 81). In this respect, if there is a biopolitics of camp, it may have more to do with the "material deviance" of the hoarder than the taste-making elitism of the queer.

A biopolitics of camp thus trades the pleasures of masquerade for the objects (and affects) of queer and crip materialism. In doing so, it is engaged in the recuperation of sincerity; it asks us to envision a mode of camp whose primary structure is not rooted in irony and whose primary affect is not humor. In the case studies that follow, I discuss the peculiar system of camp humor that emerges in *Hothead Paisan* and *The Witch*, a system that might be more accurately described as camp humorlessness. Camp humorlessness extends the "mad turn" in disability studies and the biopolitical turn in queer theory by legitimating the inability to overcome one's bad feelings, to suck it up, toughen up, or make light of those experiences that we find triggering. Without banishing comedy, camp humorlessness makes ample space for depression, despair, anxiety, self-pity, and rage. It asks that we open ourselves up to the anxiety of those figures who remain, themselves, closed off to the world. It encodes a paranoid sensibility, but requires a reparative response.

Ascending Female Mirth

Initially conceived as "rage therapy" while DiMassa was in recovery for addiction and later serialized as a comic book zine between 1991 and 1996, *Hothead Paisan* is structured as a series of queer and feminist revenge fantasies in which its defiant lesbian heroine terrorizes the heteropatriarchal world that has terrorized her. Throughout the comic, she castrates street harassers, amputates the limbs of man-spreaders, and tricks gay bashers into bashing each other. In her foreword to *The Complete Hothead Paisan: Homicidal Lesbian Terrorist*, DiMassa (1999: 9) prefaces her violent queer misandrist comic with the speculation that she may be "enhanced by some magic-powder millennium fairy dust which makes everything look as silly as it actually is! If so, I hope I'm contagious. Because life on the planet E has made the complete transition into a TV movie, and you have to learn how to float a little bit above it and laugh." Here DiMassa appears to promise her reader an experience of feminist and queer camp humor in the pages that follow. The moral of the story, we are told in advance, is that the only reasonable response to living in absurd conditions is humorous detachment.

One episode that appears about halfway through the series, titled "No

Figure 1. Diane DiMassa, *The Complete Hothead Paisan: Homicidal Lesbian Terrorist*, 241

Whining Zone," seems to bear out this message. The episode begins with a meta-reflection on the comic book's unapologetic depictions of violence against men and straight people. Amid a cacophony of disapproving voices who have taken offense at DiMassa's campy vision of queer revenge, one man directs DiMassa to "stop acting so hysterical" while another salutes a penis-shaped statue bearing a placard that reads "For God, For Country, For Penis" (ibid.: 239). Meanwhile, two feminist mischief-makers, hidden around the corner, prepare the TNT. As the statue detonates, the vandals erupt in a contagious laughter. Interspersed with Venus symbols, this endlessly unfolding chain of "hahaha's" bursts out of its initial speech bubble, becoming public (female) property. Like a witch's cackle, it stretches across the following nine panels, taking over the cityscape and terrorizing the cis-men in its wake. "Fuckin' broads laughing," one observes. "I hate that shit!!" his buddy replies (ibid.: 240). Eventually, the laughter rises, making its way up to Hothead's bedroom window in a jumble of letters that reads, "HAHAHAHAAHA ASCENDING FEMALE MIRTH" (ibid.: 241). The mirth functions like an exuberant feminist alarm clock, waking up DiMassa's protagonist, who luxuriates in bed. Curiously, a mobile in the shape of a solar system hangs above her as she awakens, suggesting that female mirth may be one ticket to maintaining a healthy distance from "life on the planet E."

This vision of camp rebellion—a celebration of "offensive," defiant, political forms of feminist mirth—resonates with those forms of camp rebellion and queer visibility that were ramping up in the early 1990s as part of activist organizations like ACT UP and Queer Nation. Sara Warner (2012: 11) refers to these politicized spectacles as "acts of gaiety," which "create a pleasurable and empowering experience out of an event or situation that is hateful or painful." Warner is especially interested in using the performance histories of "gaiety" to unearth genealogies of lesbian feminist humor that have been obscured by stereotypes of lesbian humorlessness. In her chapter on *Hothead Paisan*, Warner considers how DiMassa's pre-9/11 "lesbian terrorist" resonates with and undermines the United States' contemporary "War on Terror." Dubbing Hothead a "dissident subject who shamelessly refuses to learn the lessons of history, to relinquish utopian longings, or to cede faith in revolutionary ideals," Warner (2012: 154) reveals the way "acts of gaiety" can be just as subversive as "ugly feelings" in their capacity to disrupt the homonationalist status quo. In her account, "gaiety" emerges not as an uncomplicated description of positive feeling but as a "technology of endurance and agency for 'arranging grief'" through which feminist and queer subjects "begin to believe a better future is possible" (ibid.: xiv).

While I appreciate Warner's willingness to disrupt queer theory's antirelational attachments to negative affects, from a mad feminist perspective, I am interested in sitting a little bit longer with lesbian humorlessness. Despite the buoyant camp vision depicted in "No Whining Zone," the full context of the series unveils these moments of female mirth as an aspirational fantasy. Even when we want to, it is not always possible to "float a little bit above [the planet] and laugh." Often, we lack the resources to arrange our grief into gaiety. When we do manage to summon laughter, we may only be moments away from tears. Indeed, as Hothead's feline sidekick, Chicken, observes in the third epigraph, "First she's funny for a few minutes. . . . Then bam! She loses her shit!!" Thus in the image of the mobile described earlier, it is a notable inversion that it is the planets that hang suspended above Hothead and not the other way around. Hothead's miniaturized solar system may create perspective and relief, but it does so only through a trick of scale. As the laughter dies down, Hothead must rejoin a world to which her primary physical and affective orientation is gravity.

Hothead's grave approach is authorized, in part, by her paranoia. As Megan Milks (2010) has noted, Hothead is established from the start as a quintessentially "paranoid reader." In the first issue, Hothead is visited by a demonic figure who materializes in her living room, promising both protection and relief from the unrelenting stream of heterosexism and misogyny she encounters in both the media and her daily life: "You 'n me against the rotten stinkin' world, OK? Don't every listen to anyone again! Be really defensive all the time! You need me! Wear me like a coat! Remember, if you space out for one second the Stepfords will get you! . . . I'll always be here to protect you so you'll never feel a thing!! I'll give you all the answers!!" (ibid.: 17–20). In this brief monologue, Hothead's demon equips her with the essential tools of paranoid reading. He provides her with "strong theory" whose lack of nuance provides endless reach ("I'll give you all the answers"). He blocks negative affects rather than cultivate positive ones ("you'll never feel a thing"); the price of his protection is numbness. Placing "faith in exposure," Hothead relies on her superior knowledge of the world to develop an "anticipatory" approach to violence. She understands, in other words, that the best (or only) defense is a good offense. Accepting her demonic coat of armor with eager relief, Hothead becomes an untouchable dispenser of vigilante justice. Her paranoia inspires her to take graphically violent action against rapists, street harassers, clueless heterosexuals, medical patriarchs, and everyday bearers of male privilege.[8]

Indeed, if Hothead were a superhero, this would constitute her origin story. After her transformative encounter with the demon, the first panel of the following issue reads: "I wonder what would happen if say, some lesbian really checked out for lunch, you know, like say her brain just totally shit the bed one day, and she starts believing everything she sees on TV. So, like, while she's going about her daily queer routine, all this TV crap is seeping in, and she's getting psychotic, and like she needs therapy really bad, but she doesn't know it? I bet her boundaries would be really fuzzy. I bet she'd be lots of fun to be around. I bet she'd be a real Hothead Paisan" (ibid.: 21). On the one hand, DiMassa's framing here risks reinscribing feminist theory's problematic glamorization of madness-as-rebellion.[9] Declaring herself "nuts!" and on "permanent disability" (ibid.: 62), Hothead emerges as a "fun" "psychotic" lesbian action hero, complete with her own theme song: "This is the legend of Hothead Paisan, / no time for guilt, and packin' a gun. / Some say I'm insane but it's simply this: / Stand tall when you walk and don't take any shit!" (ibid.: 172). Saucy and irreverent, clearheaded in the face of those who would diagnose her otherwise, endowed with supernatural strength and agility, Hothead would seem to be yet another example of the camp appropriation of psychiatric disability, as the "madwoman in the attic" is rescripted as a fearless feminist crusader.

But it is important to recognize that while Hothead may appear capacitated by her "madness," DiMassa is more interested in the conditions of Hothead's precarity as a queer, a feminist, and a crip. Indeed, Hothead's struggle throughout twenty issues is precisely her failure to rise above her circumstances, to separate from the context of her oppression, to laugh at her situation instead of crying, even as she desperately wants to experience and sustain the lightness that the camp sensibility promises to provide. As her preface suggests, DiMassa does not reject the "ecstasy" of floating above one's circumstances through camp humor. She does, however, take seriously the effort required to produce these moments of mirthful detachment and the difficulty in maintaining them.

With this in mind, I would like to briefly return to Newton's ([1972] 1999: 106) observation that "when the camp cannot laugh, he dissolves into a maudlin bundle of self-pity." Newton follows this observation with an extended quote drawn from her interview with one camp performer, who explains that a camp queen "makes the other homosexuals laugh; he makes life a little brighter for them. And he builds a bridge to the straight people by getting them to laugh with him. . . . Very seldom is camp sad. Camp has got to be flip. A camp queen's got to think faster than other queens. . . . She's sort of made light of a bad situation" (ibid.: 107). In this framing, the camp queen subtly morphs into a figure that disability scholars might recognize as the "supercrip." Camp reminds us of the plucky resilience required to overcome the obstacles we encounter when navigating the homophobic world. Thus the camp queen's positive attitude and ability to maintain a sense of humor in the face of adversity dance dangerously close to the kinds of inspirational narratives we require disabled people to perform. In her humor and wit, the camp queen provides proof of her psychological well-being, her unshakeability, and even her physical stamina. Newton concludes her analysis of camp humor with the observation that a "camp queen in good form can come out on top . . . against all the competition," and her "verbal agility" furthermore "reinforces the superiority of the live performers" (ibid.: 107). Emphasizing "good form," "agility," "superiority," and "competition," Newton's camp performer is queen of the jungle, evidence that only the fittest (or wittiest) survive.

While this single interviewee's perspective in 1972 is not the definitive statement on camp, I invoke it here for the contrast it provides to Hothead's refusal to "build a bridge" to the straight world through shared laughter. Too resentful to

embody the mirthful detachment of the camp queen, Hothead is a quintessentially *bad* camp. She is not interested in or capable of making the world brighter
for anyone, including her queer comrades who express frequent concern over her
ongoing anxiety and depression. This is not to say that the series banishes comedy.
It was nominated for a 1993 Lambda Literary Award in the category of humor,
and Hothead's regular episodes of homicidal violence are interspersed with many
laughable moments. But often the humor derives precisely from Hothead's stub-
born refusal or inability to take a joke, and many of the funniest moments in the
text are those in which Hothead asserts herself as a feminist killjoy.

Responding to a therapist's suggestion that "when life gives you lemons,
make lemonade," Hothead counters, "When your shrink gives you a cliché, throw
a bomb at her!!" Against ads that declare that "a diamond is forever," Hothead's
version asserts that "a diamond is disgusting" (ibid.: 27). Finally, in one of Hothead's most memorable killjoy camp inversions, she uses a discarded bike pump
to inflate a steroid-infused jock until he floats up into the sky and explodes. As
his remains fall back to earth, Hothead opens an umbrella and sings, "It's raining
men, hallelujah!!" (ibid.: 159). In this sense, Hothead reclaims camp reclamation,
transforming (or reverting) the buoyant gay anthem into a bitter killjoy spectacle.
The joke is always tinged with too much anger and too much resentment.

In another scene, after castrating a street harasser, Hothead sets out to
determine just what use she can make of his severed penis (ibid.: 21). Attempting
to imagine its functionality as a microphone, a magic wand, a football, a dog treat,
a meditation tool, or even (in true camp fashion) as a valuable antique, Hothead
ultimately determines that this coveted commodity is, in fact, useless, and drops
it into the garbage disposal. This scene feels campy in its exaggeration, humor,
and irreverence. But it also evidences Hothead's inability to adopt camp's "trash
aesthetic," expressed in its trademark commitment to deinstrumentalized objecthood. While the camp practitioner rescues objects that have been discarded, con-
ferring new life by aestheticizing them, Hothead has no interest in salvaging or
aestheticizing the severed member. Instead, she revels in its disposability; literally
detached from its original context in ways that make it unable to function properly
as a phallus, it becomes nothing more than waste slotted for disposal.[10]

I want to be clear that, in describing Hothead's failure to adequately
embody the camp aesthetic, I am resisting queer theory's impulse to celebrate or
romanticize failure as a transgressive state. Pointing to what she calls the "bad
romance" between queer theory and disability studies, Merri Lisa Johnson (2015:
253) describes her wariness of queer "critical trends that flirt cheerfully with
precarity" and her concern that "the conflation of madness with countercultural

adventure both reflects and contributes to the cultural trivialization of psychological pain." For Johnson, this impulse largely "disregards the 'feels like shit' dimension of failure, its lightheartedness striking a dissonant note" against many of failure's graver consequences (ibid.: 255).

In a progression titled "Hothead Has the Fuck-Its," DiMassa directly confronts the "'feels like shit' dimension of failure" in ways that contend seriously with its negative affects. Hothead's "fuck-its," it is crucial to note, differ significantly from the ironic and irreverent "fuck-its" of contemporary Internet meme culture. One recent meme, for example, campily pairs an image of Maria dancing exuberantly among the Swiss Alps in *The Sound of Music* with the caption "LOOK AT ALL THE FUCKS I GIVE." By contrast, Hothead's "fuck-its" come with a complex symptomology of disordered eating, suicidal ideations, resignation, despair, numbness, and boredom. "Can't figure out what to eat, so I'll fuckin' be a skeleton. Who gives a fuck?" she tells the reader (DiMassa 1999: 294). "Whipped" and "bored," she considers masturbating, but puts it off because of menstrual cramps and bowel issues (ibid.: 295–96). Observing that coffee and food no longer "work" at keeping suicidal thoughts at bay, she explains that she "can't stand to live" and "is too tired to die" (ibid.: 349). "I can't take it anymore. There's no place left to hide," she concludes, as a miniaturized version of herself begins to slowly drown in a bucket of water (ibid.). With its life-and-death stakes, Hothead's failure to give a fuck is neither a "cheerful flirtation with precarity" nor an ironic gesture of queer rebellion; it is a snapshot of a self-defeating pattern in which she painfully accepts, and nearly enacts, those scripts that render her always already dead.

In another scene, feeling pressed out of existence, Hothead rails against a world that refuses to make space for her. "What am I supposed to do?!?!," she asks her friend Roz. "Have a cup of tea at the end of a hard day of being belittled, humiliated, berated? Held down shoved aside, mowed over, swept under, stifled, stunted, stepped on, snowed . . . hawked, stalked, smashed, bashed, and even . . . " (ibid.: 136). From here, the panel shifts to a gravestone that displays the heading "Killed." Below is a brief poem that reads: "Here lies some queer, / It don't matter who. / Cause we don't care, / And we'll get you, too!" (ibid.). As these panels progress, the previously bold font of Hothead's speech breaks down into tense scribbles, encoding her panic. In sharp contrast, the epitaph written on the nameless gravestone is etched with careful precision, revealing the hyperlegibility of homophobia and its threat to queer livelihood. As Hothead's words break down on the page, so does she, sobbing into Roz's lap. Roz holds her close, responding "I know, I know" (ibid.: 137).

One of several interludes in the series in which Hothead "dissolves into

Figure 2. Diane DiMassa, *The Complete Hothead Paisan: Homicidal Lesbian Terrorist*, 136

a maudlin bundle of self-pity," this scene is striking in the way it reconfigures the usual affects and relations of the camp sensibility. If Newton's camp queen performs a kind of resilient overcoming in her ability to make light of a bad situation, then Hothead's crip vulnerabilities are apparent in her inability to take in stride the insults of a world that would stomp her under its boot. Note, too, the grammar that separates the agency of Newton's camp queen from Hothead's feminist, queer, and crip passivity. While the camp queen "makes," "builds," "thinks," and "laughs," Hothead is "hawked, stalked, smashed, and bashed." In short, Hothead is more of a camp object than a camp subject.[11] Outside the biopolitical fold, always already "dead" or dehumanized, she is just another queer whose name is "Killed." Exhausted by her paranoia, what she requires is not laughter, parody, or demystification; she already knows everything she needs to know about her own precarity. What she needs, instead, is the reparative touch of someone who believes and accepts her reality.

Feeling like shit, in this context, is both an affective and an epistemological state. It reflects, but is not reducible to, her biopolitical status as a worthless object or disposable matter. Indeed, while Hothead may be a bad camp in her failure to salvage the "functionless" penis, in the act of disposing of it, she is engaged in the inverse work of understanding herself as recuperable. Eliminating those objects that threaten her vitality—her right to simply exist in the world—Hothead forces us to consider how her own lesbian, feminist, crip body holds the potential to persist, like Siebers's broken television, as potentially beloved trash.

Lauren Berlant (2017: 307) explores "*humorlessness* comedy" as "an aesthetics that plays out in the searing incongruities of [a character's] desire to move toward and away from himself and the world." It is related to a "fundamental intractability in oneself or in others" and "*the desire for comedy* that structures the protagonist's actions" (ibid.: 308, 309). Humorlessness happens, in other words, when incongruities are experienced as dead serious. In Hothead's case, camp humorlessness relates to the emotional strain of maintaining the disconnect between her personal reality (what she knows to be true) and the crushing weight of her social reality (what mainstream culture circulates as truth). As these mutually negating realities chafe against each other, Hothead has limited options. She can become "well-adjusted" by adjusting herself to a world that invalidates her existence; she can maintain a paranoid relation to the world; she can eliminate the enemy so that her truth reigns; or she can "learn to float a little bit above it and laugh" (DiMassa 1999: 9). Hothead adopts all these coping mechanisms, at different moments, and to different effects. As a humorless comedic subject, she moves both "toward and away from herself and the world," trapped between her desire for comedy and her inability to access the necessary space and distance that would allow her to become a flexible camp subject.

Ultimately, Hothead's relation to camp becomes a question of spatialization, as she grasps for a way to orient herself in relation to a world that has no place for her.[12] When she experiences brief moments of weightlessness, she is not defying gravity but obeying the pull of contradictory forces, vacillating between rage and retreat, violence and self-care, paranoid and depressive positions. In one issue, she occupies a personal "black hole" that allows her to "retreat" into herself "because we are all way too smart to believe that this world is real. Your blackhole is where you are when you are. It's yours, yours, yours" (DiMassa 1999: 298). Hothead's black hole is a space of humorless intractability, a refusal to make the "microadjustments" necessary to adapt to a world too ridiculous to be credible but too powerful to dismiss. As she maneuvers this impasse, she asserts her biopolitical right to exist by sliding beside, invading into, diving below, turning inward, and even, at certain brief moments, rising above. At one point in the narrative, Hothead's perpetually laughing love interest Daphne explains: "I laugh at the world cause I have such a small place in it. It keeps me sane" (ibid.: 311). Staying "sane," in this context, need not signify as an ableist injunction to "get better." It may instead name the combination of hope and resignation encoded in those small actions through which we attempt to make the world meet us where we are.

Recovering Puritans

Sometimes, in order to survive, feminists and queers need to barter with the devil. Eggers's horror film *The Witch: A New-England Folktale* ends the way *Hothead Paisan* begins, with its protagonist making a demonic pact. In the film's climatic final scene, Thomasin has withstood all that she can endure. Her family has been doubly displaced, exiled from the Puritan settlement after having already "travail[ed] a vast ocean," "leaving [their] country and kindred" on their conviction that they have been divinely chosen. As they attempt to survive alone in the wilderness, Thomasin's baby brother is murdered by a witch (who, we soon learn, gains the power of flight after bathing in the infant's blood). Thomasin's adolescent brother dies under similar circumstances, and her remaining family members suspect her as the cause of the witchcraft. After her father is gored to death by the family goat and her mother attempts to strangle her in a paranoid rage, Thomasin is forced to bash in her mother's skull with a rock in self-defense. Alone and lacking options, she summons the devil.

"Wouldst thou like to live deliciously?" he asks. "Wouldst thou like to see the world?" The only possible answer is yes. Thomasin signs a book, removes her clothes, and allows herself to be guided into the woods, where a cabal of naked women dance wildly and chant witchy incantations around a bonfire. As the magic takes hold, they slowly start to float above the ground. Pulled into the demonic circle, Thomasin, too, begins to ascend and then begins to laugh. As she laughs, a prolonged and intimate close-up on her face, bathed in the fire's orange glow, reveals the depth of her ecstasy, or perhaps just the extent of her relief. In the film's final moments, this extreme close-up is abruptly replaced with an extreme long shot of the tree-lined landscape. Thomasin's naked body floats, illuminated, in front of the peak of the tallest pine, revealing her shocking distance above the earth. Thomasin's final ascent literalizes DiMassa's (1999: 9) injunction to "float a little bit above it and laugh," as well as Newton's ([1972] 1999: 106) description of the camp practitioner as a person with the capacity to "laugh at [their] incongruous position instead of crying," and who laughs even at situations that others might find "horrifying or tragic." Levitating among the pines, Thomasin has indeed risen above her circumstances. Her laughter is possible only because of the critical distance she has managed to create and maintain (in this case, one hundred or two hundred feet) between herself and the world that has injured her. She is a good camp and, arguably, a good queer.

I believe that there are two camp readings of this scene. The first uses a traditionally queer methodology to locate camp humor and erotic transgression in Thomasin's ultimate decision to "live deliciously" as a witch. Witchcraft, after all, has long been associated with queer sexual deviance and feminist rebellion. The witch's connection to the supernatural links her to the *unnatural* and the morally perverse.[13] Marilee Lindemann (2000: 758) describes "the cultural compulsion to label certain types of (usually female) deviant behavior as witchery, a threat to social order, to bodily integrity, and to life itself." Indeed, as we watch the crone's hand drag a knife across the stomach of Thomasin's infant brother, Sam, there can be no doubt of her status as reproductive futurity's unapologetic enemy. It would seem, then, that witches are ripe for contemporary camp reclaimings, particularly in the era of what *Slate* writer Amanda Hess (2014) calls "ironic misandry." Hess explains that "feminists are ironically embracing the man-hating label: The ironic misandrist sips from a mug marked 'MALE TEARS,' frosts her cakes with the phrase 'KILL ALL MEN,' and affixes 'MISANDRY' heart pins to her lapel" and wears T-shirts proclaiming "I BATHE IN MALE TEARS." Ironic misandry, in other words, transforms female vulnerability into feminist bravado. While *The Witch*'s witch may not bathe in male tears (yet), she does concoct a levitating spell from the blood of male infants. Ironic misandry is what allow us to celebrate baby Samuel's demise, rather than mourn his loss.

These linkages make it easy to celebrate Thomasin's eventual satanic conversion as the climax of her gradual sexual awakening. She begins the narrative in prayer, apologizing to God for following the "desires of [her] own will," for which she "deserve[s] all shame." But as her perverse coming-out story culminates, Thomasin gains the courage and irreverence to speak back to patriarchal authority. Her complaints of being a "slave" to her father's laundry transform into a full-scale disobedience as she rails at him in one of the film's concluding scenes with a set of emasculating proclamations. "You are a hypocrite!" she tells him. "You cannot bring the crops to yield! You cannot hunt! . . . Thou canst do nothing save cut wood!" Soon after her verbal explosion, her father, William, is attacked by Black Phillip, the family goat, who we soon learn is Satan in disguise. Impaled by one of Black Phillip's horns, William is thrown into an enormous stack of wood, which collapses on top of him. Crushed under the weight of his own phallic inadequacies, his demise looks nothing so much as one of Hothead Paisan's scenes of gory revenge.

But there is a problem with this reading, and that is the film's banishment of irony. Like much of *Hothead*, its affects are dead serious in ways that cause our usual queer methodologies to flail. As the fate of Thomasin's baby brother reminds us, weightlessness can carry a steep price, and gaiety cannot always be sustained without supernatural aids. Though it is tempting to find camp relief in the film's ending, I would contend that its humorlessness asks us to take Thomasin's pact with the devil for exactly what it is—evidence of the compromises we make when we have run out of options. If camp humorlessness in *Hothead* had to do with DiMassa's protagonist's inability to take a joke, then camp humorlessness emerges in *The Witch*, in part, as a function of Thomasin's inability to *make* a joke. When her obnoxious younger sister Mercy follows her as she does her chores, singing about the witch of the woods, Thomasin decides to have some fun at Mercy's expense, telling her, "I am that very witch. When I sleep my spirit slips away from my body and dances naked with the Devil. That's how I signed his book. He bade me bring him an unbaptized babe, so I stole Sam, and I gave him to my master. And I'll make any man or thing else vanish I like. . . . And I'll vanish thee too if thou displeaseth me." Of course, by the end of the film, Thomasin will have performed each of the actions she names here in jest. She "dances naked with the Devil" after having "signed his book." And while she may not have willingly given up Sam to the devil, her new life as his servant will doubtless require her to bathe in the blood (or tears) of similar male children or adults. If camp irony works to dethrone moral seriousness by revealing our truths to be fictions, *The Witch* inverts these terms by revealing that what may feel like fiction has the potential to become the truth. As absurd scenarios take shape as reality, it is no longer possible to maintain a critical distance, no longer possible, in other words, to derive humor from incongruity.

There is arguably no greater enemy to queerness than Puritanism. But despite, or perhaps because of this fact, I believe that queer readings practices can be enriched by approaching Puritan paranoia reparatively, exchanging some of our attachments to perversity, irony, and transgression with new forms of faith and new suspensions of disbelief. In its sympathetic portrayal of Puritan hysteria, the film gives us a sympathetic portrait of forms of mental distress that get dismissed as merely hysterical or as overreactions to otherwise reasonable circumstances. In writing the film, Eggers lifted much of his dialogue directly from seventeenth- and eighteenth-century primary documents drawn from firsthand accounts of witchcraft. While such appropriations are often mobilized ironically, Eggers describes his attempts to remain faithful to his Puritan source material through a commitment to craft. He explains that "in every frame, it had to be like I'm articulating my own personal memory of childhood as if I was a Puritan remember [*sic*] the way my dad smelled in the cornfield that morning and the way the mist was hanging in the air." To do this required attention to "the way the saw marks look on the floorboards in the garret" or re-creating a lantern made from horn "half from scratch." In his desire to inhabit a Puritan psychology and his attunement to what it feels like to be a Puritan (its textures, colors, and even its smells), Eggers presents what we might call a humorless camp spectacle that does not unmask his source material as much as nurture it.

To take a reparative approach to Puritan paranoia might require that we focus not only on Thomasin's rebellion but on her mother's depression and anxiety. Katherine emerges throughout the film as the quintessential humorless Puritan whose repressive attitudes and narrow adherence to scriptural norms cause her to reject her own daughter. Yet she is also the character who most invites a feminist disability studies reading. In her final, and ultimately fatal, encounter with Thomasin, she shrieks at her daughter: "You are smeared of his sin. You reek of Evil. You have made a covenant with death! You bewitched thy brother, proud slut! . . . And thy father next! You took them from me! They are gone! You killed my children! You killed thy father! Witch! Witch!" This is undoubtedly antiqueer, slut-shaming moralism at its most virulent. But can we also bring ourselves to see Katherine's pain, her grief, and her sense of powerlessness in a world that has crumbled under her feet? As the film progresses, we witness her lose her community, bear the excruciating loss of her infant son, process the reality that the crop yield will not be enough to sustain them, and watch as her elder son and husband die in front of her.

Early in the film, as she grieves the loss of her son, William assures her that she "lookst too much upon this affliction," that the Lord has simply "taken us into . . . a very low condition to humble us and to show us more of his grace," and that she has "been ungrateful of God's love." But Katherine is not wrong when she declares to her husband that God "hath cursed this family." William wants her to cheerfully overcome her "affliction," to adjust to her circumstances, to laugh at her incongruous situation rather than crying, but Katherine simply cannot. Indeed, Katherine's emotional reaction to her trauma is precisely what allows her to face realities others refuse to acknowledge, making her, ironically, the most credible character in the film, even as she is the most "hysterical." Despite William's attempt to discredit her sense of fear, paranoia, and doubt, the truth remains: it is not a wolf but a witch who stole her infant son. Her family is doomed, and Christ's help is anywhere but near. When Thomasin kills her, audiences do not cheer, because there is no winning when the marginalized turn against each other.

Amplifying camp's status as a reparative and therapeutic gesture, both *Hothead* and *The Witch* excavate camp's biopolitical dimensions. I have argued that the biopolitics of camp checks our impulse to distance ourselves through humor, calling instead for forms of radical empathy and openness to a multiplicity of bodies, objects, and affective states. It asks us to cultivate, paradoxically, a nonparanoid approach to paranoia. To advocate for a reparative approach to paranoia, I want to be clear, is not necessarily to advocate a return to paranoid reading. Rather, it is to argue that anxiety is a legitimate response to trauma—particularly those forms of trauma that attach to (or form the preexisting condition of) lives lived outside the biopolitical fold.

In a *New Yorker* cartoon published prior to the election, a wolf in politician's garb appears on a billboard stationed above rolling hills dotted with sheep. The slogan next to his picture reads "I am going to eat you," prompting one sheep to observe to another, "He tells it like it is." Sometimes what looks like paranoia may simply be a matter of having learned to see what is right in front of you. We are not wrong to believe that there are monsters under the bed, witches in the woods, and big bad wolves who will blow our house down. To cope with these realities often requires that we find a way to maneuver between engagement and retreat, staring down and looking away. In these landscapes, camp requires a reparative touch. One recently developed Chrome browser plug-in, called "Make America Kittens Again," provides a campy service to those who find Trump's face triggering, by replacing every picture of our current commander in chief with cat photos. The resulting incongruities may not elicit laughter, but they do make it slightly more bearable to read the news.

Notes

I am grateful to M. Milks for thinking through these ideas with me and providing feedback on earlier drafts of this essay, and to the special issue coeditors and anonymous readers for their perceptive and useful suggestions.

1. We might here recall, with some camp irony, the self-proclaimed "little monsters" who make up the fan base of the camp icon (and "Mother Monster") Lady Gaga. But while Gaga's little monsters embrace otherness, the modified picture book banishes any trace of unruliness or "monstrosity" in Sesame Street's arguably diverse monster population.

2. Here I extend a critical genealogy of "cripping" queer representation and methodology, which began with Robert McRuer (2005) and Carrie Sandahl (2003) and has been extended in the work of Alison Kafer (2013).

3. In coining the term *crip* in 2003, Sandahl (2003: 38) explores how disabled performers theatricalize disability, including Robert DeFelice, who reveals "the telethon's latent queer campiness by spinning the pageantry of crippled children walking and talking into something akin to runway modeling." Kuppers (2002: 190) calls attention to Mat Fraser's "self-aware referencing and playful citing" of dandy style, which undermines the supposed naturalness of both disability and masculinity. And in his foundational *Crip Theory*, McRuer (2006: 31) identifies the crip value of several queer activist visions, from the parodic interventions of ACT UP to Audre Lorde's call for an "army of one-breasted women" to overtake Washington.

4. See Barounis 2013 and Siebers 2004.

5. In taking up Sedgwick's approach to camp, I am building on a genealogy of queer affect theory that centralizes shame, backwardness, depression, and other "ugly feelings." See Love 2007, Ngai 2005, Ahmed 2010, Freeman 2010, and Cvetkovich 2012.

6. See Ross 1999.

7. See Chen 2012, Herring 2014, and Kim 2015.

8. While a discussion of the comic book form is beyond the scope of this essay, it is important to note the role that graphic narrative (*graphic* in every sense of the word) plays in these violent fantasies. Ironically, for DiMassa, comics function as a way to unleash a set of affects that are not always comedic and, indeed, often humorless.

9. See Johnson 2015, 2013, Donaldson 2011, Mollow 2014, and Prendergast 2008.

10. For a reading of Hothead's relationship to the Phallus, see Dean 1997.

11. Newton and her participants refer to individuals as "camps," employing a somewhat outdated but intriguing use of the term, which gestures toward its slippery grammar as both subject and object.

12. As Dana Heller (1993) observes of the comic, Hothead's primary mission is to "clear a space" for lesbian existence in an oversaturated heterosexist culture.

13. In her canonical "Thinking Sex," Gayle Rubin ([1984] 2007) repeatedly uses the term *witch hunts* to describe the moral panics that lead to the scapegoating and persecution of erotic deviants.

References

Ahmed, Sara. 2010. *The Promise of Happiness*. Durham, NC: Duke University Press.

Barounis, Cynthia. 2013. "'Why So Serious?': Cripping Camp Performance in Christopher Nolan's *The Dark Knight*." *Journal of Literary and Cultural Disability Studies* 7, no. 3: 305–20.

Berlant, Lauren. 2017. "Humorlessness (Three Monologues and a Hairpiece)." *Critical Inquiry* 40: 305–40.

Chen, Mel. 2012. *Animacies: Biopolitics, Racial Mattering, and Queer Affect*. Durham, NC: Duke University Press.

Chen, Mel, and Dana Luciano. 2015. "Introduction: Has the Queer Ever Been Human?" *GLQ* 21, nos. 2–3: 183–207.

Cvetkovich, Ann. 2012. *Depression: A Public Feeling*. Durham, NC: Duke University Press.

Dean, Gabrielle N. 1997. "The 'Phallacies' of Dyke Comic Strips." In *The Gay '90s: Disciplinary and Interdisciplinary Formations in Queer Studies*, edited by Thomas Foster et al., 199–223. New York: New York University Press.

DiMassa, Diane. 1999. *The Complete Hothead Paisan: Homicidal Lesbian Terrorist*. San Francisco: Cleis.

Donaldson, Elizabeth J. 2011. "Revisiting the Corpus of the Madwoman: Further Notes toward a Feminist Disability Studies Theory of Mental Illness." In *Feminist Disability Studies*, edited by Kim Q. Hall, 91–114. Bloomington: Indiana University Press.

Freeman, Elizabeth. 2010. *Time Binds: Queer Temporalities, Queer Histories*. Durham, NC: Duke University Press.

Heller, Dana. 1993. "Hothead Paisan: Clearing a Space for Lesbian Feminist Folklore." *New York Folklore* 19, nos. 1–2: 27–44.

Herring, Scott. 2014. *The Hoarders: Material Deviance in Modern American Culture*. Chicago: University of Chicago Press.

Hess, Amanda. 2014. "The Rise of the Ironic Man-Hater." *Slate*, August 8, 2014. www .slate.com/blogs/xx_factor/2014/08/08/ironic_misandry_why_feminists_joke_about _drinking_male_tears_and_banning.html.

Kafer, Alison. 2013. *Feminist, Queer, Crip*. Bloomington: Indiana University Press.

Kim, Eunjung. 2015. "Unbecoming Human: An Ethics of Objects." *GLQ* 21, nos. 2–3: 295–320.

Johnson, Merri Lisa. 2013. "Label C/Rip." *Social Text Online*, socialtextjournal.org /periscope_article/label-crip.

———. 2015. "Bad Romance: A Crip Feminist Critique of Queer Failure." *Hypatia* 30, no. 1: 252–67.

Kuppers, Petra. 2002. "Image Politics without the Real: Simulacra, Dandyism, and Disability Fashion." In *Disability and Postmodernity*, edited by Mairian Corker and Tom Shakespeare, 184–97. London: Continuum.

Lindemann, Marilee. 2000. "Who's Afraid of the Big Bad Witch? Queer Studies in American Literature." *American Literary History* 12, no. 4: 757–70.

Love, Heather. 2007. *Feeling Backward: Loss and the Politics of Queer History*. Cambridge, MA: Harvard University Press.

McRuer, Robert. 2006. *Crip Theory: Cultural Signs of Queerness and Disability*. New York: New York University Press.

Meyer, Moe. 1994. Introduction to *The Politics and Poetics of Camp*, edited by Moe Meyer, 1–19. New York: Routledge.

Milks, Megan. 2010. "So I Want to Kill This [Spritzhead]: Paranoia in Tori Amos, Hot-head Paisan, and Reading/Writing Generally." *Montevidayo*, montevidayo.com /2010/10/so-i-want-to-kill-this-spritzhead-paranoia-in-tori-amos-hothead-paisan-and -readingwriting-generally/.

Mollow, Anna. 2014. "Criphystemologies: What Disability Theory Needs to Know about Hysteria." *Journal of Literary and Cultural Disability Studies* 8, no. 2: 185–201.

Newton, Esther. [1972] 1999. "Role Models." In *Camp: Queer Aesthetics and the Performing Subject—a Reader*, edited by Fabio Cleto, 96–109. Ann Arbor: University of Michigan Press.

Ngai, Sianne. 2005. *Ugly Feelings.* Cambridge, MA: Harvard University Press.

Prendergast, Catherine. 2008. "The Unexceptional Schizophrenic: A Post-Postmodern Introduction." *Journal of Literary and Cultural Disability Studies* 2, no. 1: 55–62.

Ross, Andrew. 1999. "The Uses of Camp." In *Camp: Queer Aesthetics and the Performing Subject—a Reader*, edited by Fabio Cleto, 308–29. Ann Arbor: University of Michigan Press.

Rubin, Gayle. [1984] 2007. "Thinking Sex: Notes for a Radical Theory of the Politics of Sexuality." In *Culture, Society, and Sexuality: A Reader*, 2nd ed., edited by Richard Parker and Peter Aggleton, 150–86. New York: Routledge.

Sandahl, Carrie. 2003. "Queering the Crip or Cripping the Queer? Intersections of Queer and Crip Identities in Solo Autobiographical Performance." *GLQ* 9, nos. 1–2: 25–56.

Sedgwick, Eve Kosofsky. 2003. *Touching Feeling: Affect, Pedagogy, Performativity.* Durham, NC: Duke University Press.

Siebers, Tobin. 2004. "Disability as Masquerade." *Literature and Medicine* 23, no. 1: 1–22.

———. 2009. "Sex, Shame, and Disability Identity." In *Gay Shame*, edited by David Halperin and Valerie Traub, 201–16. Chicago: University of Chicago Press.

Sontag, Susan. [1964] 1999. "Notes on Camp." In *Camp: Queer Aesthetics and the Performing Subject—a Reader*, edited by Fabio Cleto, 53–65. Ann Arbor: University of Michigan Press.

Tinkcom, Matthew. 2002. *Working like a Homosexual: Camp, Capital, Cinema.* Durham, NC: Duke University Press.

Warner, Sara. 2012. *Acts of Gaiety: LGBT Performance and the Politics of Pleasure.* Ann Arbor: University of Michigan Press.

Wiegman, Robyn. 2012. *Object Lessons.* Durham, NC: Duke University Press.

The Witch: A New-England Folktale. 2015. Dir. Robert Eggers. New York: A24 Films.

OFFSETTING QUEER LITERARY LABOR

Samuel Solomon

"You're an electronic technician,
not a typesetter. You're lucky
to be shut out of the union."

I know that typesetters
grow more capillaries
in our fingertips
from all that use.

here's a test: cut my fingers
and see if I bleed more.
—Karen Brodine, *Woman Sitting at the Machine, Thinking*

This article works through the poems of Marxist-feminist writer Karen Brodine in order to explain how LGBTQ+ people and other feminists in the United States navigated late twentieth-century changes in print technology between 1965 and 1990, and to explore how this navigation shaped literary production in this period. During these years typesetting was computerized and then all but abandoned as part of the preprint process. Brodine was one of many working-class LGBTQ+ people, especially, but not only, lesbians and transmasculine workers, who found employment as typesetters in the 1970s and 1980s. While she is not the only writer whose work navigates the feminized and racialized class politics of new forms of printing labor, Brodine is singular in the extent to which the labor relations of typesetting are in full view at the surface of her writing. An excerpt from her 1981 poem "Woman Sitting at the Machine, Thinking" provides my epigraph. Even from this short excerpt, it is easy to see how this poem takes contested

GLQ 24:2–3
DOI 10.1215/10642684-4324801
© 2018 by Duke University Press

labor relations as sites for the development and elaboration of bodily capacities and skills, and not only of those that are a part of "work." Brodine's reference to the capillarization of fingers is not only clinically descriptive; it also evokes other possible uses of digital strength and dexterity and of bloodletting, including those that might be more properly considered the domain of a pulp novel. Brodine accounts for the intertwining of intimacy and labor; her writing brings together the material production of literature with late twentieth-century working-class lesbian and queer life in the United States.

In the 1960s and 1970s, typesetting for large-run print jobs in the United States underwent an unevenly distributed but rapid shift from "linotype" (a popular brand-name for "line casting," heavy machinery that casts hot metal "slugs") to phototypesetting (basically two dimensional). This shift in prepress technologies complemented the slightly earlier transition in large-scale printing from letterpress to photo-offset lithography. In each case, the technology shifted from three-dimensional impressions to two-dimensional photographic processes for creating printing plates and for getting ink onto the final printing surface.[1] Phototypesetting technologies were constantly innovating during this period, and they involved the computerized storage of layout and copy data, whether in punched tape or microchips, to create film negatives that could be developed onto metal plates for printing.

By the 1990s, typesetting as a distinct phase in the printing process was superseded by desktop and online publishing, while offset lithography remains to this day the go-to method for large-scale print runs of newspapers and books. The expansion of phototypesetting in the 1960s and 1970s had required that the mostly white and male linotype operators be retrained or else that new workers be drafted to take their place. These new workers were frequently women who could be paid less. Both the materials for and the relations of origination (prepress) work were dramatically changed by this process, which involved the painful busting of old trade unions dominated by white males and the opportunistic employment by industrial bosses of nonunion workers previously excluded from these jobs. In other words: the politics of these new labor relations were deeply ambivalent.

It was also in the wake of this transition that "lesbian and gay" literature came into prominence as a category among publishers, booksellers, printers, educators, and activists. This was the period in which the particular complex of text, labor, collectivity, and printed matter that we might call "LGBT literature" was quite literally composed. In this essay I consider how gender and sexual categories, as well as queer forms of intimacy, were forged through the material relations of print-related wage work. Rather than claim to "queer" these texts or this history,

I would suggest that the category of LGBT literature came about partly through the feminized and racialized labor that still attends literary technologies.[2] I weave together three strands of argument: (1) a broad claim in the history of sexuality, that the growth of feminized labor in a previously masculine printing industry was part of the development of lesbian and protoqueer identities, collectivities, and structures of feeling; (2) a more tentative and implicit literary historical argument, that the shifting labor relations brought on by phototypesetting technologies contributed to the development of queer print cultures and of LGBT literature as a category; and (3) a more specific and definite argument about the work of Brodine, which not only illustrates these developments but also provides a queer and Marxist-feminist politics that is responsive to the history of literary production.[3]

Brodine's writing has not received much critical attention, even as it has been important to a range of poets and activists and received substantive literary recognition during her lifetime.[4] One of my aims is to correct for the critical neglect of Brodine's work by looking at some of her published poems and also by making reference to archival materials: personal journals, published political writings, and memos that she circulated in a more limited fashion to her comrades as part of their organizing work. The most relevant critical treatment of Brodine for my purposes comes from Karen Kovacic, in "The Poetry of Pink Collar Resistance," which features nuanced readings of Brodine's work. Kovacic (2001: 23) notes that in "Pink Collar" poetry, "secretaries and waitresses emphatically call attention to their presence as individuals and as members of a collective." Her article proceeds to read Brodine's work as counterposing "the worker's alienated and instrumental performance of her body on the job with her emotional and physical engagement during lovemaking" (ibid.). Kovacic emphasizes the alienating aspects of Brodine's work, although she also notes the fact that Brodine imagines a potentially revolutionary offshoot of pink-collar work. That is to say, Brodine works to show how women and other feminized workers might take control of the production and reproduction of the textual processes that are meant merely to pass through them. Kovacic's is a precise and skillful reading of Brodine's work, and it also bears extending. Indeed, Brodine's descriptions of lesbian intimacy are not simply *opposed to* the "instrumental performance of her body on the job"; they are not *only* there as evidence of the alienating nature of word-processing labor. Rather, the labor relations that surround the typesetting computer are part and parcel of the revolutionary working-class and queer socialist-feminist politics that Brodine elaborates across her writing and that she worked for tirelessly in her life. Brodine (1947–1987) was born in Seattle into a radical family (her secular

Jewish maternal grandmother, Harriet Pierce, who features in many of Brodine's writings, was a member of the US Communist Party, as were other members of Brodine's immediate and extended family) and was raised in Woodinville, Washington. She moved to the San Francisco Bay Area in the mid-1960s to study dance at UC Berkeley, where she suffered a knee injury, at which point her creative efforts switched to poetry. In the mid-1970s, having studied for a master's of fine arts in writing at San Francisco State University, Brodine (along with her then lover and fellow student Sukey Durham as well as the writers Roz Spafford, Frances Phillips, and others) cofounded the SFSU Women's Caucus. The caucus, which later came to be known as the Women Writers Union (WWU), was originally formed in an effort to change the structure of the English master's oral exams so that they might include women and nonwhite writers ("Creative Writers Seek New Degree Policy" 1975). Through her work with the WWU, Brodine, along with Nellie Wong, Merle Woo, and others, joined Durham as members of Radical Women and the Freedom Socialist Party, two affiliated socialist-feminist organizations in the Trotskyist tradition; these women launched the Bay Area branches of these organizations.

Brodine also helped found the Berkeley Poets Cooperative and Kelsey St. Press, which respectively published her first two books of poetry, *Slow Juggling* (1975) and *Work Week* (1977). Her third book, *Illegal Assembly* (1980), was published by the New York–based Hanging Loose Press, and her final book, *Woman Sitting at the Machine, Thinking* (1990), was published posthumously by the Freedom Socialist Party's (FSP) affiliate, Red Letter Press, after several feminist presses had rejected the manuscript (Brodine 1986: 4). It is perhaps no surprise that Red Letter Press embraced the book, in light not only of the politics of the work itself but also of the extent to which Brodine had focused her energies on organizing with FSP and Radical Women. She took on many leadership roles, including as an organizer of the San Francisco branch of Radical Women and of FSP. She also did extensive work on various defensive campaigns as the organizations' communist radicalism came under legal attacks.[5] Brodine also produced, designed, edited, and wrote the introduction for Gloria Martin's *Socialist Feminism: The First Decade, 1966–1976*, the first book to be published by Red Letter Press.

The rejection of Brodine's more militant Marxist arguments by some cultural feminists fed into a wider theme throughout Brodine's work: the multiple sources of silencing and censorship that she faced. She was acutely aware of how her writing was prevented from reaching potential readers, and she experienced her terminal illness as continuous with these forces of silencing and repression. Brodine died in 1987 from advanced breast cancer that had gone undiagnosed as a result of medical negligence (her journals and her poetry testify to feelings of serious illness years prior to her diagnosis).[6] Her personal papers, and some of her published works, indicate an awareness of the limited audiences for which she wrote. She resented the ways in which her writing was deemed irrelevant or uninteresting by some other feminists because it was by a working-class Marxist lesbian. Censorship in these many modes is a central problem for Brodine's poetry. At the same time, her poetry teases out how capitalist literary technologies, in the moment of their feminization, might be expropriated, shared, and liberated against censorship. This complex intertwining of literary labor, technology, and lesbian existence is as thoroughly imagined in Brodine's work as it is anywhere else.

In what follows, I begin by providing a more detailed account of the feminization of typesetting after 1965; I read Brodine's work to see how, in her account, this feminization conditioned some late twentieth-century forms of queer life. I then take a detour through other queer and feminist responses to technological shifts in printing labor, in order to outline some alternative practices of LGBTQ+ literary production in this period. Finally, I synthesize these various strands in an extended reading of the "thinking" that Brodine's work takes as its subject. Her dialectical approach to poetics can model how we engage the history and politics of queer literary production.

The Feminization of Typesetting and Queer Literary Labor

The introduction of phototypesetting (a metonymic name for the larger process of photocomposition) brought with it major changes in the demographic composition of printing and prepress labor. Management could either allow for the retraining of mostly white male linotype workers in new photocomposition jobs or else spring for new workers to be hired, often women who could be paid less and who, in many cases, already had facility with the QWERTY layout used for photographic composition (linotype keyboards had been laid out differently, did not afford touch-typing, and were understood to require sustained physical strength and the risk of burn injuries).[7] The QWERTY layout—that of a typewriter—was not an inevitable feature of phototypesetting design. As Cynthia Cockburn argues in her 1983 study of London male newspaper compositors, *Brothers: Male Dominance and Techno-logical Change*, "The continued use of QWERTY has been to enable the integration of office and printing technologies and to enable the use of relatively cheap female typists on both" (Cockburn [1983] 1991: 99–100). In *Brothers*, a socialist-feminist study of masculinity at work, Cockburn focuses on the experiences of men who were "deskilled" by the transition to photocomposition.[8] The attitude that these men had toward typing labor was, Cockburn explains, deeply infused with feelings about feminized labor more generally and with what might be called the psychological wages of white masculinity.

Cockburn explains that the transition to photocomposition was not only about increasing productivity but also about control and the breaking of workers' political power (ibid.: 91). The introduction of phototypesetting took place within a larger horizon of industrial transformation, and the direct input of copy (by writers and editors—bypassing typesetting as a profession altogether) was the writing on the wall. Few workers—and perhaps fewer managers—seem to have believed that photocomposition would be a permanent fixture of origination work. Computerized typesetting was a stopgap, and digitization was understood to be around the corner (Marshall 1983: 69–70). The feminization of typesetting, then, was part of a longer trajectory in its elimination as a form of steady wage work.

Because of union protections and negotiations, some linotype operators were retrained in computerized typesetting rather than laid off. In the United States, the International Typographical Union also tended to approach the rise of phototypesetting and the threat it posed to workers' power with a rearguard craft unionist strategy: the ITU leadership would be loyal to its "men" as "skilled" workers. National policy focused on negotiating contracts that guaranteed lifetime employment or early retirement for composition workers in exchange for allowing their existing jobs to be phased out by automation. This approach won out, on the whole, over efforts to unionize the women, queers, and people of color (including women and queers of color) who were increasingly finding employment at nonunion shops. Such people were soon to be employed as typesetters in new, open-shop typesetting businesses, and many pieced together work as freelancers. Perusal of ITU publications and mainstream media coverage from the period show this clearly, as do Brodine's writings (think, for example, of my opening epigraph) and other literary texts more widely recognized to be central to the canon of LGBT literature. Leslie Feinberg's pathbreaking *Stone Butch Blues*, for example, includes in its closing pages a common historical narrative about Bertram Powers's industrial strategy as president of ITU Local 6 in New York City:

> I told him I'd stopped taking hormones and moved to New York City and now I was a typesetter.
>
> "Nonunion?" he asked.
>
> I nodded. "Yeah. When the computers came on the scene, the own-

ers could see first how it was going to transform the old heat-lead industry. So they hired all the people the old craft union didn't realize were important to organize. That's how they broke the back of Local 6. (Feinberg 1993: 298)[9]

While Cockburn focuses on the experiences of men who were losing craft control of labor relations, Brodine's poetry sets out from the position of already feminized and "deskilled" workers. The feminization of typesetting labor took place in an era when the waged workplace tacitly facilitated some expressions of same-sex desire after a brief retrenchment of employment opportunities for many women immediately after World War II.[10] The fact that phototypesetting could form an important basis for the development of queer print cultures was not a reflection of the technology itself; rather, it was partly because of the flexibility of the labor relations and management styles that the technology facilitated in a period of deindustrialization. There were more and less busy times of year, for example, enabling artists and activists to work intensely for a few months and then to take longer chunks of time off for artistic and political projects. Phototypesetting was somewhere between blue-, white-, and pink-collar work—it was sometimes, although not always, done in an office environment, but was shift work all the same, and it did not always require the consistent affective labor (or white femininity) of, for example, much corporate secretarial work.

The "visibility" that some versions of lesbianism achieved in the 1980s and 1990s, largely through the growth of the "professional managerial class" and of feminist and lesbian women's inclusion in it, then, does not explain the working-class lesbian lives that are elaborated in Brodine's work. Nor does phototypesetting work quite line up with what various theorists and historians have called the "gay economy," or "queer work," or "camp labor," insofar as phototypesetting did not necessarily mark one as queer.[11] Phototypesetting and related jobs were, rather, attainable skill sets for people with good enough vision, typing know-how, and the capacity to learn new skills and adjust to technological changes.[12] This was appealing for many artists and writers who needed to make a living but who wanted to have flexible wage-work schedules. Of course, such flexibility was also often part and parcel of feminized jobs. As Brodine writes at the end of her long essay-poem "Money and Land":

My mother always said, "A woman has to have some independent means of income, independent of marriage, I mean, Karen . . ."

> In the back of my mind, a practical little hand taps out, 'she can type, she can type, and fast too.' I count the jobs I've been somewhat paid for—berry-picker, baby-sitter, dance-teacher, writer, secretary, bread-baker, art model, waitress, house-cleaner, old woman's companion, slide-mounter, writing teacher, dish-washer, paste-up person, typesetter, house-painter, inventory-taker, label-maker. . . . And I have plans for a big garage sale. (Brodine 1980: 37–38)

Most of the jobs enumerated here were marked as feminized (many also involve heavy manual labor, including those that might be called "care" work). Most of these jobs required that a worker, either by choice or else by economic compulsion, would pick up work as and where possible without strong (or any) union protections. For Brodine, the fact that "she can type" provides an alternative to marriage (she herself had been married to a man in her early twenties), and it might allow her to scrape by. In this sense, flexible, feminized jobs could be linked to the prospect of combating compulsory heterosexuality.

Indeed, in her journals from November 1975, Brodine wrote, having secured a job in a typesetting shop:

> I think the job for me is an instant element of centeredness, sureness. Just to know I will have enough money for once in my life. . . . I fantasize coming home that I come home to a woman, strong + a working person I come home + we are warm in a warm house + perhaps she has just walked in the door. . . . Yet the truth is, I watch the moon leaning backwards in the sky right above my own little place. I live alone + cook for myself + after sleep alone. + now that is good. . . . I don't <u>know</u> how to live. But oh I want to be the strongest and happiest [and] perhaps finally I am learning this. (Brodine 1970–87)

It should not come as a surprise that the reality of a new job is linked, here, to Brodine's capacity to thrive as a working-class lesbian. The fact that the job was in a nonunion typesetting shop does not diminish this fact, even as Brodine cannot yet find a clear path to everything she desires. Still, with this job—and, implicitly, with her newfound involvement in political organizing—she feels that she may be learning how happiness and strength are made.

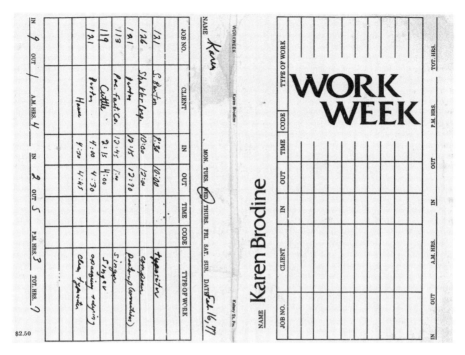

Figure 1. Back and front cover of *Work Week* (1977). Courtesy Karen Brodine estate

Skills for Assembly

Brodine wrote the above words in the same journal in which she composed many of the poems that would appear in her second book, *Work Week* (1977). Indeed, Brodine's work as a typesetter, and the kinds of organizing she did in relation to her job, coincided with her development as a gay woman, a communist, and a poet. Brodine was employed at the time by the magazine *Communication Arts, Inc.*, where she was part of an ultimately successful effort to unionize those who worked in typesetting and related prepress work. But this effort does not really show up until the later *Illegal Assembly* (1980); *Work Week*, for its part, foregrounds in a primarily descriptive mode the relations between feminized labor and the critique of political economy. The book is framed by a cover featuring the calculation of clients and jobs, including a range of different origination tasks from typesetting to pasteup to offset plate preparation ("opaquing and dyeing"). The book is named for one of the mechanisms by which the capital-labor relation subsumes the worker's life. The title suggests that all aspects of life are structured by the calculation of labor time, including the writing of "poetry" and the sharing of private intimacy.

Alongside this reduction of duration to the calculation of labor time, *Work*

Week investigates the relations among women in feminized workplaces that require or encourage feminine self-presentation. The book's third poem, for example, is titled "The receptionist is by definition" and closes as follows:

> 2. the receptionist is by definition underpaid to lie
>
> remember the receptionist with the lovely
> smile, with the green eyes, the cropped
> hair, big feet, small knees, with the
> wrinkled hands, the large breasts, with
> the husky voice, the strong chin?
>   She takes her breaks
> In the washroom, grimacing, waving her fists
> At the blurred reflection of her dress.
> (Brodine 1977: 11)

This receptionist is marked by stereotypical feminine descriptors ("the lovely / smile"), but the poem pushes past this, presenting a much more detailed physical description, followed by the acknowledgment of her time *off* the clock: time that is stolen away from capital's demands for feminized self-presentation. The description points to the tacit forms of attention that women pay to each other, and the book as a whole features tentative relationships between women that might be described as part of what Adrienne Rich (1980) called the "lesbian continuum." The first section of *Work Week*, "On the Job," opens with an untitled poem that reads in its entirety:

> new to this office, we watch
> the faces of the other women
> for clues, to discover which tribe,
> we watch their soft faces
> for the quick glance, the laugh
> of recognition, what we call
> the understanding
> (ibid.: 9)

In this office, women work together for low wages and communicate through coded looks and silences. *Work Week* presents itself, as well as the dreams that it narrates, as an alternative or escape. The possibility of relationships between women at work is presented as a puzzle or challenge, as in the following excerpt from the opening of "Jigsaw Riddle":

who's that woman avalanching down the street?

setting the margins
doesn't justify, but
I can frame her face   the word
with my hands, what
we both dreamt, a jig-
saw puzzle of planes,   floats down through
welded cold steel
in a sky that would   the memory
not rain
(ibid.: 22)

Women's faces are sources of fascination here, and they are framed by the time-line of the workweek (as in the case of the receptionist) and by the restrictions of the typeset page. But "setting the margins" and justifying the lines cannot frame this relationship in the same way that *hands* would. Indeed, the column on the left-hand side of the page is typographically disrupted by the skillfully set (by Brodine) "floating" words to the right. In *Work Week*, wage labor is a barrier, and women try to breach it with imagined and furtive connections—glances, words, and touches—but it remains a sort of limiting partition. Not all the poems confine themselves to silence and noncommunication—there are moments of overt conversation between women, but many of these seem to be reported dreams.

By the time of *Illegal Assembly* (Hanging Loose Press, 1980) and especially *Woman Sitting at the Machine, Thinking* (Red Letter Press, 1990), Brodine had developed new ways to think about feminist political agency in the workplace—through, on the one hand, acts of sabotage, and, on the other hand, the collective development of political skill and power. If *Work Week* engaged with typesetting labor in terms of the silences imposed by technology and management, it was in *Illegal Assembly* that Brodine moved toward building collective power in the context of the feminized workplace. The book is less obviously about work than about forms of collectivity and the changes that both legal and illegal assemblies can bring about. "Making the Difference," for example, discusses organizing a union (presumably at *Communication Arts, Inc.*): "in two weeks we will have a union election. we will vote yes and no. we will win or lose. it will make a difference" (Brodine 1980: 50). Brodine has developed confidence in her political and her technical skills, and she explores the pleasures that come from acquiring and playing with new skills: "when I learn something new at work, even when it is very minor, and could in time become drudgery, the hours shrink. / I like the clean slice of the exacto blade against the drawing board." (ibid.: 56). Here, skill is presented as a source of pleasure and as an aspiration—it is a generative part of being with others. This entails a rejection of the rhetoric of "deskilling" that accompanies the encroachment of feminized labor and that amounts to a *political* assault on feminized versions of skill: "I have skills and they attach to what I need or love / there are skills I don't have and I mean to learn them" (ibid.: 61).[13] These lines appear in *Illegal Assembly*, and they were taken directly from Brodine's June 29, 1977, journal entry. In the journal, they are preceded by an indication of the political nature of Brodine's thinking about skill as a typesetter, a writer, and an organizer: "Skill is a hand-up toward power when it is applied toward our (+ I mean the group's) own ends" (Brodine 1970–87: n.p.).

Simultaneously, *Illegal Assembly* begins to reflect in detail the extent to which these skills can turn the worker into a sort of word-processing machine: "at work I have to let the brutality of language turned against us flow thru my hands—typing, 'a relatively senseless robot will be marketed under the name, "the Helen Keller robot"'" (Brodine 1980: 55).[14] Similar sharp reportage of management discourse shows up in the tongue-in-cheek lunch-break discussions that run throughout "Opposites That Bleed One into the Other or Collide":

> at lunch I sit with other office workers sunning on a small scrap
> of sidewalk
> it's so nice to work in the arts
> it's so laid-back we don't have to dress up
> & they don't even mind gays working here
> her supervisor said she was only half a woman
> (ibid: 53–54)

As its title implies, this poem is typographically rendered as a picture of dialectics. Right- and left-aligned portions of text are "opposed" on the page but also show themselves to be the flip sides of each other through their alternations down the page. The typographically opposed portions of this text are no longer quite divided into reality and dream, as they were in *Work Week*; they are instead processes of change and movement through antagonism and opposition. The poem's final section documents the materials for revolutionary assembly that have been built by the concentration of feminized office work in the deindustrialized core of San Francisco, and it moves from left- to right- to center-aligned text:

and leaning out the window, I watch the small fist of a three-month strike
up the street flowering into bright turning signs and shouting people, circling, circling

and staring up the street I see hundreds of green streetcars stopped now backed
up stockstill unbudging for blocks. a disruption in service. a stoppage.

and people rushing and tumbling out of the cars like water—

we could shut this city down.

(ibid.: 54)

The last line is centered, as is, in a sense, the book as a whole. This growth of Brodine's confidence and transformative vision is a result not only of the passage of time or of simply having written or worked more. It is clear from her journals that coming out as a lesbian, and doing so in the context of organizing with the Women Writers Union, Radical Women, and the Freedom Socialist Party changed her day-to-day understanding of her life. Each of these organizations prioritized the training of women, queer people, and people of color for revolutionary political leadership. This experience of leadership—and of using and developing her skills, including those that she learned at work, for political purposes—may explain Brodine's facility in writing about alternative, humane ways to organize the activity of making and distributing printed texts and other forms of information.

Collectivity, Autonomy, and Uncertainty

Brodine's poetry, of course, was not the only development in LGBTQ+ literary production that was enabled by the era of photocomposition. Before turning to Brodine's landmark poem, "Woman Sitting at the Machine, Thinking," I take a detour through some of the other queer consequences of new printing technologies, specifically the development of new typesetting, printing, and publishing collectives. I do so to locate the specificity of Brodine's queer and Marxist-feminist poetic project in a broader context of queer and feminist literary production: Brodine's first two books had, after all, been published by the Berkeley Poets Cooperative and Kelsey Street Press (she had helped found and did voluntary origination and publishing work for each).[15] Kelsey Street had its early titles printed at the West Coast Print Center, a community endeavor that donated typesetting and printing equipment to small presses, especially within avant-garde poetry circles. Collectives of this sort, including a range of alternative and underground presses and other feminist and gay liberation publishing ventures, were widespread, if often short-lived, during this period.

A rich body of work on feminist and LGBT print culture (scholarly and otherwise) has shown that for LGBTQ+ publishers—including those committed to feminist and gay liberation politics—there was a pervasive tension between ambitions for political autonomy and the instability of the printing and publishing industries that undergirded them.[16] For publishers, access to affordable computerized typesetting and small offset lithography did indeed allow for large-run prints of materials that might otherwise have been censored or else produced by necessity using more-limited duplicating machines. This advantage is noted repeatedly in reflections by gay and lesbian publishers, such as Gay Sunshine Press's Winston Leyland (1975: 8), who reports that the printer for John Wiener's pioneering *Hotel Wentley Poems* "was so uptight that he deliberately left out the word 'cock' in 'Cocksuckers,' and a second printing with the unexpurgated title had to be done almost immediately."

But if access to phototypesetting and offset printing allowed for greater control over content, it also brought up the more complicated but equally critical question of control over the means of production of printing. While phototypesetting equipment was within reach for some LGBTQ+ and feminist presses and typesetting collectives, large-scale offset-printing machinery was usually out of reach. Autonomous publishing collectives still needed to manage print production. This presented distinct challenges for feminist, lesbian, and gay publishing and printing ventures that sought to maintain nonhierarchical and collective decision-making and production processes, as it did for the "underground press" more broadly.[17]

For some print collectives, and particularly for lesbian-feminist groups, the key challenge was in maintaining both autonomy and nonhierarchical relationships, and this involved skill sharing and job rotation. In some cases, autonomy and equality were understood to be mutually reinforcing.[18] Barbara Smith, a trailblazing black feminist and supporter of Brodine, Merle Woo, and Nellie Wong, located her impetus for cofounding Kitchen Table: Women of Color Press in autonomy and control, referring to "our need for autonomy, our need to determine independently both the content and conditions of our work" (Jones and Eubanks: 2014: 155). But Smith also reflected on the political difficulties of managing such a project *as a business*.[19] Running presses autonomously and collectively did not guarantee their survival, if survival was dependent on profitability, which it was for many presses and publishers such as Kitchen Table that did not have wealthy patrons or people able or willing to live without steady wages.[20] While, on the one hand, the expansion of photo-offset printing and of queer and feminist typesetting collectives helped more people produce and distribute on a large scale, these technological developments also accelerated the organizational and political problems of functioning as businesses. When asked by Matt Richardson if Kitchen Table was a collective, Smith remarked, "That was what was said on the piece of paper. . . . We had a commitment to people having non-hierarchical roles and relationships, but it can be very difficult, particularly if you are running what is essentially a business, to operate in that way" (ibid.: 2014: 157).

Charley Shively, a central member of the staff of the Boston-based anarchist periodical *Fag Rag*, recalled how changes in typesetting technology affected the labor relations of the collective. This was the case, for example, when it started having to pay for typesetting: "Seeing the need for typesetting in the gay community, [David Stryker] started a part-time business. Ken Sanchez, who worked for Stryker, was able to type out *Fag Rag* text (with some volunteer help) after hours; we paid a dollar an hour for using the machine. . . . Stryker charged basically at cost per issue; still our typesetting costs quadrupled. He saw it as a sacrifice for the movement; others saw it as an inroad of capitalism" (Wachsberger 2012: n.p.). Shively's account, while detailed, is hardly exceptional. Cheap print and typesetting machinery were not always readily available through community print centers and personal contacts, and most radical and underground collectives had little starting capital with which to pay for origination and printing. While new typesetting technologies could allow for more efficient and sophisticated control over typesetting, Shively notes that constant shifts in technology also made ideals of autonomy and collectivity more difficult to attain than they otherwise might have been. The expertise required for operating the machinery as it continually developed posed challenges to the collective's anticapitalist and nonhierarchical aspirations. Moreover, as Shively notes, by the end of the 1980s, "Desktop publishing almost instantly wiped away all the skills learned on the Compugraphic."

In other words, the use of new typesetting technologies (including piecemeal methods of origination, e.g., laying out and photographing typewriter copy) in radical egalitarian collectives can only be understood as an uneasy development in the face of the feminization and racial-ethnic diversification of the typographical labor force. That is, such collective efforts, and particularly LGBTQ+ and feminist businesses that depended on making ends meet (if not on making profits), were the flip side of the feminization and casualization of much printing labor in the deindustrializing global North, and they stood on shaky ground.

Brodine's work pushes past this tension between the ideal of autonomy and the need for profit. Unlike some separatist and cultural feminists, Brodine never wanted to abandon the feminized waged workplace as a site for feminist struggle, even as she certainly did not idealize such wage work or see it as liberating in itself. Brodine's poetry centers feminized labor—including waged literary labor—as a site of *struggle and elaboration* rather than something to be abandoned in favor of separatist or nonhierarchical ideals. Through her writing, Brodine showed that all work, but particularly undervalued and feminized work, was as suitable a topic for feminist poetry as was anything else; she raged at the economic and racial privileges of those feminist writers who argued that the workplace was a masculine domain from which women should remove themselves. She refused feminist dismissals of wage labor, that is, and wanted instead to think about feminized work in the context of an ever-changing social totality.

Thinking at the Machine

Following on this exploration of some alternative forms of queer literary labor, I close with an extended reading of Brodine's "Woman Sitting at the Machine, Thinking," the title poem from the 1990 book of the same name. Originally written in 1981, the poem is the most sustained of Brodine's poems that engage with phototypesetting labor. If *Work Week* indicated the ways in which feminized wage labor might facilitate tacit expressions of lesbian desire, and *Illegal Assembly* began to theorize the revolutionary potential of feminized workers, "Woman Sitting" returns to these problems, mediated this time by a dialectical approach to the material conditions of its own writing. In my reading, I track "thinking" as an abstraction that Brodine's materialist poetics renders concrete: this thinking is conditioned by and responsive to the social conditions of feminized, queer literary labor. Thinking is not a collective escape from but a *communist elaboration of* feminized labor.

Brodine wrote this poem while she was working as a typesetter for Howard Quinn Co., a unionized, family-run, all-service print shop. Brodine herself was initially kept out of the union because she was an "electronic technician" rather than a typesetter; she contested this and eventually won membership in GAIU Local 280, only to be placed in a partitioned room, separated from the other nonunion phototypesetters (Brodine c. 1981: 2). The poem moves through the everyday work experiences of a typesetter in a small shop, and it weaves into the description of these routines bits of dreams, memories, and fantasies: about animals, about other women, about spontaneous insurrection, and about organized revolutions.

The poem's composition tracks "thinking" across the processes that make up the daily routines and expropriations of photocomposition. This includes the selection and placement of characters, the justification of lines, and the manipulation of codes to call up and store different jobs:

> Call format o five.   Reports, Disc 2, quad left
> return.   name of town, address, zip.   quad left
> return.   rollalong and there you are.
> done with this one.   start the next.
>
> call format o five. my day so silent yet taken up with words.
> floating through the currents and cords of my wrists
> into the screen and drifting to land, beached pollywogs.
> all this language handled yet the room is so silent.
> everyone absorbed in feeding words through the machines
> (Brodine 1990: 5)

Kathleen Fraser (1991: 24) writes of this passage that "as Brodine keeps a mental tally of her mechanical tasks, she simultaneously notes the deep silence soaking up her fellow workers and pulling her into mental drift."[21] I would add to Fraser's account that, despite or because of so much silence, the poem presents its own activities, including the thinking that it weaves through the computer, as sites of struggle: the thinking is not simply a product of the machine but is conditioned by it all the same. Thinking emerges alongside the peculiar collective social experience of phototypesetting, and it describes an unvoiced choreography, a kind of silent communication around the machines.

In the lines that follow on the same page, a different kind of thinking—and of communication—is slotted in among the codes:

> Call file Oceana.   name of town, Pacific.   name of street, Arbor.
> thinking about lovemaking last night, how it's another land,
> another set of sounds, the surface of the water, submerged,
> then floating free, the delicate fabric of motion and touch
> knit with listening and humming and soaring.
> never a clear separation of power because it is both our power
> at once.   hers to speak deep in her body and voice to her own
> rhythms.   mine to ride those rhythms out and my own,
> and call them out even more. a speaking together from body
> to mouth to voice.
> (ibid.)

Thoughts "sneak through," here—the silent room is filled with the memories of a different arrangement of bodies and modes of speaking and thinking together. As in *Work Week* and *Illegal Assembly*, however, the poem demonstrates that "women's work" and "lesbian love" are not simply opposed bodily experiences. Indeed, there is a sort of "speaking together from body" in the typesetters' subaltern modes of communication with regard to their racist and sexist bosses:

> because they must think we are stupid in order
> to push us around, *they* become stupid.
> knowing "something's going on," peering like moles.
> how can they know the quirk of an eyebrow behind their back?
> they suspect we hate them because they know
> what they are doing to us——but we are only
> stupid Blacks or crazy Puerto Ricans, or dumb blonds.
>
> we are their allergy, their bad dream.
> they need us too much, with their talk of
> "carrying us" on the payroll.
> we carry them, loads of heavy, dull metal,
> outmoded and dusty.
>
> they try to control us, building partitions,
> and taking the faces off the phones.
> they talk to us slow and loud,
> HOW ARE YOU TODAY? HERE'S A CHECK FOR YOU.
> As if it were a gift.
>
> we say—even if they stretched tape
> across our mouths
> we could still speak to one another
> with our eyebrows
> (Brodine 1990: 7–8)

While the regular exchange of raised eyebrows is not identical to "lovemaking last night," both involve the building of coordinated skills and perhaps of political power in the face of a generalized disregard for the embodied lives of working-class women. Speaking through eyebrows is, of course, not any kind of guarantee of solidarity among the feminized workers—and certain versions of female solidarity at work are premised on the expulsion of gender nonconforming people.[22] All the same, the knowledge conveyed in these exchanges, that "we carry them, loads of heavy, dull metal, / outmoded and dusty," is a small advantage that the typesetters have over management. Management is figured here as the heavy, metal linotype machines whose white male operators were prioritized by labor leadership over the women and queer people increasingly finding work in the industry. Management is also figured as having a disadvantage in terms of both technical and political skill. Brodine has learned that there is some power on the flip side of her downgraded status. The conditions of her work allow for the generation of skills, and these are skills that must be taken into the hands of those who have been silently collectivized.

Again, this dialectic between technical deskilling and political power is rendered through the movement of "thinking" across the poem. The woman who is "thinking" is not simply shaped by lovemaking and wage labor: she is shaped by the Marxist-feminist praxis that Brodine developed with comrades in the WWU, Freedom Socialist Party, and Radical Women. Brodine described the genesis of the project in a 1984 letter to her good friend Edgar Poma, a gay Filipino writer: "Do you know what inspired that poem? (I mean besides the job I was working at then). A talk on Marxist economics by [an FSP comrade]. It was that talk that spoke of human labor hours stored up in machines, and so on, and really got me thinking." This explanation of machinery by way of Karl Marx's labor theory of value also inflects the significance of the word *thinking*: it appears not quite to belong to the woman in the title: "Woman Sitting at the Machine, Thinking." *Thinking* posits a dimension of freedom from work, but it is a freedom conditioned by the choreographic constraints of typesetting labor: code, rhythm, gesture, posture, manipulation of text as seen on the monitor or video display terminal, and transfer of data to the mainframe. The placement of "thinking" after the comma affords some ambiguity about the agent of the thinking: woman, machine, or woman-machine. That is, thinking is *conditioned by* rather than simply *outside or beyond* the relations of feminized wage labor.

Take the opening lines of "Woman Sitting at the Machine, Thinking":

she thinks about everything at once without making a mistake.
no one has figured out how to keep her from doing this thinking
while her hands and nerves also perform every delicate complex
function of the work. this is not automatic or deadening.
try it sometime. make your hands move quickly on the keys
fast as you can, while you are thinking about:

the layers, fossils. the idea that this machine she controls
is simply layers of human workhours frozen in steel, tangled
in tiny circuits, blinking out through lights like hot, red eyes . . .
(Brodine 1990: 3)

Thinking is something that emerges through the material discipline of work, alongside the silences and solidarities that accompany it. Brodine grasps at the hierarchical and networked relations and forces that determine her life, and she delineates the contradictions that underpin and threaten this ordering of relations. Thinking happens despite apparent attempts to prevent it from taking place ("no one has figured out how to keep her from doing this thinking") and especially to *prevent it from being shared.*

At the same time, at least some of this thinking also enters *into* the machine and is thereby destined for expropriation by the bosses; it does not simply escape the relations of production. The mainframe computer and the information that it stores are the private property of the bosses and of their clients. This is the literal transfer of feminized human labor power (quantified "thinking") to an expropriating machine. In this sense, the poem literalizes the fact that capitalism recuperates and appropriates feminized interventions in technique:

> we sell ourselves in fractions. they don't want us all
> at once, but hour by hour, piece by piece. our hands mainly
> and our backs. and chunks of our brains. and veiled expressions
> on our faces, they buy. though they can't know what actual
> thoughts stand behind our eyes.
> (ibid.: 3)

These "actual / thoughts . . . behind our eyes" are cold comfort if the means for their communication and preservation are not "ours." And writing and reading poetry—sharing these thoughts—cannot resolve this problem.

That is, while the poem comprehends at once the machine, the feminized work, and the thinking that stream into it as social material, it also expresses a wish that the computer *could* hold and convey all the thinking that takes place in front of it. Brodine writes a demand for the machine and a wish to store meaning and labor in the machine in a way that is *not* an expropriation:

> what if you could send anything in and call it out again?
> I file jobs under words I like—red, buzz, fury
> search for tiger, execute
> the words stream up the screen till tiger trips the halt
> search for seal   search for strike
> search for the names of women

we could circle our words around the world
like dolphins streaking through water their radar
if the screens were really in the hands of experts: us.
think of it—our ideas whipping through the air
everything stored in an eyeflash
our whole history, ready and waiting.
(Brodine 1990: 17)

Here the machine becomes an enabling condition of joy and desire precisely because of all it has absorbed of collective feminized labor, of unspoken conversations, of women rolling their eyes at management and glaring into the machine, and of women looking longingly at one another over the machines. The contradictory labor relations of computerized typesetting, and the social antagonisms that these relations entail, make up Brodine's vision of feminized labor (and of thinking) as concrete activity. The poem calls for efforts to make it so—to appropriate the machine so that "our whole history, ready and waiting" can be readily available to "experts: us."

For this to be possible, the woman at the machine has to engage in various forms of resistance, including, but not limited to, collective industrial action. Brodine did just this, as I have already noted. But the context of Brodine's work—the relatively brief historical window during which typesetting was simultaneously feminized and computerized—potentiated other, complementary but distinct forms of organizing and resistance. Stealing time or just using machines after hours to typeset poems about feminized labor certainly falls into this category of resistance. A single typewritten sheet of paper archived among Brodine's teaching materials is titled "Sabotage." The page seems to be Brodine's notes for a public reading or performance. She has typed:

writing about work is a form of sabotage.

stealing, another: running off my poems on the company
xerox machine, or copying material about the union

saying the way things really are

. . . .

sneaking words into the memory of the machine . . .
(Brodine c. 1980: n.p.)

Brodine, unlike some of the "Language" poets who were her San Francisco contemporaries, did not expect formal linguistic experimentation on its own to resolve or even intervene directly in the contradictions of capitalist society.[23] Rather, she saw poetry learning from and being shaped by collective struggles against capitalism as a total system, struggles coordinated and led by those whose labor has most often been undervalued because it is racialized and feminized. As she wrote in a controversial essay, "The Politics of Women Writing":

> The poem I write, *by itself*, will not organize for affirmative action, or abortion. Action, organizing with other people, has to do that. New different poems come out of that organizing experience. I can give a new poem, copied secretly on the office machine, to my fellow workers. Because the images in it come from us, our anger, our resistance, my co-workers care for the poem, and it become[s] a part of the gathering force of our solidarity. For that poem can collect on one page a record of the contradictions we experience every day. I have yet to know the use of a poem the way I know the use of a hammer. Yet I feel a poem is surely a tool. (Brodine 1979: 9)[24]

The arguments that Brodine makes here for the "use" of poetry are not about the creation of revolutionary forms of subjectivity in an abstract reader. Rather, poems are materially situated in the production and distribution of literary language, and Brodine sees "the poem" as a technology that affords particular uses. The poem "Woman Sitting at the Machine, Thinking" has a range of such possible uses, one of which is to share it with her coworkers as part of the collective development of political skill.

Brodine's "sabotage" is not (or is at least not only) intended to ironize the labor relations that condition it, to make irreverent fun out of her work for sharing with professional writers who are not her comrades. This is not to say that the poems are not fun and funny (they are), and that others would not want to read them (many do); rather, they are geared toward the collective transformation of queer literary labor. This is not simply a matter of Brodine's moral decision making or of some special individual attitude that she held toward poetry—rather, it has everything to do with the objective, feminized labor relations of typesetting work in this period. And it also has to do with Brodine's political orientation, as a leading member in socialist-feminist organizations, toward a revolutionary strategy that takes as its basic condition of possibility the feminization and racialization of the US working class. Thinking and writing can be individually engaged activities, but when they are also part of the conditions of labor, they can line up with ways to feed collective disruption into the management machine and to enlist technologies (screens, memory, and even deadly chemical processes) to aid in this resistance.

Such resistance, it must be added, was framed by the fact that prepress and printing labor would be further outsourced in the years to follow through the explosion of logistics and the outsourcing of much microchip fabrication and computer manufacturing, a story that might profitably be explored in relation to the global feminization of literary and printing labor all the way down the supply chain. By contrast, in Brodine's work, the machine comprises both the terminal and the mainframe—the machine and the information that it stored were on-site, and the point of production was relatively centralized. That this particular combination of access to the means of print production and Marxist-feminist praxis under discussion in this article was localized and relatively brief does not, however, limit its purchase for thinking about and engaging in the concrete activities that are abstractly called "LGBT literature" today. In a journal entry from October 7, 1983, Brodine wrote out a plan to perform "the working poem" at a reading and to introduce it according to these indications: "Explain: from one shop—wouldn't let in union—call by another name. found poem—word stretches out. Thinking in and out of the gaps of the work itself . . . . The poem in the form that material <u>goes</u> into the machine. //files// . . . resistance the prime ingredient" (Brodine 1970–87: n.p.). Brodine's work shows us how this kind of queer poetic resistance—getting it into the machine—was made distinctly possible, for a relatively brief time, by the feminization of typesetting labor in the United States.

Notes

This article benefits from the work of too many people to name, including some who have worked in typesetting and print and many who knew Karen Brodine. Helen Gilbert, Toni Mendocino, Mark Solomon, Nellie Wong, and Merle Woo all generously provided crucial information and guidance at various stages; special thanks are due to Helen and Toni for sharing materials from their personal archives. I am grateful to Tim Wilson and Andrea Grimes at the San Francisco Public Library for help during my visit to the Karen Brodine papers. I am indebted to Ramzi Fawaz, Shanté Paradigm Smalls, and two anonymous reviewers for suggestions about the shape and scope of the article.

1. In offset lithography, positive images on a photographically developed metal plate are inked (as in lithographic processes more broadly, the adhesion of the ink on some parts of the plate but not others is based on the repulsion of oil and water). Ink is

transferred from the plate as a negative image onto a "blanket" and then transferred again from the blanket onto a printing surface.

2.   I use the terms *feminized* and *racialized* labor in the sense of work that is marked by the politically distorted sense of the value of the labor power of the workers who do it. Conversely, "feminized" work tends to further feminize those who do it. In this, I follow Rosemary Hennessy's (2013: 171) account of feminized "second skins."

3.   I understand these claims to be in conversation with recent work in queer Marxism, particularly the work of Hennessy and Holly Lewis on feminization, labor, and nonnormative sexual practices. See Hennessy 2013, Lewis 2016, and also Floyd 2009, Liu 2015, Tinkcom 2002, and the still-unpublished work of Nat Raha on queer labor and trans social reproduction. For recent accounts of the gay Left and of gays and lesbians in the labor movement, see Hobson 2016 and Frank 2014, respectively.

4.   Brodine's work has received renewed critical appreciation from poets and editors; see especially Buuck 2014 and Boyer 2015.

5.   For an outline of one legal and political campaign that Brodine organized in the early 1980s, see "Merle Woo vs. UCB: The History." Woo was Brodine's lover and comrade for many years.

6.   It is possible that some of the chemical processing involved in photocomposition may have contributed to Brodine's cancer. Many of her journal entries contain retrospectively upsetting notes along the lines of one typed entry dated "July 30" and likely from 1979 or 1980: "I'm afraid of how my chest hurts. It must be the fumes. Nothing else could make it feel this way" (Brodine 1970–87: n.p.). For an extended consideration of sickness and labor in relation to Brodine's poem, see also Boyer 2015.

7.   The paradigmatic literary representation of this attitude and situation can be found in Updike 1990.

8.   For a recent study of masculinity in the transition from letterpress to offset lithography (for which masculinity remained a marker of privilege and skill), see Stein 2016.

9.   Feinberg hirself was not only a revolutionary communist and a transgender icon: ze also made a living as a typesetter and was intimately acquainted with this history; *Stone Butch Blues* can, in fact, be read as a novel that narrates the processes that allow for butch and transmasculine experiences to be *asserted in print*. For earlier management and journalistic accounts of Powers's industrial strategy, see "The 'Revolution' on Park Avenue" 1973 and Montgomery 1974.

10. This history is, of course, of consequence in most of the workplaces in which Jess Goldberg finds herself in *Stone Butch Blues* (particularly in the binderies, where Feinberg narrates the open secret of butch and femme women workers flirting and developing relationships—binderies, of course, have long been the most feminized workplaces in the print and publishing industries).

11. On "camp labor," see Tinkcom 2002; on "queer work," see Bérubé 2011; on the "gay economy," see Rubin (1984) 1994.

12. The eyestrain that often came from spending long shifts in front of video display terminals is the subject of Susan Meurer's poem "Have You Ever Considered . . .": "My VDT tortured eyes, twitching again / begged for a break from green letters / and glare eyed hours a day" (Wayman 1991: 98).

13. Alan Marshall (1983: 105) argues that computerized typesetting was not, in and of itself, any less "skilled" than linotyping had been: "The inherent capabilities of computer-typesetting do not, however, necessarily imply deskilling. . . . But in general they are being used by management to break up the work sequence into simplified and more easily quantifiable sections."

14. For the material and metaphorical history of "word-processing" in late twentieth-century American literature, see Kirschenbaum 2016. For a brilliant exploration of typing and copyediting as exemplary feminized modes of "not reading," see Cecire 2015.

15. Kelsey Street was formed out of a split in the Berkeley Poets Cooperative: "Patricia Dienstfrey recalls her impetus for breaking away from the Berkeley Poets Cooperative and forming KSP: She remembers the critique of a particular poem by Karen Brodine and the sense that the vocal, male members of the Berkeley Poets Cooperative had reduced the poem to its domestic subject matter, to its apparent femininity, and nothing more" (Kelsey Street Press Blog).

16. See Streitmatter 1995 on gay and lesbian publishing, Baim 2012 for scholarly and oral histories from LGBTQ+ print ventures, and Hogan 2016 on the crucial role that "feminist bookwomen" played in the economy of gay and feminist publishing in the late twentieth century.

17. For accounts of the "underground press" that take on the problem of management, see Lewis 1972, Marshall 1983, and McMillan 2011.

18. "The structure of job sharing allowed a variety of women to learn different skills in the phases of printing, and it also expressed an important philosophical commitment of feminism in the early 1970s: the refusal of hierarchical structures, associated with patriarchy, and the egalitarian belief that all women could learn all types of skills" (Beins and Enszer 2013: 205).

19. Many of Smith's reflections on running Kitchen Table are collected in Jones and Eubanks 2014. To support Smith's ongoing work, visit fundly.com/barbara-2.

20. The same was true of for-profit feminist typesetting businesses. WGC Typesetting and Design was founded in the early 1980s to fund the operations of the Women's Graphic Centre at the Woman's Building in Los Angeles. The business ran almost entirely in the red, however, and by March 1988 had declared bankruptcy and suspended operations (Wolverton 2002: 168–232).

21. Fraser, who taught at SFSU when the WWU was formed, dedicated the 1988 issue of the avant-garde feminist poetry journal *How(ever)* to Brodine.

22. Indeed, in Feinberg's *Stone Butch Blues*, Jess is subjected at a typesetting shop to painful transphobic suspicions by cisgendered women coworkers, who, while confer-

ring with each other in a manner reminiscent of the raised eyebrows in Brodine's poem, identify Jess as "a psycho," "effeminate," "gay," and "the kind you gotta watch out for" (Feinberg 1993: 265). Jess leaves work and never returns to that particular shop.

23. See "Response to L-A-N-G-U-A-G-E," in *Illegal Assembly*. Brodine (1980: 51–52) writes: "I say blow the house down / the whole house, not just the words" and later "it's true I want things to mean / it's true I mean things / to change."

24. This article caused significant controversy among the radical feminist readership of the feminist journal *Second Wave*, not least for Brodine's blunt criticisms of Adrienne Rich and of radical feminism more broadly. Brodine's comrades wrote letters to the editor in defense of Brodine in subsequent issues, as did the science fiction writer Joanna Russ. Rich, for her part, wrote movingly about Brodine's work on numerous occasions (e.g., Rich 1991).

References

Baim, Tracy, ed. 2012. *Gay Press, Gay Power: The Growth of LGBT Community Newspapers in America*. Chicago: CreateSpace Independent Publishing Platform.

Beins, Agatha and Julie R. Enszer. 2013. "'We Couldn't Get Them Printed,' So We Learned to Print: *Ain't I a Woman?* And the Iowa City Women's Press." *Frontiers: A Journal of Women's Studies* 32, no 2: 186–221.

Bérubé, Allan. 2011. *My Desire for History: Essays in Gay, Community, and Labor History*. Chapel Hill: University of North Carolina Press.

Boyer, Anne. 2015. "Woman Sitting at the Machine, Thinking." *Poetry Is Dead*, no. 12: 6–9.

———. 1970–87. Notebooks. Boxes 1–3, Karen Brodine Papers, LGBTQIA Center, San Francisco Public Library.

———. 1975. *Slow Juggling*. Berkeley: Berkeley Poets Workshop and Press.

———. 1977. *Work Week*. San Francisco: Kelsey Street.

———. 1979. "The Politics of Women Writing." *The Second Wave: A Magazine of Ongoing Feminism* 5, no. 3: 6–13.

———. 1980. *Illegal Assembly*. New York: Hanging Loose.

———. c. 1980. "Sabotage." Box 3, Karen Brodine Papers, LGBTQIA Center, San Francisco Public Library.

———. c. 1981. "Getting into Graphic Arts Intl Union Local 290." Private collection of Helen Gilbert. Seattle, Washington.

———. 1984. Letter to Edgar Poma. Box 3, folder 15, Karen Brodine Papers, LGBTQIA Center, San Francisco Public Library.

———. 1986. "Women Writers Telling the Truth from All Its Sides." Box 3, Karen Brodine Papers, LGBTQIA Center, San Francisco Public Library.

————. 1990. *Woman Sitting at the Machine, Thinking*. Seattle: Red Letter.

Buuck, David. 2014. "40x40x40: David Buuck on Karen Brodine." *Small Press Traffic* (blog). smallpresstraffic.org/2436 (accessed February 16, 2017).

Cecire, Natalia. 2015. "Ways of Not Reading Gertrude Stein." *ELH* 82, no. 1: 281–312.

Cockburn, Cynthia. [1983] 1991. *Brothers: Male Dominance and Technological Change*. London: Pluto.

"Creative Writers Seek New Degree Policy." 1975. *Zenger's*, October 22.

Feinberg, Leslie. 1993. *Stone Butch Blues*. Ithaca, NY: Firebrand Books.

Floyd, Kevin. 2009. *The Reification of Desire: Toward a Queer Marxism*. Minneapolis: University of Minnesota Press.

Frank, Miriam. 2014. *Out in the Union: A Labor History of Queer America*. Philadelphia: Temple University Press.

Fraser, Kathleen. 1991. "Personal Computing." Box 4, Karen Brodine Papers, LGBTQIA Center, San Francisco Public Library.

Hennessy, Rosemary. 2013. *Fires on the Border: The Passionate Politics of Labor Organizing on the Mexican Frontera*. Minneapolis: University of Minnesota Press.

Hobson, Emily K. 2016. *Lavender and Red: Liberation and Solidarity in the Gay and Lesbian Left*. Oakland: University of California Press.

Hogan, Kristen. 2016. *The Feminist Bookstore Movement: Lesbian Antiracism and Feminist Accountability*. Durham, NC: Duke University Press.

Jones, Alethia, and Virginia Eubanks, eds. 2014. *Ain't Gonna Let Nobody Turn Me Around: Forty Years of Movement Building with Barbara Smith*. Albany: State University of New York Press.

Kirschenbaum, Matt. 2016. *Track Changes: A Literary History of Word Processing*. Cambridge, MA: Harvard University Press.

Kovacic, Karen. 2001. "Between L=A=N=G=U=A=G=E and Lyric: The Poetry of Pink-Collar Resistance." *NWSA Journal* 13, no. 1: 22–39.

Lewis, Holly. 2016. *The Politics of Everybody: Feminism, Queer Theory, and Marxism at the Intersection*. London: Zed Books.

Lewis, Roger. 1972. *Outlaws of America: The Underground Press and Its Context*. London: Penguin.

Leyland, Winston, ed. 1975. *Angels of the Lyre: A Gay Poetry Anthology*. San Francisco: Gay Sunshine.

Liu, Petrus. 2015. *Queer Marxism in Two Chinas*. Durham, NC: Duke University Press.

Marshall, Alan. 1983. *Changing the Word: The Printing Industry in Transition*. London: Comedia.

Martin, Gloria. 1986. *Socialist Feminism: The First Decade, 1966–1976*. Seattle: Red Letter.

McMillan, John. 2011. *Smoking Typewriters: The Sixties Underground Press and the Rise of Alternative Media in America*. New York: Oxford University Press USA.

Montgomery, Paul. 1974. "Printers Approve New Contract, 1009–41." *New York Times*, July 24.

"Merle Woo vs. UCB: The History." 1989. *Freedom Socialist Newspaper*, June. socialism.com/drupal-6.8/articles/merle-woo-vs-university-california-berkeley -history?q=node/2529.

"The 'Revolution' on Park Avenue." 1973. *CIS Newsletter*, May 15. Bertram Powers Papers and Photographs, WAG 173, box 1, folder 7, Tamiment Library/Robert F. Wagner Labor Archives, New York University.

Rich, Adrienne. 1980. "Compulsory Heterosexuality and Lesbian Existence." *Signs* 5, no. 4: 631–60.

———. 1991. "Books: Poetry for Daily Use." *Ms. Magazine* 11, no. 2: 74.

Rubin, Gayle. [1984] 1994. "Thinking Sex: Notes for a Radical Theory of the Politics of Sexuality." In *The Lesbian and Gay Studies Reader*, edited by Henry Abelove, Michèle Aina Barale, and David M. Halperin, 3–44. New York: Routledge.

Stein, Jesse Adams. 2016. "Masculinity and Material Culture in Technological Transitions: From Letterpress to Offset Lithography, 1960s–1980s." *Technology and Culture* 57, no. 1: 24–53.

Streitmatter, Rodger. 1995. *Unspeakable: The Rise of the Gay and Lesbian Press in America*. Boston: Faber and Faber.

"Tender Benches: Making the Park & HAIR-RAISING (1976)." 2014. Kelsey Street Press Blog, March 12. www.kelseyst.com/news/2014/03/12/tender-benches-making -the-park-hair-raising-1976/.

Tinkcom, Matthew. 2002. *Working like a Homosexual: Camp, Capital, Cinema*. Durham, NC: Duke University Press.

Updike, John. 1990. *A Rabbit Omnibus*. London: Penguin Books.

Wachsberger, Ken, ed. 2012. *Insider Histories of the Vietnam Era Underground Press, Part 2*. East Lansing: Michigan State University Press.

Wayman, Tom, ed. 1991. *Paperwork: An Anthology*. Madeira Park, BC: Harbour.

Wolverton, Terry. 2002. *Insurgent Muse: Life and Art at the Woman's Building*. San Francisco: City Lights.

BESIDE WOMEN

Charles Dickens, Algernon Charles Swinburne, and Reparative Lesbian Literary History

Natalie Prizel

Repair

QUEERS READ THIS: queers read Matthew Arnold? To what queer purpose could the Victorian stalwart be put? To begin with lines of poetry that have been well worn, whose cultural effects have endured long past the Victorian period that produced them, near to the point of cliché, is to recover words that have never been lost, and to put them to new use. Arnold writes ([1867] 1994: 29–37):

> Ah, love, let us be true
> To one another! for the world, which seems
> To lie before us like a land of dreams,
> So various, so beautiful, so new,
> Hath really neither joy, nor love, nor light,
> Nor certitude, nor peace, nor help for pain;
> And we are here as on a darkling plain
> Swept with confused alarms of struggle and flight,
> Where ignorant armies clash by night.

Arnold's "Dover Beach" might be read as a melancholic rebuke to Victorian positivism or a sally into the darker realms of Victorian apocalyptic thinking, but it does not signal resignation. The poem circulated widely on social media among my many queer Victorianist friends responding to the election of Donald Trump. Imagining it might be useful, they read it to their students. Ian McEwan ([2005] 2006: 278) incorporates "Dover Beach" into his novel *Saturday*, by having a character wield it as a way to disarm her would-be rapist. As a plot device, it feels cheap in

GLQ 24:2–3
DOI 10.1215/10642684-4324813

its suggestion that sexual violence can be overcome by recourse to a shared canon that awakens humanist identification. But the poem does do work—it imagines a possible future, born out of and against the darkness of violence. This essay argues that this insistence on what might endure the mass destruction of modernity is essentially reparative, following Eve Kosofsky Sedgwick (2002: 149) insofar as it "assemble[s] and confer[s] plenitude on an object that will then have the resources to offer an inchoate self."

The question of repair has been at the heart of many of the central debates in queer theory over the past decades. In perhaps the most forceful articulation of queer antisociality and concomitant rejection of the reparative, Lee Edelman (2004: 4), rejecting reproductive futurity also "refuse[s] the insistence of hope itself as affirmation." This essay argues for a version of queer repair that both draws on Sedgwick's reparative reading and expands on, perhaps beyond, the paradigms of reproductive futurity to think about the future, understood by José Esteban Muñoz (2009: 1) as the "warm illumination of a horizon imbued with potentiality." Queer reparativity is more similar to *regeneration*—a word that, according to the *Oxford English Dictionary*, like *repair* dates back to the late fourteenth century—than to the later term *reproduction*. To regenerate or repair is not to make new things but to make things new and better—again and again. I want to suggest that it is our capacity to regenerate, to imagine and restore, in the face of the abjection that would seem to be our inheritance that marks the act of "queering." The capacity to queer is aesthetic, ethical, and erotic. Queering demands not a break from the past but a twisted relation to it.

The term *relating* is of particular importance: the relationship between past and present is affective, akin to Elizabeth Freeman's (2010: 95) *erotohistoriography*, which "admits that contact with historical materials can be precipitated by particular bodily dispositions, and that these connections may elicit bodily responses, even pleasurable ones, that are themselves a form of understanding." I suggest in this essay the usefulness of an affective return to a particularly Victorian past, not in service of reifying Michel Foucault's ([1976] 1990: 3) reductive inauguration of a new period—"the monotonous nights of the Victorian bourgeoisie"— but rather to think about how the period queered itself, offering what I am calling a reparative lesbian literary tradition.

This essay considers two male authors—Charles Dickens and Algernon Charles Swinburne, alongside a series of intertexts and continuations—to suggest that the two participate in, if not inaugurate, a tradition of lesbian repair. Whereas Dickens participates actively in the discourse of romantic friendship between women, Swinburne focuses on Sapphic erotics more explicitly. Despite such differences, Swinburne ([1902] 1972: 224) deeply admired Dickens, whom he called "the greatest Englishman of his generation." This essay focuses on Swinburne's 1866 volume *Poems and Ballads, First Series*, which the *Saturday Review* described that year as evidence of "a mind all aflame with the feverish carnality of a schoolboy" (Morley [1866] 1995: 34), in conversation with Dickens's *Bleak House* (1853). In a series of close readings of these widely divergent texts, I demonstrate how the authors use similar structural paradigms in characterizing relationships between women. Elizabeth Freeman (2010: xvi–xvii) most effectively makes a queer case for close reading: "To close read is to linger, to dally, to take pleasure in tarrying, and to hold out that these activities can allow us to look both hard and askance at the norm. . . . the queerest commitment of my own book is also close reading: the decision to unfold, slowly, a small amount of imaginative texts . . . and to treat these texts and their formal work as theories of their own, interventions upon both critical theory and historiography." What is most generative in Freeman's approach is the idea that literary texts articulate and anticipate theory; accordingly, I argue that Dickens's and Swinburne's texts become a kind of lesbian theory and attest to the cultural pervasiveness of the aesthetics and ethics of lesbian repair.

I make a claim for a renewed transhistorical use of the word *lesbian*, not to suggest a return to Adrienne Rich's model of the lesbian continuum, which has been rightfully critiqued for "desexualiz[ing] lesbianism" (Marcus 2007: 10). My use of the term is focused on present need more than historicity: I argue that these texts constitute an important part of a usable archive that is needed today in thinking about lesbian literary history. Lytton Strachey ([1918] 1970: viii) argues, "Human beings are too important to be treated as mere symptoms of the past," but perhaps their fictional counterparts can be guides for the present. Dickens and Swinburne engage in a particular structural way of thinking about erotics between women that continues to mark what might be called lesbian writing.[1] I use the term not only to claim a structure that was *then* but also to reclaim a category for the *now* that I worry is in danger of disappearing back into the musty closet from which it emerged.

One primary reason for the disappearance of *lesbian* has been, unsurprisingly, the insurgence of the term *queer*. The term degenders lesbianism in ways that may be useful to coalitional politics and noncategorical thinking but not necessarily to the formation of a literary tradition grounded in the Victorian period. Critics have argued that lesbian erotics in Victorian literature are often written "primarily within the male literary tradition" in which "lesbian fantasies allow male writers to indulge . . . the 'wish to be a woman'" (Dellamora 1990: 85, 75). I am not willing to cede the lesbian as a code for male-male desire. As Rich ([1982] 1993: 239) has said: "Lesbians have historically been deprived of a political existence through 'inclusion' as female versions of male homosexuality." Similarly, Terry Castle (1993: 12) asserts that the lesbian "is not a gay man." One should read erotics between women as just that, refusing the assumption that the presence of women is always already in service of something else.

Furthermore, to the extent that the relationships in these texts are queer, they are only so in relation to the most banal versions of Victorian intimacy and ethics. Therefore, to the extent I use *queer* in this essay, I do so following the paradigm set forth by Robyn Wiegman and Elizabeth Wilson (2015: 11) in their special issue of *differences* on queer theory without antinormativity. Whereas much of queer theory has imagined itself according to the preposition *against*, we have yet to appreciate what Wiegman and Wilson call "the more intimate and complicit gesture of moving *athwart*." (Prepositions, it seems to me, are as important a contested grammatical site through which queerness might be articulated as pronouns.) *Athwart* suggests an attitude that is oblique even as it is complicit, and it is this obliqueness that I see in Dickens's and Swinburne's portrayals of erotic attachments between women.

To use the term *lesbian* is to invite the charge of ahistoricism or anachronism, either one reckless. In naming a lesbian literary history, I maintain an interest in the historical points in which iterations of lesbian repair emerge but not necessarily in connecting a line between them. Valerie Traub (2013: 26) argues against such an approach, calling it "queer unhistoricism": "By offering either a synchronic analysis or one that paratactically juxtaposed and connected modernity with premodernity, they could bracket the question of any intervening time span—indeed the point was to bracket it." This essay does precisely what Traub fiercely condemns. While I focus on the Victorian period, I foray forward: while the essay is grounded in the 1850s and 1860s, the 1950s and 1960s—periods associated with a stifling regime of the normative and its disruptions—provide continuities that are worth exploring.

I understand the relationships among these multiple-points according to Eve Kosofsky Sedgwick's (2002: 8) concept of *beside*, which "seems to offer some useful resistance to the ease with which *beneath* and *beyond* turn from spatial descriptors into implicit narratives of, respectively, origin and telos." *Beside* is the relational preposition that constructs, contracts, expands, and rewrites something like a lesbian literary history based on a particular ethical stance rather than teleological movement. In Zadie Smith's (2000: 227) *White Teeth*, a character is admonished by her teacher, "Never read what is old with a modern ear." The admonishment, however, is no more or less than a colloquial version of "always historicize!" Those of us who read literature outside what we immediately work on do not read in periods or even in sequence. Furthermore, queer readers scour archives for traces of ourselves, however anachronistic, and suspicious, such a practice might be.[2] Without disavowing history, we might come to texts with an attitude that, however subconsciously, follows Madhavi Menon's (2013: 783) response to Traub: "History is not always historicist."

Dickens and Swinburne participate in a version of a literary history, then, based on ideas of perverse sympathy and intersubjectivity as foundational to a newly imagined world. In contrast to the antisociality endorsed by Edelman and others, the kind of empathy that unites these works might be considered hypersocial—social to the point that self and other become messily conflated.[3] The joke about lesbian couples' "urge to merge" is well worn, but whereas that urge is usually presented as a sign of complacency, or relational frumpiness, I argue that that urge is not only profoundly imbricated in Victorian culture but also profoundly radical for imagining a lesbian literary history that might fortify us for the future.

(Lesbian) Bed Death

"Nothing is better, I well think, / Than love" (Swinburne [1866] 2000b: 1–2). So Swinburne begins his necrophiliac poem, "The Leper," in a mode redolent of Arnold's speaker, lost on a plain with nothing left but the possibility of love. "The Leper" imagines a physically intimate encounter between a medieval scribe and his aristocratic mistress, first dying, then dead, of leprosy. After she is taken ill, the lady is rejected by her royal companions and her lover, at which point the scribe takes her into his home, cares for her, embraces her, and engages in an intimate and likely sexual relationship with her. As she approaches death, the question of her ability to consent to his attentions, sexual and otherwise, becomes more pressing. By the time of the poetic utterance, the speaker has himself contracted leprosy, as he has continued to embrace his beloved's diseased body for six months after her death. The speaker's statement and the poem's sentiment can, I argue, be assimilated into a Victorian culture in which radical sympathetic identification was the basis for moral, even heroic, self-making. The poem enacts what might be called, perversely, ethical necrophilia.

Through acts of love and identification one might become more, or better, than one once was. Sympathy, however, could go too far precisely at the moment in which the subject threatened to be subsumed into another. George Eliot's narrator in *Middlemarch* ([1872] 2008: 182) famously warns against the dangers of excessive fellow-feeling (sensitivity to others' experiences): "If we had a keen vision and feeling of all ordinary human life, it would be like hearing the grass grow and the squirrel's heartbeat, and we should die of that roar which lies on the other side of silence." Mary Ann O'Farrell (2004: 152) theorizes Eliotic sympathy using the term *susceptibility*, which points to "preparedness and receptivity" as well as, more ominously, "a vulnerability—a state of endangerment." Excessive susceptibility might blur the divide between subject and object. Swinburne ([1877] 1894: 13) delights in this sort of ontological confusion, as he praises the Brontës for prose that partakes in such blurring, noting their "power to make us feel in every nerve, at every step forward which our imagination is compelled to take under the guidance of another." Such absorption of subject into object and vice versa might look like that moment in Emily Brontë's *Wuthering Heights* ([1847] 2003: 87), so beloved by Swinburne, when one of the central lovers, Cathy, declares that she and her beloved are one: "I *am* Heathcliff." "The Leper" exemplifies the danger that Eliot warns of. By the time of his speaking, the speaker of "The Leper" has contracted leprosy himself: the poem's title, then, may refer to its speaker or his beloved. The embrace described in the poem seems to follow the logic of sympathetic intimacy to its perverse conclusion.

Despite the era's reputation for prudishness, to embrace, to touch in the Victorian period was a moral imperative. In his 1843 polemical volume *Past and Present*, written in one of the most tumultuous decades of Victorian history, Thomas Carlyle ([1843] 1965: 151) lambastes the Victorian passer-by who refuses to touch: "The forlorn Irish Widow applies to her fellow-creatures, as if saying, 'Behold I am sinking, bare of help: ye must help me!' They answer, 'No, impossible; thou art no sister of ours.' But she proves her sisterhood; her typhus-fever kills them: they actually were her brothers, though denying it! Had human creature ever to go lower for proof?" If by looking past the Irish widow Carlyle's readers hope to maintain distance, the transmissibility of disease attests to the futility of such endeavors, dismantling a strict subject-object divide. For touch to count as such, it must imply intimacy; moreover, the risk of contagion, transmission, and disease does not stand as an ethically permissible barrier. The speaker of "The Leper," then, passes the ethical test by taking in the beloved; however, the fact that the beloved's sickness and ultimately her death allows the speaker of "The Leper" the access to her body that he enjoys complicates the question of motive and consent. The speaker recognizes that it is only because of her abject state that his beloved allows him to touch her, but he persists:

> She might have loved me a little too,
> Had I been humbler for her sake.
> But that new shame could make love new
> She saw not—yet her shame did make.
> (Swinburne [1866] 2000b: 113–20)

In suggesting that "new shame could make love new"—that the shame of the interclass love might reinvent the shame of the leprosy that has caused the beloved to be rejected by her noble friends—Swinburne makes a case for the regenerative power of love. Heather Love (2007: 32) warns critics to be careful about the redemption of shame in writing queer genealogies: "By including queer figures from the past in a positive genealogy of gay identity, we make good on their suffering, transforming their shame into pride after the fact." What is most provocative about Swinburne's notion of transformed shame is that he suggests it can happen in the moment without historical distance. If the speaker's love cannot create pride where shame once was, at least shame might be transformed. It is as if to say, "shame gets better."

How can one read a poem about shame and necrophilia, with its explicitly invoiced dubitable consent, within a history of Victorian moral aspirations understood through the locus of sympathy? A contemporaneous review ("Mr. Swinburne's New Poems" 1866) of Swinburne's volume in the *New York Times* suggests that Swinburne's work represents the same kind of sexual depravity already seen in both literary novels and popular ones. The critic uses the novel as the generic benchmark against which Swinburne's poem might be critiqued, a genre he imagines to be dangerously instructional, "in the hands of every girl." Insofar as the novel is understood as the genre of common life and a frequently didactic one, the critic demonstrates that the sexual depravity that characterizes Swinburne's oeuvre lies within a continuum, even a condemnable one, of the normal. If the *Times* reviewer implies that the everyday can accommodate interclass necrophiliac love, what is everyday life coming to?

The necrophiliac embrace appears not infrequently in the fiction of the period. Jane Eyre—the literary creation of Swinburne's much-beloved and admired Charlotte Brontë—lies with the body of her deceased schoolgirl friend, Helen Burns. After promising to stay with the dying Helen, Jane falls asleep: "When I awoke it was day: an unusual movement roused me, I looked up; I was in somebody's arms. . . . a day or two afterwards I learned that Miss Temple, on returning to her own room at dawn, had found me laid in a little crib; my face against Helen Burns's shoulder, my arms around her neck. I was asleep, and Helen was—dead"

(Brontë [1848] 2001: 70). This scene is remarkable in its awareness of the implications of this act of touching. Like the speaker of "The Leper," Jane seems aware of the potential public reaction to the revelation of her necrophiliac embrace. By recounting herself as unconscious of the fact that the body in her arms had died, Jane paints herself as blameless and innocent, and indeed the school mistresses seem to find her so as well, since Jane tells us, "I was not reprimanded" (ibid.: 70). But Jane's need to defend herself thus, along with the two-day delay in telling Jane where and how she was found, indicates that this is indeed a momentous revelation and one that might be potentially damning. The touching of the sick and dying and dead that Swinburne's poem describes also echoes the necrophiliac embrace in *Wuthering Heights*, however—the result of an obsessive myopia that has turned pathological. Recounting the act of digging into Cathy's grave, Heathcliff dreams "of dissolving with her, and being more happy still!" (Brontë [1847] 2003: 247). If Heathcliff and Swinburne's speaker seem extreme, their actions lie on a continuum of behavior in which even a bourgeois heroine such as Jane Eyre can engage and remain morally unscathed.

The daily bourgeois life of the Victorian period, I contend, is expansive. Sharon Marcus (2007: 13) warns of the tendency in queer studies "to downplay or refuse the equally powerful ways that same-sex bonds have been acknowledged by the bourgeois liberal public sphere." Bourgeois public life in the period can, I argue, reluctantly include the necrophiliac embrace. Even the paragon of bourgeois normativity in the Victorian period, Queen Victoria herself, was not so different from Swinburne's speaker.[4] When Prince Albert died in 1861, the queen's doctors were disturbed at an outpouring of grief so extreme that she refused to leave his body for three days. For the rest of her days, the royal widow had her husband's chamber pot emptied (Weintraub 1997: 436).

My placing Swinburne's speaker in the context of bourgeois probity risks endorsing a politics of respectability. As Lauren Berlant and Lee Edelman (2013: xiv) warn in *Sex, or the Unbearable*, "Sex, as a locus for optimism, is a site at which the promise of overcoming division and antagonism is frequently played out. But the consequences of such efforts to resolve our social and psychic contradictions can include the establishment of sexual norms and the circumscription of sex for socially legitimated ends. This warning does not apply to Swinburne's poetic project, however, because it imagines a limited range of social legitimation. Wiegman and Wilson (2015: 13) argue, "Antinormative stances project stability and immobility onto normativity. In so doing, they generate much of the political tyranny they claim belongs (over there) to regimes of normativity." Taking the historiography we have inherited from Foucault as a given, we imagine a normative monolith beginning in the Victorian period—described by Virginia Woolf's ([1928] 1973: 225–26) queer narrator, Orlando, in terms of a seismic shift: "A turbulent welter of cloud covered the city. All was dark; all was doubt; all was confusion. The Eighteenth century was over; the Nineteenth century had begun." This darkness extends, the story goes, to our own time—the "quagmire of the present," to use José Esteban Muñoz's (2009: 1) phrase, in which Foucault's "we other Victorians" are stuck. The norm, however, in addition to having been historically contingent over the past two hundred years, is as contingent as its outliers, and, as Wiegman and Wilson (2015: 15) argue, *"averages are synecdochal measures of the entire group. Averages don't exclude anyone."* From this, they conclude that "antinormativity misses what is most engaging about a norm: that in collating the world, it gathers up everything" (ibid.: 17). Even, at its fringes and despite *Poems and Ballad's* largely hostile reviews, a mind as perverse as that of Algernon Charles Swinburne.

The Urge to Merge

Despite the apparent heterosexuality of the pairing in "The Leper," structurally the poem follows a particularly lesbian erotic formation, one frequently mocked as the "urge to merge." One could easily imagine the speaker in a position of what Love (2007: 29) celebrates as abjection that has been—and perhaps is—essential to the making of queer identity. She writes, "Rather than disavowing the history of marginalization and abjection, I suggest we embrace it, exploring the ways it continues to structure queer experience in the present." Such abjection is frequently associated with the position of the butch in a lesbian pairing; as Eve Kosofsky Sedgwick (2002: 63) suggests, "butch abjection" is one manifestation of "shame consciousness and shame creativity." Sedgwick's association of butch abjection with shame is significant in regard to "The Leper" because the shame the speaker feels seems to vacillate wildly. When the speaker does invoke shame and his own doubt, the speaker suggests that the beloved, unable to see shame made new, is herself constituted by shame: "Yet her shame did make." Furthermore, in her discussion of butch-femme aesthetics, Sue-Ellen Case (1988–1989: 56) argues that "the butch-femme couple inhabit the subject position together." This kind of merge is structurally similar to the one in "The Leper," though Swinburne's poem takes intersubjectivity to its perverse extreme by suggesting that it is in the transmission of disease that two become one.[5] Even without lesbians per se, the poem leaves us with a lesbian structural paradigm characterized by a mutual subsumption of one subjectivity into another's in which both subjects share in abjection and power, in shame and glory.

The "urge to merge," while a trope used both derisively and playfully to characterize lesbian relationships, is of course not limited to lesbians but is essentially queer. But it seems that lesbians are seen to particularly embrace this stance, even as it is rhetorically weaponized against them. That said, this kind of merge does appear in a gay male tradition, literary and otherwise. Tim Dean's work on barebacking subcultures within the gay community, for example, is particularly relevant because of his focus—as well as Swinburne's and Dickens's—on the transmission of disease. Dean (2008: 82) writes, "What particularly interests me is how unprotected sex has given rise to a discourse of kinship, based on the idea that the human immunodeficiency virus may be used to create blood ties." He goes further to argue, "Gay men have discovered that they can in some sense reproduce without women. In breeding a virus, these men are propagating also a way of life" (ibid.: 86). But sero-converting another is replication without regeneration. It makes more virus but it makes nothing new. The alternative kinship networks of caretaking during the AIDS crisis would be a more apt comparison to the relationships under discussion, despite Dean's focus on transmission.

William Empson ([1951] 1979: 78), in his assessment of "The Leper," writes, "both characters are humane, and indeed behave better than they think." In a rare nineteenth-century defense of the poem, one "Sylvanus Urban," writing in the *Gentleman's Magazine* in 1889, argues that "the poem which represented the triumph of mind over matter, of affection over loathing, was spiritual and not animal" (Urban 1889: 104). Swinburne's speaker reaches an ethical goal that puts him or her higher than those who refuse to touch Carlyle's Irish widow on the street. But the end is still death, with only the language of the poem left to do the work of repair. And the speaker is uneasy about his own ability to do such work: "It may be all my love went wrong— / A scribe's work writ awry and blurred, / Scrawled after the blind evensong— / Spoilt music with no perfect word" (Swinburne [1866] 2000b: 129–32). Doubt, it seems, is part of the ethical process.

Swinburne's leper ends his speech with a rhetorical appeal to God's justice rather than a direct address to a reading public or to God himself. "Will not God do right?" extends the ethical question beyond the realm of the human. This moment is comparable to the story in the Gospel of John in which Jesus resurrects Lazarus, dead four days since. When Jesus asks Martha to uncover her brother's grave, she responds with the disgust that accompanies taboo: "By this time he stinketh: for he hath been dead four days" (John 11:39).[6] Jesus chastises her, "Said I not unto thee, that, if thou wouldest believe, thou shouldest see the glory of God?" (John 11:40). The leper has not, over six months, given in to disgust and yet still waits for God's justice. The speaker is perhaps too pious to complain to God directly; therefore, he asks the question of the reader. If God will not do right, he seems to say, might you, reader, do me the justice of looking kindly upon my love?

In this cry for justice, the leper sounds not so different from the outraged narrator of a Victorian novel, faced with the social consequences of failed intimacies. In *Bleak House* (Dickens [1853] 2003: 180), the death of one character provokes such outrage on the part of the third-person narrator:

> With houses looking on, on every side, save where a reeking little tunnel of a court gives access to the iron gate—with every villainy of life in action close on death, and every poisonous element of death in action close on life—here, they lower our dear brother down a foot or two: here, sow him in corruption, to be raised in corruption: an avenging ghost at many a sick-bedside: a shameful testimony to future ages, how civilization and barbarism walked this boastful island together.

The ethical burden, in Dickens's prose and Swinburne's poem, lies with us. It is up to us to read the "shameful testimony" and recognize the source of the shame—not in the diseased and corrupted body itself but in a response that distances that body.

Dickens's *Bleak House* has its own share of disease and questions of transmission and the ethics of intimacy. At the center of the novel, its protagonist, Esther Summerson, contracts what is presumably smallpox from her maid, Charley, who has in turn contracted it from the orphan crossing-sweeper, Jo, to whom Esther has tended. Jo, despite himself and the fact that he is to much of the world "stone blind and dumb!" (ibid.: 257), functions as a kind of Patient Zero—blamed in a manner that belies the fictionality of his blameworthiness—the locus around which connections in the novel are made. The idea of connection is made explicit when the third-person narrator asks, rhetorically, anticipating his or her reader's question:

> What connexion can there be, between the place in Lincolnshire, the house in town, the Mercury in powder, and the whereabout of Jo the outlaw with the broom, who had that distant ray of light upon him when he swept the churchyard-step? What connexion can there have been between many people in the innumerable histories of his world, who, from opposite sides of great gulfs, have, nevertheless, been very curiously brought together! (ibid.: 256)

The "connexions" become clear through plot but also through the transmission of disease. Jo has left the scene by the time Charley and then Esther acquire their illnesses, leaving the exchange to be particularly between women. When Esther falls ill, Esther commands that under no circumstance should Ada Clare, her companion and beloved, be admitted to see them: "And in the morning, when you hear Miss Ada in the garden, if I should not be quite able to go to the window-curtain as usual, do you go, Charley, and say I am asleep. . . . let no one come" (ibid.: 503). She later reiterates this demand, "if you let her in but once, only to look upon me for one moment as I lie here, I shall die" (ibid.: 504). Esther presents the threat to Ada as a threat to herself and uses it as a threat against Charley in an act of triangulation between the three women.

Is keeping Ada from her the ultimate act of love—the refusal of touch and the risk of transmission? And would such refusal be possible if Esther did not have the now-immune Charley to take care of her? During her illness, Esther "had heard my Ada crying at the door, day and night; I had heard her calling to me that I was cruel and did not love her; I had heard her praying and imploring to be let in to nurse and comfort me, and to leave my bedside no more; but I had only said, when I could speak, 'Never, my sweet girl, never!'" (ibid.: 556). Shortly after she makes her final demands to Charley, Esther asks her, "And now come sit beside me for a little while, and touch me with your hand" (ibid.: 504). Esther's use of the term *beside* can be understood in the sense that Sedgwick uses it: within the context of the chapter, the hierarchy between maid and mistress (who is also a paid housekeeper) is collapsed; furthermore, the chapter simply sees the reproduction and transmission of disease, with no teleological movement toward cure or death. In fact, this chapter is the last of Esther's narration in the tenth monthly number of the serial publication; therefore, Dickens's readers would have had to wait to see if Esther recovered. Because Esther immediately contracts the disease from Charley, the latter's healing becomes a pyrrhic victory because the promise of reunion with Ada is thwarted and Esther can speak to Ada only through a curtained window.

Before their reunion, the revelation of her newly scarred face to Ada worries Esther, and she hides behind a door when Ada comes to see her, hesitating to unveil herself. There is a similar moment of unveiling in "The Leper." As a servant in the mistress's house, the scribe "plucked his clerk's hood back to see / Her curled-up lips and amorous hair"; similarly, as she lies dead in his cottage, he "plait[s] up her hair to see / How she then wore it on the brows" (Swinburne [1866] 2000b: 11–12, 16–17). Both acts performed by the speaker enable his gaze in acts of unveiling that potentially deconstruct the boundary between the speaker and his love-object, unfettering the gaze in such a way as to allow unmediated access to the beloved. In the first act, however, he is in a position only to control his own unveiling, while in the second he is master of his beloved's body as well as his own. The act of mutual unveiling is suggestive, albeit obliquely, of a marriage ceremony between women, even though it is only with her future husband, Allan Woodcourt, that Esther literally unveils her scarred visage. Nonetheless, Esther has far more of a lover's anxiety about seeing Ada; in her first interaction with Woodcourt after her illness, she becomes "so comfortable with [herself] now not to mind the veil, and to be able to put it aside" (Dickens [1853] 2003: 705). In a much more fleshy encounter, when Esther and Ada reunite, Esther describes their passionate embrace: "O how happy I was, down upon the floor, with my sweet beautiful girl down upon the floor too, holding my scarred face to her lovely cheek, bathing it with tears and kisses, rocking me to and fro like a child, calling me by every tender name that she could think of, and pressing me to her faithful heart" (ibid.: 588). To read the women down on the floor together as erotic requires no great leap of imagination.

The chapter in which Esther falls ill is called "Nurse and Patient," and as the title of "The Leper" does, refers to both Charley and Esther interchangeably (Jo is also a patient earlier in the chapter). Once again, the deliberate confusion of personages, of the subject and object of care, results in muddied subjectivity. Esther's subjectivity, however, frequently seems indeterminate in the novel, making her a strange protagonist—one who must share the narration of the novel with a third person. En route to the eponymous Bleak House, Esther drifts somewhere between wake and sleep: "I began to lose the identity of the sleeper [Caddy Jellyby] resting on me. Now, it was Ada; now, one of my old Reading friends from whom I could not believe I had so recently parted. Now, it was the little mad woman worn out with curtseying and smiling; now, some one in authority at Bleak House. Lastly, it was no one, and I was no one" (ibid.: 63). This passage suggests the contingency of Esther's subjectivity, which only seems to gain strength in relation to those around her, particularly Ada, whom she at this point has only just met but has already become "my darling," while to Ada, Esther is already "my love" (ibid.: 45).

Esther and Ada are easily assimilated under the rubric of the Victorian romantic friendship, and it would be simple to begin and end the inquiry into their relationship there. But the merge of subjectivities that occurs between the women exceeds that of the romantic friendship trope and suggests, if not a sexual relationship per se, a lesbian literary and erotic structure. Anne Carson (1986: 16) argues that Eros's "activation calls for three structural components—lover, beloved, and that which comes between them." Esther and Ada's loving relationship is defined quite literally by what comes between them, Ada's impending marriage to her hapless cousin Richard. When Ada and Richard announce their marriage to Esther, Esther responds in a manner almost as morbidly perverse as that of the leper. She listens at a barrier, at the door of the newlyweds: "I listened for a few moments; and in the musty rotting silence of the house, believed that I could hear the murmur of their young voices. I put my lips to the hearse-like panel of the door, as a kiss for my dear, and came quietly down again, thinking that one of these days I would confess the visit" (Dickens [1853] 2003: 790). The "hearse-like panel" to which Esther refers contributes to the sense of muddled subjectivities: is it she who lies within the tomb or Ada and Richard? Perhaps this is another sort of lesbian bed death—one in which lesbian intimacy is buried and the bed is converted into the heterosexual marriage bed.

Richard, soon after his marriage to Ada, does indeed go to his grave. Though Esther marries, her attachment to Ada becomes no less central, as is most evident perhaps by her striking assertion that the younger Richard, Ada's son, "says that he has two mamas, and I am one" (ibid.: 988). At the end of the novel, she reflects: "I think my darling girl is more beautiful than ever" (ibid.). The famous last lines of *Bleak House* are Esther's response to her husband's question, "And don't you know that you are prettier than you ever were?" to which she thinks, "I did not know that; I am not certain that I know it now. But I know that my dearest little pets are pretty, and that my darling is very beautiful, and that my husband is very handsome, and that my guardian has the brightest and most benevolent face that ever was seen; and that they can very well do without much beauty in me—even supposing—" (ibid.: 989). By ending with two paeans to Ada's beauty—her darling's beauty—Esther in effect externalizes herself and projects herself onto and through Ada. Her beauty, "even supposing—," becomes irrelevant because it has come to occupy another's body.

Possession

The kind of radical empathy that was idealized in the Victorian period—and taken to its perversely logical extreme by Swinburne—serves at once as an ideal and a disturbance. The disturbance lies in the convergence of identification and desire in such a way that renders clear subject-object divisions moot. Marcus (2007: 135) refutes the notion "that the beholder must choose between desire and identification." The amalgamation of desire and identifications might seem to straddle the line between the eroticism and narcissism, between self-worship and worship of the other that might render one abject. And the convergence of the two—the two women, the states of identification and desire—is both titillating and disturbing. For example, in Todd Haynes's 2015 adaption (*Carol*) of Patricia Highsmith's 1952 lesbian romance *The Price of Salt*, Carol says to her lover, Therese, on seeing her naked body for the first time, "I never looked like that." This moment, even as it highlights the age difference between the women, signifies a mode of erotic attachment in which the female form is a site through which to glance backward, for comparison as much as longing, for identification as much as desire.

Disturbance, however, is abundantly evident in Swinburne's ([1866] 2000a) Sapphic poem "Anactoria," in which Sappho describes how the two women might merge.

> I feel thy blood against my blood; my pain
> Pains thee, and lips bruise lips, and vein stings vein.
> Let fruit be crushed on fruit, let flower on flower,
> Breast kindle breast, and either burn one hour.
> (11–14)

As Swinburne ([1866] 2000c: 407) imagines Sappho—and he admits that "it is as near as I can come; and no man can come close to her"—consumption, cannibalism even, is the scorned lover's dearest wish:

> That I could drink thy veins as wine, and eat
> Thy breasts like honey! that from face to feet
> Thy body were abolished and consumed,
> And in my flesh thy very flesh entombed.
> (Swinburne [1866] 2000a: 111–14)

The enjambment between lines 111 and 112 suggests that the desire to consume and the desire to praise "Thy breasts like honey" (does "like" mean Anactoria's breasts are sweet like honey or simply edible?) are messily conflated. The speaker is at once violently possessive and undone by her lover's body. Despite the will to power of the speaker, moreover, the same speaker is abject in the face of a lover who has spurned her; she begins the poem by stating "my life is bitter with love" (ibid.: 1). Sappho partakes in a kind of abjection that Love associates with the queer subject position. Nonetheless, abjection is not synonymous with destruction, nor is it beyond repair. Carson (1986: 14) argues that Sappho experiences no jealousy of the man present in fragment 31, on which "Anactoria" is founded, and "were she to change places with the man . . . she would be entirely destroyed." Swinburne, in contrast, does see jealousy but suggests that Sappho is destroyed regardless;

she only hopes to take Anactoria down with her. The stanza's subjunctive mode ("That I could . . .") suggests that doing such to Anactoria is essential to Sappho's regeneration, not to her ultimate downfall. It is in her abjection that, Sappho prophesies (Swinburne [1866] 2000a: 276–90), she will survive, as will her love, outliving the mortal Anactoria and the fickleness of the heart:

> I Sappho shall be one with all these things,
> With all high things for ever; and my face
> Seen once, my songs once heard in a strange place,
> Cleave to men's lives, and waste the days thereof
> With gladness and much sadness and long love.
> Yea, they shall say, earth's womb has borne in vain
> New things, and never this best thing again;
> Borne days and men, borne fruits and wars and wine,
> Seasons and songs, but no song more like mine.
> And they shall know me as ye who have known me here,
> Last year when I loved Atthis, and this year
> When I love thee; and they shall praise me, and say
> "She hath all time as all we have our day,
> Shall she not live and have her will"—even I?
> Yea, though thou diest, I say I shall not die.

In suggesting how she, and the manifestation of her love as poetry, will outlive Anactoria, and "borne days and men," Sappho locates power not in lesbian love itself but in its structure and, particularly, in a kind of abjection that is sublime and poetically enabling. Sappho announces the end of regeneration through her polemic: "Yea, they shall say, earth's womb has borne in vain / New things, and never this best thing again" (ibid.: 281–82). And yet, Swinburne's envoicing of Sappho is a literal manifestation of regeneration and repair, imagining a past literary tradition that is useful, even needful, in the present. In recognizing that no man can come close to Sappho, however, Swinburne suggests that his act of repair will not render invisible the rents and tears that Sappho's fragments have been subjected to over the years but might allow for the making of a new kind of fabric, beautiful in its brokenness.

In addition to her argument that eros contains what comes between the two lovers, Carson (1986: 30) contends that "Eros is an issue of boundaries. . . . And it is only, suddenly, at the moment when I would dissolve that boundary, I realize I never can." There is, however, seepage across boundaries through the act of touch.

This is essential not only in thinking about lesbian relationships in the Victorian period but also in thinking about one's relationship to (lesbian) literary history as well. Carolyn Dinshaw (1999: 39) defines queer literary history as "a history of things touching. . . . Beyond the basic understanding that a queer history will be about the body because it is about sex, my queer history has a relation to the tactile." The absence of touch has been the forcible condition of many same-sex pairings. In his novel *Giovanni's Room*, James Baldwin ([1956] 2000: 56) reflects on the problem of "all touch, but no contact." Similarly, in *The Price of Salt* ([1952] 1991: 256), Carol relocates the meaning of that stinging word, *degeneration*, from the queer touch to the absence of intimacy: "It is true, if I were to go on like this . . . never possessing one person long enough so that knowledge of a person is a superficial thing—that is degeneration." *Possession* and its knowledge and *degeneration* are conceived of as naturally and necessarily in opposition; similarly, in Sappho's case, her possession of and by Anactoria constitutes Sappho and makes her immortal in poetry. Furthermore, her poetry "cleave[s] to men's lives" and is thus transportable from context to context, even beyond the lesbian context from which her words emerge. She also comes to be possessed by the male poet: as Yopie Prins (1999: 17) argues, "Swinburne's Sappho . . . is a rhythmicized body that disappears and reappears in the rhythms of its own scattering, according to a logic of disintegration and figurative reconstitution." Through such possession and the abjection it implies, she regenerates in verse to be repeated indefinitely.

Esther Summerson is no Sappho, but she most frequently refers to Ada using the possessive *my*. It is through this process of claiming that Ada becomes less than a fully realized character and more a projection of Esther's desire. Ada is often conceived as a flat character, if not a boring one, the blond foil in a novel where the brunette is centralized. Ada seems to be a blank, a palimpsest, a surface. An understanding of Ada as boring, however, obscures the very structure of lesbian literary erotics. Ada seems empty because the novel is not concerned with her subjectivity but with Esther's mind in relation to her. This structure, in its own queer, twisting way, anticipates the obsessional, possessive erotic lesbian structure in *The Price of Salt*. Carol's suitability is less important than Therese's construction of her. Rooney Mara (2015), who plays Therese in *Carol*, says that most of Highsmith's novels are about the criminal mind, whereas *The Price of Salt* is about the amorous mind. In an interview, Haynes (Davis 2015) recounts the claustrophobic experience of reading *The Price of Salt*, being "stuck with Therese inside her own consciousness." The sections of *Bleak House* narrated by Esther feel this way also, though they are broken by the entrance of the third-person narrator, just as in the screenplay of *Carol*, the writer Phyllis Nagy disrupts the hegemony of

Therese's consciousness to include glimpses into Carol's inner life. That said, if Ada is merely a projection or a possession of Esther's, it is the structure of possession that defines the relationship more than the psychology of the two characters.

Highsmith once said that her title came from her investment in the biblical story of Lot's wife, who looks back at Sodom and Gomorrah in flames and is turned into a pillar of salt (Schenkar 2009: 272). Heather Love (2007: 5) writes of this same biblical moment, "In turning back toward this lost world she herself is lost: she becomes a monument to destruction, an emblem of eternal regret." What is most notable in these Victorian texts, characterized by a structure of lesbian repair, is how productive, in fact, turning back is, for us as readers but also for the various speakers and characters discussed. What if it were possible to look back not in regret but in search of something usable for the here and now?

Regeneration

Elizabeth Bishop went through a "brief Swinburne phase" (Brown 1996: 21). While she was referring to her imitations of the poet in her juvenilia, Swinburne also seems like a sexual identity one could put on or dispense with. But Bishop—private, reticent, restrained, perfected Bishop—was no Swinburne, and fleshly eroticism remains obscured in her work, if present in the margins. "Close, close all night" is an unpublished poem dated to the late 1960s, during her time in Brazil with her lover, Lota de Macedo Soares. Bishop gave the poem to the artist José Alberto Nemer on the occasion of his marriage: it is a queer poem presented as a gift to sanction that most normative of institutions, heterosexual marriage. Nemer inscribed it to his wife along with an etching, described by Lloyd Schwartz (1991: 90) as "an image of two lovers entwined on a bed: an arm reaches around a woman's body and under her breast; the second figure is hidden behind her, unidentifiable, androgynous."

Bishop's poem invites such an image. It reads:

> Close close all night
> the lovers keep.
> They turn together
> in their sleep,
> close as two pages
> in a book
> that read each other
> in the dark.

Each knows all
the other knows,
learned by heart
from head to toes.
(Bishop [n.d.] 2007: 1–12)

As they read each other, the lovers do not create knowledge; rather, they attend to each other's. There is nothing new; everything is already "learned by heart" down the length of their bodies. But the conjunction of the two pages, the one with the other, creates new meaning, whether lyrical or narrative.

In the fall of 2012 I taught a classroom of first-year students Bishop's ([1955] 2008: 13–18) poem "The Shampoo," which concludes:

The shooting stars in your black hair
in bright formation
are flocking where,
so straight, so soon?
—Come, let me wash it in this big tin basin,
battered and shiny like the moon.

This shocked my students, who I thought were inured to shock. The idea of a person washing another person's hair was intimate beyond imagination, much more intimate than sex, they said. They might be right: it is not sex itself but the fear of being subsumed into a radically empathetic intimacy that is terrifying and sublime, threatening but regenerating. Radical empathy, particularly the radical empathy of the sexual encounter, may be too much; it may be, in Berlant and Edelman's (2013) words, "unbearable." Nonetheless, this archive has shown again and again that it is essential for the "making new" that characterizes queer repair. Walt Whitman (1855: 17) famously wrote, "Who need be afraid of the merge?" It turns out, much of the time we all are. In a moment that reflects her courage throughout *The Price of Salt*, Therese thinks to herself, "How was it possible to be afraid and in love" (Highsmith [1952] 1991: 209). When Carol and Therese are separated, Carol writes to her, "I remember your courage that I hadn't suspected, and it gives me courage" (ibid.: 245). This is the courage to repair, to regenerate, to imagine, if not a new world, a new way of being in it.

Notes

This essay is in honor of the late Linda H. Peterson, who introduced me to Swinburne and made me love him.

1. Nonetheless, one should be careful not to too quickly dismiss the "lesbianism" of Swinburne's Sappho. Nicholas Shrimpton (1993: 64) compares Swinburne's rendering of Sappho to those of his (male) contemporaries: Swinburne "insists that Sappho cannot be assimilated to the polite assumptions of a male, nineteenth-century, North West European, middle-class, Christian heterosexual." Similarly, Catherine Maxwell (2001: 182) has argued that "Swinburne's portrayal of Sappho as a lesbian can be seen as decisive in helping determine the term's modern sexual meaning."

2. Perhaps the term *anachronism* does not do justice to the richness of this approach. As Peter Coviello (2013: 14) points out, an approach to sexuality that does not use the advent of sexology as symbolic of a "great divide" allows us to understand "the degree to which the emergence of modern sexuality was a movement, a slowly unfolding *process*, rather than an event."

3. I want to insist on the radical nature of this kind of intimacy: though the politics of intimacy might be deservedly open to the critique of reifying a privatized politics of sympathy that resists structural transformation, such a critique misunderstands the political philosophy underlying social transformation in the nineteenth century. In an era when social care became ever more institutionalized, the invocation of intimacy maintains a more radical—if at times reactionary—politics than structural approaches of Victorian reform.

4. Enlisting Queen Victoria in an essay on lesbianism is at least a little perverse, given that she is rumored, when it was suggested that she expand the Criminal Law Amendment Act to include women, to have been unable to fathom the possibility of sex between women (Castle 1993: 11).

5. Yopie Prins (1999: 116) locates a similar gesture in the beginning of Swinburne's Sapphic poem "Anactoria"; however, she locates an only partial merge therein: "whose body? Sappho's or Anactoria's? 'I' and 'thou' suffer in a mutual subjection that divides subject from object, rendering them apart yet also rendering them interestingly interchangeable." Richard Dellamora (1990: 71) similarly argues, "The descriptions of sexual interaction often leave unclear who is doing what to whom, an indefiniteness that includes rather than excludes the imaginable alternatives."

6. All biblical quotations are from the King James Version.

References

Arnold, Matthew. [1867] 1994. "Dover Beach." In *Dover Beach and Other Poems*. New York: Dover Thrift Editions.

Baldwin, James. [1956] 2000. *Giovanni's Room*. New York: Delta.

Berlant, Lauren, and Lee Edelman. 2013. *Sex, or the Unbearable*. Durham, NC: Duke University Press.

Bishop, Elizabeth. [1955] 2008. "The Shampoo." In *The Complete Poems: 1927–1979*, 84. New York: Farrar, Straus and Giroux.

———. [n.d.] 2007. "Close, close all night." In *Edgar Allen Poe and the Juke-Box: Uncollected Poems*, edited by Alice Quinn, 141. New York: Farrar, Straus and Giroux.

Brontë, Charlotte. [1848] 2001. *Jane Eyre*. Edited by Richard J. Dunn. New York: W. W. Norton.

Brontë, Emily. [1847] 2003. *Wuthering Heights*. Edited by Linda H. Peterson. New York: Bedford St. Martin's.

Brown, Ashley. 1966. Interview with Elizabeth Bishop. In *Conversations with Elizabeth Bishop*, edited by George Monteiro, 18–29. Jackson: University Press of Mississippi.

Carlyle, Thomas. [1843] 1965. *Past and Present*. Edited by Richard D. Altick. Boston: Houghton Mifflin.

Case, Sue-Ellen. 1988–1989. "Towards a Butch-Femme Aesthetic." *Discourse* 11, no. 1: 55–73.

Castle, Terry. 1993. *The Apparitional Lesbian: Female Homosexuality and Modern Culture*. New York: Columbia University Press.

Coviello, Peter. 2013. *Tomorrow's Parties: Sex and the Untimely in Nineteenth-Century America*. New York: New York University Press.

Davis, Nick. 2015. "The Object of Desire: Todd Haynes Discusses *Carol* and the Satisfaction of Telling Women's Stories." *Film Comment*, November–December. www .filmcomment.com/article/todd-haynes-carol-interview/.

Dean, Tim. 2008. "Breeding Culture: Barebacking, Bugchasing, Giftgiving." *Massachusetts Review* 49, nos. 1–2: 80–94.

Dellamora, Richard. 1990. *Masculine Desire: The Sexual Politics of Victorian Aestheticism*. Chapel Hill: University of North Carolina Press.

Dickens, Charles. [1853] 2003: *Bleak House*. Edited by Nicola Bradbury. New York: Penguin.

Dinshaw, Carolyn. 1999. *Getting Medieval: Sexualities and Communities, Pre- and Postmodern*. Durham, NC: Duke University Press.

Edelman, Lee. 2004. *No Future: Queer Theory and the Death Drive*. Durham, NC: Duke University Press.

Eliot, George. [1872] 2008. *Middlemarch*. Edited by David Carroll. Oxford: Oxford World Classics.

Empson, William. [1951] 1979. *The Structure of Complex Words*. Totowa, NJ: Rowman and Littlefield.

Foucault, Michel. [1976] 1990. *Introduction*. Vol. 1 of *The History of Sexuality*. Translated by Robert Hurley. New York: Vintage.

Freeman, Elizabeth. 2010. *Time Binds: Queer Temporalities, Queer Histories*. Durham, NC: Duke University Press.

Highsmith, Patricia. [1952] 1991. *The Price of Salt*. New York: W. W. Norton.

Love, Heather. 2007. *Feeling Backwards: Loss and the Politics of Queer History*. Cambridge, MA: Harvard University Press.

Mara, Rooney. 2015. Commentary on Cate Blanchett. iTunes Extras. *Carol*, directed by Todd Haynes.

Marcus, Sharon. 2007. *Between Women: Friendship, Desire, and Marriage in Victorian England*. Princeton, NJ: Princeton University Press.

Maxwell, Catherine. 2001. *The Female Sublime from Milton to Swinburne: Bearing Blindness*. Manchester, UK: Manchester University Press.

McEwan, Ian. [2005] 2006. *Saturday*. New York: Anchor Books.

Menon, Madhavi. 2013. "Historicism and Unhistoricism in Queer Studies: Response to Valerie Traub." *PMLA* 128, no. 3: 782–84.

Morley, John. [1866] 1995. Review of *Poems and Ballads*. In *Algernon Swinburne: The Critical Heritage*, edited by Clyde Hyder, 33–40. New York: Routledge.

Muñoz, José Esteban. 2009. *Cruising Utopia: The Then and There of Queer Futurity*. New York: New York University Press.

"Mr. Swinburne's New Poems." 1866. Review of *Poems and Ballads* by Algernon Swinburne. *New York Times*, November 3.

O'Farrell, Mary Ann. 2004. "Provoking George Eliot." In *Compassion: The Culture and Politics of an Emotion*, edited by Lauren Berlant, 145–58. New York: Routledge.

Prins, Yopie. 1999. *Victorian Sappho*. Princeton, NJ: Princeton University Press.

Rich, Adrienne. [1982] 1993. "Compulsory Heterosexuality and Lesbian Existence." In *The Lesbian and Gay Studies Reader*, edited by Henry Abelove, Michèle Aina Barale, and David M. Halperin, 227–54. New York: Routledge.

Schenkar, Joan. 2009. *The Talented Miss Highsmith: The Secret Life and Serious Art of Patricia Highsmith*. New York: St. Martin's.

Schwartz, Lloyd. 1991. "Elizabeth Bishop and Brazil." *New Yorker*, September 23.

Sedgwick, Eve Kosofsky. 2002. *Touching Feeling: Affect, Performance, Pedagogy*. Durham, NC: Duke University Press.

Shrimpton, Nicholas. 1993. "Swinburne and the Dramatic Monologue." In *The Whole Music of Passion: New Essays on Swinburne*, edited by Rikky Rooksby and Nicholas Shrimpton, 52–72. Aldershot, UK: Scolar.

Smith, Zadie. 2000. *White Teeth*. New York: Vintage.

Strachey, Lytton. [1918] 1970. *Eminent Victorians*. London: Collins.

Swinburne, Algernon Charles. [1866] 2000a. "Anactoria." In *Poems and Ballads and Atalanta in Calydon*, edited by Kenneth Hayes, 47–55. New York: Penguin.

———. [1866] 2000b. "The Leper." In *Poems and Ballads and Atalanta in Calydon*, edited by Kenneth Hayes, 95–100. New York: Penguin.

———. [1866] 2000c. "Notes on Poems and Reviews." In *Poems and Ballads and Atalanta in Calydon*, edited by Kenneth Hayes, 403–18. New York: Penguin.

———. [1877] 1894. *A Note on Charlotte Brontë*. London: Chatto and Windus.

———. [1902] 1972. "Charles Dickens." In *Swinburne as Critic*, edited by Clyde K. Hyder, 223–42. London: Routledge and Kegan Paul.

Traub, Valerie. 2013. "The New Unhistoricism in Queer Studies." *PMLA* 128, no. 1: 21–39.

Urban, Sylvanus. 1889. "Table Talk: Mr. Swinburne's Poems and Ballads." *Gentleman's Magazine*, no. 267: 103–4.

Weintraub, Stanley. 1997. *Uncrowned King: The Life of Prince Albert*. New York: Free Press.

Whitman, Walt. 1855. *Leaves of Grass*. Whitman Archive. whitmanarchive.org/published /LG/1855/whole.html.

Wiegman, Robyn, and Elizabeth A. Wilson. 2015. "Introduction: Antinormativity's Queer Conventions." *differences* 26, no. 1: 1–25.

Woolf, Virginia. [1928] 1973. *Orlando*. London: Harcourt.

MATERNAL FAILURES, QUEER FUTURES

Reading The Price of Salt (1952) and
Carol (2015) against Their Grain

Jenny M. James

$\mathcal{I}$n 1941 Virginia Kent Catherwood, a Pennsylvania socialite, lost custody of her only daughter after a bitter divorce from her husband, Cummins Catherwood, a wealthy banker. Catherwood's maternal loss was a result of her adulterous relationships with other women—her lesbianism was used as legal evidence of her unfitness as a mother. Five years later, Catherwood met the young, aspiring novelist Patricia Highsmith at a party in Manhattan, and the two became lovers. While their relationship lasted for only a year, Catherwood made a deep impression on Highsmith, which resurfaces in the novelist's portrait of the fictional character Carol Aird, the focal point of her 1952 novel *The Price of Salt* (Wilson 2003: 132). This lesbian cult classic depicts the love affair between Carol and Therese Belivet, two women who meet across a children's toy counter in Frankenberg's department store one December morning in Manhattan as Carol shops for Christmas gifts for her eight-year-old daughter, Rindy. Spurred by this fanciful meeting, the narrative delineates the women's torturously long intergenerational courtship, which includes a romantic American road trip, the dramatic outing of Carol by a private eye that is used to deny her parental rights to her daughter, an epistolary cross-country breakup, and the novel's surprising, concluding scene of the two women's reconciliation. Yet what is not made much of in the novel, but should be made much of today, is the fact that the novel's fantasy of lesbian romance relies on Carol's loss of maternal custody and the subsequent erasure of her experience as a queer mother—a plotline of love and loss often easily overlooked.

GLQ 24:2–3
DOI 10.1215/10642684-4324825
© 2018 by Duke University Press

In the past fifteen years Highsmith's life and work have witnessed a revival in academic and cultural circles; this new interest was ushered in by the 2004 Norton reissuing of *The Price of Salt* and *Strangers on a Train* and a series of biographies published in the early 2000s by Andrew Wilson, Joan Schenkar, and Marijane Meaker. However, Highsmith's transgressive literary oeuvre received little attention in queer cultural and academic circles until the recent 2015 film adaptation of *The Price of Salt*. Upon its release, Todd Haynes's *Carol* invited viewers to remember the plots and motifs of the mother-daughter relationship in Highsmith's novel, tasking audiences with looking backward through the literary to consider the unspoken history out of which the novel emerged—a past prior to gay liberation where gay and lesbian parenthood existed but remained undocumented in the legal or historical record. The following reading shows how each text, in varying ways, incorporates strategies of metaphorical substitution and narrative replacement to imagine the love affair between two white women of different ages, ethnicities, and classes during an era where their queer love often remained unimaginable. Yet the portrayals of queer maternity most notably diverge in the affective experiences each text inspires in its audiences. While Highsmith's postwar pulp novel satirizes the mother-daughter bond in its camp machinations, Haynes's lyric period film inspires viewers to grieve the loss of Carol's queer motherhood. These affective differences reveal a vital knot of queer history that mirrors our contemporary moment. Thus Highsmith's novel and Haynes's film reflect how the narrative arc of lesbian romance is often represented in and against parent-child bonds; mother-daughter erotic fantasies may be sexy, but they operate in the necessary absence of true parentage.

By reading the film and novel alongside each other and taking part in the comparative mode of textual reception that the palimpsestic quality of artistic adaptation requires, this essay draws attention to the absent presence of the queer parent-child relation in these narratives of postwar lesbian life (Hutcheon and O'Flynn 2012: 116). The knots and burls that arise in the dialogic space between novel and film thus offer the opportunity to cultivate a critical openness to intersecting texts, identities, and histories in a continuing intertextual process of creative and interpretive re-vision. This interpretive capacity to think otherwise and against the grain of the texts themselves emerges, then, from the "repetition with variation" that characterizes filmic adaptation as well as the principal cycle of replacement and substitution that formally defines both texts (ibid.: 116). Attending to the melancholia that the narrative's foreclosure of queer maternity inspires, the following reading asks us to conceive a more radical vision of family that might incorporate reproductive notions of futurity and also embrace the beauty, intimacy, and care that chosen queer families have cultivated for decades. For in holding on to the events and outcomes that might have been in *The Price of Salt* and *Carol*, we arrive at a renewed understanding of queer kinship by reading the texts against their own grain.

Carol and *The Price of Salt* envision a world narrowly defined by a white subculture of postwar queer bohemianism. In my reading of these two texts, I argue against a critical approach to queer parenthood that understands it as metonymic of class assimilation and neoliberal ascendancy for a twenty-first-century white queer elite, asking the question, how might stories of queer maternity work to resist, rather than reconfirm, the forces of white privilege that currently define queer family and community within homonormative, exclusionary frames? By failing to recognize the diversity of queer families and the relative socioeconomic marginalization that most of them face, queer textual cultures risk upholding the same institutions of white heteropatriarchy that have oppressed queer communities for centuries. An intersectional analysis of queer kinship today must therefore reckon with the primacy of the Euro-American meta-narrative of mid-twentieth-century gay and lesbian history.

This essay's attention to kinship and queer maternity asks more of Highsmith's novel and Haynes's filmic adaptation than they can give. Spanning sixty years of queer history, this textual comparison evinces a troubling continuity between the 1950s and today, where despite the "progress" of the Stonewall riots, AIDS activism, the Supreme Court's ruling against antisodomy legislation, and the recent legalization of gay marriage, queer maternity remains an unnarratable experience within the story of lesbian romance. Even in my love of the twists and turns in Carol and Therese's intergenerational affair, I remain disappointed in the narrative's deficient vision of queer kinship that inscribes lesbian desire within neoliberal values while maintaining the lie that family is by definition straight, white, and economically stable. The novel and film thus present a negative model, which I choose to interpret not just as paranoiac evidence of the ubiquity of white heteronormativity but also as an opportunity to attend to a more capacious textual archive. For although it may be impossible to repair these representational failures, they provide a crucial window onto the insufficiencies of the past and present of queer kinship. To shed light on their seductive privations reanimates a range of expectations and hopes for future stories of queer love and kin making—stories that imagine erotic desire and parenting as mutually constitutive while bringing voice to the racial, ethnic, and class diversity of queer families.

Contextualizing the Postwar Past of Queer Parenthood

Before embarking on a comparative analysis of Highsmith's novel and Haynes's film, I take a brief look at the postwar history of queer parenting in the United States, which offers a helpful context to fully understand the irreconcilability of queer maternity and desire at work in these texts. Recent historical studies of postwar LGBTQ life illustrate that Catherwood's experiences of parental loss were not unique. In *Radical Relations: Lesbian Mothers, Gay Fathers, and Their Children in the United States since WWII*, Daniel Winunwe Rivers (2013: 25) notably claims that during the 1940s and 1950s, "denial of parental rights to anyone who openly loved someone of the same sex was part of the legal and social policing of same-sex relationships and the enforcing of heterosexuality, though this danger was often extrajudicial." The extent to which an individual's pursuit of queer desires in the 1950s brought with it a rejection of parental identity was greatly dependent on class and race. For although the character of Carol Aird may prove a provocative subject of identification and attraction for readers and viewers alike, her life trajectory was decidedly different from a great percentage of queer women living in working-class, butch-femme, and racially diverse communities where children often remained with their mothers and were raised within postwar lesbian collectives (ibid.: 34–42).

Rivers's research suggests that this is a history not easily articulated, for news of pre-Stonewall gay and lesbian parenting as well as queer custody battles often circulated only by word of mouth, because of the absence of any legal record of private family court proceedings (ibid.: 28, 53).[1] His study documents the complicated story of 1950s women like Blue Lunden, a butch, working-class lesbian mother who lived with her daughter in a racially, ethnically, and sexually diverse community in Manhattan's Lower East Side, yet faced stigmatization, prejudice, and instability that no bohemian underground could fix. Postwar queer mothers of color, such as Vera Martin, experienced even more serious threats to their families and children; the triple jeopardy of being black, female, and queer created hurdles that made parenting a potentially dangerous enterprise (ibid.: 25–31). With the rise of gay liberation in 1968, lesbian mothers and gay fathers began to "come out," only to become victim to a homophobic backlash in a series of antigay custody cases that gathered force from 1967 to the mid-1980s and made national headlines. While common memory of gay liberation highlights the risks that queer individuals took to pursue their sexual desires, few contemporary accounts of the era recognize that the homophobic institutions against which liberation activists fought were equally fixed on dismantling queer parent–child bonds.

As queer parents sought to find community and new modes of sexual identity without risking the safety of their families, second-wave feminists and gay liberation activists struggled over the place of family and reproductive parenthood in movement ideology and strategy. For LGBTQ people in the process of coming out, children often served as an inopportune reminder of life in the closet and the pre-Stonewall path of assimilating to straight, nuclear norms while often maintaining a double life.[2] And for many in the radical lesbian feminist movement, motherhood was understood to be part and parcel of the patriarchal servitude that heterosexuality demanded. In Martha Shelley's "Notes of a Radical Lesbian," originally published in 1969, the rejection of maternity is a key component of radical lesbian feminism's rejection of patriarchy. She writes that the lesbian "is freed from fear of unwanted pregnancy and the pains of childbirth, and from the drudgery of child raising. On the other hand, she pays three penalties. The rewards of child raising are denied her. There is a great loss for some women, but not for others" (Shelley 1970: 307). As Shelley articulates, the ideology underlying radical lesbianism saw "women loving women" as a way out of "dependence on men" and the domestic and reproductive labors associated with heterosexual partnership, most notably "the drudgery of child raising." She does, however, concede that "for some women" the loss of child raising might be "great." Radicalesbians co-organizer Rita Mae Brown was known to tell women to give up their children in order to fully invest in the movement (Nelson 2015: 75). For others, though, especially single mothers who were socioeconomically marginalized, rescinding parenthood was impossible.

In place of an authentic recognition of queer mothers in the movement, and in lesbian culture more broadly, mother-daughter bonding became a popular cultural feminist metaphor to imagine same-sex love between women. As the poet Sue Silvermarie attests in Adrienne Rich's (1995: 232) classic *Of Woman Born*: "In loving another woman I discovered the deep urge to both be a mother to and find a mother in my lover."[3] Reappropriating the midcentury psychoanalytic discourse that saw "mother fixation" as the etiology of homosexual pathology (Bohan 1996: 76), Silvermarie and other lesbian feminist authors celebrated the love and erotic union between women in essentialist, maternal terms—thereby obfuscating the actual lived experience of queer mothers. While there were sustained efforts within feminist circles to protect lesbian motherhood and fight back against the rise of homophobic custody suits, such as the revolutionary work of the Berkeley Lesbian Mothers Union in the 1970s, the antimaternal ideology of radical lesbianism remained a central component of queer women's coming-out experiences since 1968—and continues to subtly overshadow the flourishing of radical forms of queer parenthood today (Rivers 2013: 80, 83).

Highsmith's Maternal Erotics and the Elision of Difference

Adumbrated by this complex history, Highsmith's *Price of Salt* and Todd Haynes's *Carol* metaphorically and narratologically illuminate how motherhood and lesbian romance are often understood as incompatible and incommensurate desires. In 1952 Highsmith published *The Price of Salt* under the pseudonym Claire Morgan to an expanding pulp fiction readership. Becoming the first mass-market American novel to outwardly depict lesbian romance with a somewhat "happy ending," the novel did much to expand the cultural archive of gay and lesbian life for which so many midcentury queer readers were hungry. According to Highsmith's biographer Andrew Wilson (2003: 172), it sold over one million copies in its first years of printing. The brief 1952 *New York Times* review of the novel speaks to the paucity of literature devoted to queer subject matter: "Obviously, in dealing with a theme of this sort, the novelist must handle his explosive material with care. It should be said at once that Miss Morgan writes throughout with sincerity and good taste" (Rolo 1952). Highsmith's novel was published and reviewed in the *New York Times* precisely because its representation of sex and love between women remained "sincere" and in good "taste."[4] Despite its representational obfuscations, the novel challenged readers, as it still does today, to recognize the real desires of two women in search of queer selfhood and sexual relation, yet faced with the absence of a common language or cultural framework in which to fully articulate their experience.

Turning to a traditional plotline in literature representing women's lives, Highsmith draws on the figure of motherhood in her development of Therese and Carol's love affair, crafting the plot of lesbian romance and potential cohabitation from the ruptured plot of closeted maternity. The author's narratological strategy to substitute Carol's intimate bond with Therese for her primary relationship to her daughter late in the novel calls on camp tropes of the pathological and menacing older lesbian. This logic of replacement, which creates an almost smooth progression from Carol's tainted motherhood to a redeemed queer romance with Therese, is complemented by Highsmith's use of an erotic motif of mother and girlhood to represent lesbian desire. By doing so, the novel underscores the femininity and relative middle-class respectability that the characters share, building on the femme-on-femme relationship depicted in schoolgirl love affairs popular in pulp fiction, yet sidestepping the working-class butch-femme culture that defined much of postwar lesbian life.

While Carol is the novel's focal point, the narrative is usually focalized through the viewpoint of nineteen-year-old Therese; like many mother-daughter plots, Carol's maternal perspective remains often underdeveloped in the text (Hirsch 1989). Therese's occupation selling "Drinky-Wetsy" dolls by day and crafting set models by night speaks to her queer, extended girlhood. Highsmith's eerie symbols of girlhood align Therese with Carol's daughter, Rindy, posing them as competitors for Carol's maternal love. Ironically, Therese appears just as child-like, if not more so, as Rindy, even if she is at least ten years older; while Rindy is described as "conservative" and "serious," Therese's ignorance and sexual naïveté are hyperbolized to the point of infantalization. This portrayal amplifies the age difference between Therese and Carol and their subsequent erotic tension, as their thirteen-year difference adds a frisson of sexual subversion and power play. Whether it be the dolls Therese sells at Frankenberg's or her own capacity to become one in Carol's eyes, Highsmith uses this motif to invoke the erotic tensions between mother and daughter on which their romance turns.[5]

Playing on the discriminatory postwar psychology that saw lesbianism as a mental pathology arising from a girl's unhealthy relationship with an overbearing or absent mother, the maternal metaphor is integral to a host of postwar lesbian fiction and memoirs. In her 1955 nonfiction "insider" report on lesbian culture titled *We Walk Alone*, Ann Aldrich drew on traditional psychoanalytic and ethnographic accounts of homosexual development to discuss the important role of the mother in catalyzing same-sex desire in women. Underscoring the "little-girl-ness" of lesbian abnormality, she writes:

> The lesbian is the little girl who couldn't grow up. Whether she is a per-petual tomboy who has yet to don high heels, a silk dress, and lipstick to brave the world of grownups, or whether she is a charming and very femi-nine "adult child," she is an immature and abnormal woman. Her world is self-centered and centered on her other selves. As a lesbian, she looks in an eternal mirror for a reflection of her own image, in the image of mother substitutes, child substitutes, and substitute sisters (Aldrich 2006: 24).

Aldrich, otherwise known as Marijane Meaker, later briefly became High-smith's lover, meeting her at a Greenwich Village lesbian bar four years after the publication of this account. In this passage, she plays into the stereotypes of lesbians being "immature" "adult children" and therefore narcissistically focused on themselves. Interestingly, Aldrich describes the lesbian looking for "mother substitutes, child substitutes, and substitute sisters," the repetition of "substitute" not so subtly illuminating the unspoken rationale of replacement in *The Price of Salt*.[6]

Highsmith's portrait of mother-daughter love stays true to the Cold War fears of mental pathology and the dangers that maternal failure supposedly produced, crafting mother-daughter scenes between Carol and Therese steeped in the author's characteristic maudlin irony. Upon Therese's first visit to Carol's opulent country house in New Jersey, conventional activities usually assigned to mother and daughter frame their initial flirtation. Once Therese arrives, Carol offers her lunch, then asks her what she would like to do, taking her up to the second floor for a "nap"; finally, Carol asks Therese if she would like something to drink—like water or scotch, but Therese requests warm milk. From this line, a discomforting erotic exchange ensues, where Highsmith (2004: 67) describes Therese's infantile tastes: "The milk seemed to taste of bone and blood, of warm flesh, or hair, saltless as chalk yet alive as a growing embryo. . . . Therese drank it down, as people in fairy tales drink the potion that will transform, or the unsuspecting warrior the cup that will kill." This hilarious episode turns on the shared femininity of Carol and Therese, their corporeal similitude symbolized in the abject reproductive figure of milk. The diction of reproduction bears this out, as terms like *bone*, *blood*, *flesh*, and *embryo* transport Therese into a womblike world of symbolic transformation, but also one of possible spoiling; as Highsmith notes, the warmed milk had scalded, leaving a "scum" that disgusted Carol. The passage also echoes the title *The Price of Salt* by invoking the complex taste of milk that is "saltless as chalk" but also, underneath the surface, perhaps salty from the strains of blood and flesh embedded there. As the novel reveals in the chapters to follow, this scene awakens Therese's queer desires, as she cultivates a taste for Carol's domineering, domestic femininity.

While this moment illuminates the characters' shared feminine tastes and comportment, their gendered similarity masks the more precarious forms of difference embedded in their same-sex bond. The women's desire that crosses more than a ten-year age difference highlights the potential psychic aggression and competition the women share; this is true as well for their vast social differences in class, ethnic background, and potential levels of intellectual and sexual education. And yet their romance seems to thrive on these modes of difference, which add suspense and melodrama to the story. If we look more closely at Highsmith's motif of the maternal erotic, however, readers may notice the one mode of difference that truly cannot be sustained in Carol and Therese's bond: the social reality of racial difference. Within the racial imaginary that is foundational to the women's growing intimacy, the previous image of Therese drinking warm milk symbolizes the cultural and phenotypic whiteness that underlies the women's desire for each other. Whiteness is a defining condition for their love, and like this abject image, it is the impossible, social norm that haunts the imagined lesbian union across age, class, and ethnic differences.

Consequently, Highsmith's use of mother-daughter metaphors for lesbian desire produces an implicit assumption of racial and genetic similarity that structures the novel's conception of lesbian romance. The struggle over racial privilege is further legible in the ethnic conflicts that are elemental to the two white lovers' opposing social worlds. Therese's interest in Carol stems, in part, from the economic and cultural privilege embodied in the latter's "Nordic" features and sophistication. While Carol remarks on the originality of Therese's Czech surname "Belivet," Therese is attracted to Carol's blond beauty that seems inseparable from her opulent home and dress (ibid.: 51, 52). As Highsmith writes of their first meeting in Frankenberg's: "[Carol] was tall and fair. . . . Her eyes were gray, colorless, yet dominant as light or fire, and, caught by them, Therese could not look away" (ibid.: 39). Lacking color, Carol's complexion and light gray eyes entrance Therese. The women's romance thus arises from the class tensions alive in midtown New York City's consumer society, where the class struggle over whiteness is emblematized in tense encounters between wealthy, suburban shoppers and staff from historically more disadvantaged white ethnic backgrounds. The fact that Therese meets and immediately falls for Carol while at work speaks to her desire to flee the monotonous drudgery of shopgirl life and enter a different, whiter world of adventure, untethered by class or marital responsibility.

Out of the collection of staff members with names like "Santini," "Martucci," "Zabriskie," and even Therese's current German American boyfriend Richard Semco, it is Mrs. Ruby Robichek who is the true abject foil to Carol Aird's class superiority and allure. Described as "exhausted," "greedy," "ugly," and "creeping," Mrs. Robichek is coded as Jewish. She befriends Therese across a cafeteria table at lunch; a couple of days later, she invites Therese to her gloomy brownstone, offers her dinner, proceeds to dress her in one of the dresses she had designed as a former dressmaker, and finally spoons some kind of medicine between Therese's lips after the girl falls suggestively on her unmade bed. Caught in a nightmarish reverie, Therese becomes frightened by Mrs. Robichek's abject maternal body and erotic threat—her "heavy body with the bulging abdomen"—and eventually escapes the grip of the character that Highsmith describes as "the hunchbacked keeper of the dungeon" (ibid.: 20, 23). Without the presence of a white, upper-class veneer of respectability, Mrs. Robichek's queer desires become monstrous, casting lesbianism as a grotesque aspect of Jewish American, working-class widowhood. With the inclusion of this scene prior to the lovers' meeting, Highsmith sets out the extreme limit of abject maternal eroticism that Carol and Therese's loving bond must resist. To escape Mrs. Robichek's horrific fate, and the loneliness that it presumes, Carol and Therese will seek solace in a solidly middle-class future, filled with art, travel, and beauty.[7]

Up until the novel's partial resolution in the women's scene of reconciliation, Carol's white and straight-passing privilege as a closeted suburban femme is conceived through, and in many ways watched over by, Rindy, an embodied metonym of the normative postwar family and Carol's femininity. Highsmith's portrayal of Rindy and Carol's relationship upends traditional notions of mothers reproducing gender norms in their daughters, as Rindy polices the boundaries of her mother's "proper" gender and sexuality. Described as having "white-blond hair" and loving big houses, Christmas, new toys, and horseback riding, Rindy becomes the symbol of not just the forms of relation but the forms of privilege that Carol will lose if she falls into the trap of her own queer desires (ibid.: 128). Traveling between Rindy's and Therese's haunts, Carol and her movements highlight the vast distance between her daughter's suburban elite lifestyle and Therese's downtown bohemianism. Highsmith underscores this point in one scene where Therese is shopping in Chinatown with Carol and spots some "sandals with platform heels that she thought were beautiful, rather more Persian-looking than Chinese." As Therese indicates her desire to purchase them for Carol, Carol resists, saying that Rindy would not like her wearing them. Highsmith writes: "Rindy was a conservative, and didn't like her even to go without stockings in summer, and Carol conformed to her" (ibid.: 110). This short line speaks to the way Carol's tastes are moderated by Rindy's presence and opinion; her daughter is "conservative" in her desire to make sure Carol conforms to more modest dress and by extension a white cultural norm that would look down on any "Persian-looking" pair of shoes.

Described at one point as Carol's "property," the loss of Rindy, then, will bring with it a loss of suburban class and economic privilege (ibid.: 224). Carol's assessment of Rindy as an object of value, rather than a subject worthy of sharing a deep, intimate relationship, prefigures the deleterious vision of queer kinship that contemporary neoliberal discourse has produced. Although Rindy Aird protects the boundaries of white heteronormativity in the text, I choose to read her ironic "conservatism" as belying the potential tender feelings of need and care that she might share with her mother—a more complex emotional landscape than is hinted at in the pulp novel, but rendered fully manifest in the filmic adaptation. Yet as figures of queer economic mobility and cultural assimilation, textual representations of children growing up in queer families often contribute to the centering of white experience within queer culture and social thought. As David Eng (2010: 29) writes in *The Feeling of Kinship*, "We cannot underestimate the ways in which neoliberalism and its proliferating modes of consumer capitalism underpin the historical evolution and transformation of capitalism and of gay identity into queer family and kinship." The consumptive forms of whiteness structuring love and sex in *The Price of Salt* point to how "family and kinship" are still metonymic of white, middle-class society, whether they refer to "straight" or "queer" kin. The novel's intimation of a queer past where parenthood and gay and lesbian life were in tense opposition, however, complicates the assumption that children equate a homonormative lifestyle. Even though the novel's portrait of queer motherhood is foreclosed, its absent presence points to the need for the contemporary LGBTQ movement to radically resist the whitewashing of family ties that is inevitable under contemporary neoliberalism. For we must remember the inassimilable modes of family that queers have always held close—and especially to honor the queer families of color that are statistically the "norm."

Narrative Replacement and Its Losses

Highsmith's invocation of erotic maternal metaphor facilitates the novel's plot of lesbian romance, helping further the sinister erasure of Rindy as a threat to Carol's desire for a relationship with Therese. Resembling the plot of identity theft, the narrative replacement of Therese for Rindy is similar to the plots of doubles, mistaken identities, and forgeries that we see in Highsmith's other pulp suspense novels like *Strangers on a Train* and the *Ripley* series. In Highsmith's oeuvre, authentically sustaining bonds of relation are rare; instead, relationships often are vehicles for psychic manipulation or physical violence. By halfway through *The Price of Salt*, Rindy's minimal presence in the text all but disappears, her role taken up by Therese. While not necessarily a murder, this loss is crucial to the plot. Only in the uncanny traces of Carol and Rindy's primary filial bond, which is now transmuted in the women's intergenerational romance, does the devaluation of the straight, suburban mother-daughter bond even register to readers.

In the 2015 filmic adaptation of Highsmith's novel, by Todd Haynes (director) and Phyllis Nagy (screenwriter), the more sinister tones of Carol and Therese's pulp romance are neutralized, the novel's stark ironies transformed into melancholic ambivalence. A historical narrative film that looks back to a pre-Stonewall moment, *Carol* evokes a sense of what Patricia White (2015: 9) calls "belatedness," inspiring in viewers a longing for, rather than rejection of, a past where queer life was under constant threat. This belatedness suggests the complex timescape that the novel and its filmic pairing produce: a queer temporality that inspires viewers to identify with the familial losses and sexual defeats of the past, but in the service of animating a different, queer future beyond the present reliance on white, homo-normative family frames. If in *Carol* Nagy and Haynes play Highsmith's "melo-drama straight," as the *Rolling Stone* editor David Fear notes, the filmmakers are thus better able to dramatize the incommensurability of queer motherhood and desire (quoted in Haynes 2015, Supplemental Interviews).

While *Carol* pictures Carol and Therese's sexual relationship, it also fore-grounds Carol's bonds with Rindy, producing in viewers a melancholic desire for an alternative kinship that can embrace both queer sex and actual maternity (Haynes 2015). Deepening and extending the plot of Carol's custody battle for Rindy, it thereby offers a screen through which viewers can attend to the foreclosure of motherhood. Notably, Highsmith's most farcical instances of maternal metaphor are absent from *Carol*, which subsequently emphasizes the importance of the strat-egy of narrative replacement. The mother-daughter erotics of the novel are also quieted; no longer sinister doubles or competitors, Therese (played by the diminu-tive Rooney Mara) and a very youthful Rindy remain linked in the mutual love and feelings of possession that Carol directs toward them. They are even depicted in the same scene, when Therese visits Carol on Christmas Eve and undertakes nanny-like duties in helping care for Rindy. Yet as the film progresses, Rindy and Therese do not meet again—a filmic choice that metaphorizes the conflicting plots of motherhood and romance that center on Carol, played deftly by Cate Blanchette.

Never fully replacing the character of Rindy or the plot of maternity, this narrative strategy of replacement accentuates the sense of melancholic substitu-tion at work in the romance between Carol and Therese while also inspiring in the viewer an expectation of future substitutions and projections of characters, objects, and images. Haynes and the film's cinematographer, Edward Lachman, collabo-rate to cinematically capture the threat of replacement and dissolution by using visual motifs that link Therese and Rindy and position them in similar relation to Carol, facilitating the film's strategy of replacing plots of queer motherhood for les-bian romance. There are two key motifs that illuminate the conceit of replacement within the narrative: Carol and Therese's encounters with photographic portraits of children and scenes of Carol brushing another's hair at vanity mirrors. The visual content found in these motifs illuminates the white, domestic, feminine atmosphere of *Carol*, which is embellished by the period sets and wardrobes that make up the mise-en-scène. One distinct difference between the film and novel is the film's sidestepping of the tensions over ethnic whiteness at work in *The Price of Salt*; the film does include an African American couple early on, but an actual working through of racial difference is notably absent, even in the film's visual landscape.

Photography, particularly documentary photos, plays a crucial role in the film's cinematic style, which Haynes modeled after the work of midcentury photographers such as Vivian Maier and Saul Leiter. It is not surprising, then, that in the first scene of Therese and Carol's meeting in Frankenberg's, one of the first moments of exchange between the women occurs when Carol shows Therese a wallet-sized portrait of Rindy. The photo's subject and size both highlight Rindy's youthful innocence, for in the film, Rindy is four years old, rather than eight years as in the novel. The photograph creates the opportunity for the women to touch across the shop counter, the exchange foreshadowing Carol's purchase, and unspoken proposition, that will complete the scene. The shot moves in on each woman holding the photograph at opposite edges; Carol's age and maturity can be seen in her red manicured nails and elegant wedding and engagement ring, while Therese's hands, in contrast, seem small, young, and slightly unkempt. As both women grasp the photo, a substitute for the child, the scene conveys a sense of triangulation, where the photograph is the threshold for future intimacy between the women. Rindy is thus both the catalyst for their meeting—she is the future recipient of the toy that inspires Carol's visit, after all—and also the key impediment to their romance.

This photographic imagery continues in the early days of the women's affair, as Therese takes candid, dreamy snapshots of Carol. Notably, on her first visit to Therese's apartment a couple of weeks later, Carol gives Therese a belated Christmas gift of a new camera and encounters a new photo. Here Haynes incorporates a shot that revises the earlier scene in the store while playing up the sentimentality of Carol's recent realization that she may in fact lose Rindy to her husband, Harge. Looking up at and tenderly touching a photograph of a young girl on Therese's kitchen wall, Carol soon realizes that this is in fact a portrait of Therese when she was about the same age as Rindy—a fact that inspires Carol to tearfully confess the reality of her circumstances to Therese. In this replacement of one photo for another, the triangulation is gone, the barrier removed. What is significant, though, about Carol's connection with this snapshot on the wall is that the childhood photograph of Therese is not presented on its own but appears at the end of a shot that pans across a wall of Therese's own street photography. A window onto a broader (white) public sphere, this seemingly private domestic scene thus sheds light on the larger structures of power that shape Carol and Therese's fate. The series of photographs illuminates the heteronormative social conditions that made pre-Stonewall lesbianism, and by association lesbian motherhood, not just "immoral" but all but invisible.

While Therese's photographs ask the film's viewers to look outward, to the broader social landscape that *Carol* seeks to reflect, the pattern of visual replacement continues in two scenes that turn inward, to illuminate the realm of lesbian fantasy and same-sex intimacy. These scenes focus on mirrors, and thus metatextually reflect each other. In the first scene, early in the film, Carol sits in front of her bedroom vanity with her daughter, lovingly brushing Rindy's hair. The camera approaches them from the side, and thus the two are never fully captured in any single frame of the hinged three-paneled mirror, although their hairstyles and mannerisms mirror each other. We learn moments later that this shot is from the viewpoint of Harge, who enters the room and interrupts their reverie, a symbol of patriarchal judgment and surveillance intervening in the mother-daughter bond. Both visually and narratologically, Carol and Rindy's relationship is fragmented in this scene; their faces are not held within any single panel of the hinged mirror, nor can they hold each other's gaze.

By the time we arrive at the second iteration of a shot of Carol in front of a vanity mirror, her efforts to recognize herself as an independent queer woman are progressing, but not without new risks. In a climactic scene just prior to Therese and Carol's first sex scene, the women are in a hotel room on their road trip west, now finally on the brink of consummating their affair after a lengthy narrative deferral. The camera first directs our gaze toward Carol standing above Therese, who is sitting in front of a beveled vanity mirror, almost as if we were looking through the mirror; here Carol gently plays with her hair. As they gaze into each other's eyes through the mirror's mediating frame, the characters become available to viewers as an erotic couple, as they are to each other. They are now completely included within the mirror's frame and regard this portrait of themselves together, no longer interrupted or fragmented. The mirror, then, finally reflects a fantastical world where Therese and Carol can be together, their mimicking of the earlier scene underscoring the mommy-daughter kink that contributes to their subsequent sexual play. However, this fantastic world of sexual pleasure is temporary and not without rough edges, for as we later learn, their bliss will be ruptured the following morning, when they discover that they have been followed by a private investigator and their entire evening tape-recorded, to be used against Carol in court.

Mirrors, as metatextual figures in film, reveal the potential worlds in which characters may find themselves. In this sequence, we see that Carol's ability to remain connected to, and thus imagine a future with her daughter, is increasingly fraught, while her connection to Therese conversely blossoms. The vanity mirror in some ways symbolizes Carol's narcissistic fantasy or efforts at self-identification, yet it only offers a "mirror-image" of Carol at this moment. Passing off a reversed, illusory view as authentic truth, this motif reminds viewers that the modes of identification and forms of relation that Carol—and by extension audience members—

have access to are constrained by the incommensurability of maternity and queer desire. These opposing scenes and reflections cannot be reconciled, leaving a sense of loss that the film's "happy ending" never quite fully redeems.

The Melancholia of Living "against One's Grain"

The necessary losses of maternal attachment and identity, and the melancholia they produce in character and viewer alike, culminate in the climactic turn that both texts share. After Carol learns that she is losing custody of Rindy, she breaks off her romance with Therese, creating the obstacle that the narrative seeks to resolve and catalyzing the replacement of the plot of motherhood with the plot of lesbian romance. These events begin while the two women are traveling and Carol abandons the younger Therese in a Sioux Falls motel to go home to face her custody woes (a foreshadowing of her secondary abandonment of Rindy). From this point the novel and film take quite different paths. In the novel, Highsmith emphasizes the characters' separation and diverging viewpoints through the inclusion of a long-distance epistolary breakup, while Haynes's film dramatizes Carol's plight through the addition of scenes not present in the text, deprioritizing the conflict between the women to illustrate their common suffering. Central to each is a heart-wrenching moment where Carol gives up motherhood to escape the deep suffering she has experienced in living "against [her] own grain" of queer desire (Haynes 2015). Unable to perceive the structural causes of her own double bind, Carol chooses her sexual identity over her maternal identity—a decision emblematic of the postwar fantasy that self-discovery leads to an authentic and coherent identity.

In *The Price of Salt*, Highsmith intensifies the negative consequences of Carol's absence by shifting to an epistolary structure that opens up the narrative viewpoint to both Therese and Carol. Told at first through phone calls and then epistolary fragments, Therese becomes depressive and then angry at her inability to directly challenge the news. As Therese awaits Carol's phone call, she feels a sense of despair: "For a while, the sound of Carol's voice was in her ears. Then a melancholy began to seep into her. She lay on her back with her arms straight at her sides, with a sense of empty space all around her, as if she were laid out ready for the grave, and then she fell asleep" (Highsmith 2004: 241). Here Therese hovers in a void, listening to Carol's lamenting "voice in her ears" but unable to respond. Highsmith's description of the heartbroken Therese as a corpse "ready for the grave" depicts queer desolation as a state of near abjection, echoing a previous moment where Therese worries silently, "Would Carol ever want to leave her?," and Carol, seeing the concern in her eyes, curtly responds to Therese that she was getting too "melancholic" (ibid.: 194). Since Carol rarely occupies a position of depression or recognizable grief in the novel, Therese serves as the affective register of the two women's sufferings and fears of being cast out.

By reading these letters, we accompany Therese in her feelings of abandonment as she misinterprets Carol's decision to leave as a rejection of their love, understandably unable to appreciate the reasons behind her departure. Carol's letters counter this assumption, however, in their complex portrayal of her "surrender" to patriarchal authority, describing her acquiescence to the lawyers' demand that she promise to stop seeing Therese, and people like her, in order to retain visitation rights with Rindy. Carol states: "I said I would stop seeing you. I wonder if you will understand, Therese, since you are so young and never even knew a mother who cared desperately for you. For this promise, they present me with their wonderful reward, the privilege of seeing my child a few weeks of the year" (ibid.: 254). Seeing Rindy as her competitor for Carol's love, Therese responds with jealousy: "Carol loved her child more than her" (ibid.: 255). Therese's victimization obscures her capacity to recognize Carol's similar defeat, their romantic losses clearly outplaying any maternal loss imagined in the text.

And yet, when set in dialogue with the film's more emotionally visceral portrayal of Carol, twenty-first-century readers of the novel can also perceive what Therese, and even Carol, cannot: that Carol's complex feelings of loss indicate a broader patriarchal system that limits the horizon of possibility for sexual relation and familial configurations between two women. Even as she seems to give in to the lawyers' demands for her to repress her sexuality in order to maintain custody of Rindy, the text of Carol's final letter to Therese defies the discourse of pathology and foreshadows Carol's eventual rescinding of any parental claim. Instead of registering shame or humiliation at her supposed degeneracy, Carol eloquently reflects on her queer desires, celebrating the joy of lesbian erotics, albeit as more an aesthetic than sexual experience:

> I wonder do these men grade their pleasure in terms of whether their actions produce a child or not, and do they consider them more pleasant if they do. It is a question of pleasure after all, and what's the use of debating the pleasure of an ice cream cone versus a football game—or a Beethoven quartet versus the *Mona Lisa*. . . . Someone brought "aesthetics" into the argument, I mean against me of course. I said did they really want to debate that—it brought the only laugh in the whole show. But the most important point I did not mention and was not thought of by anyone—that the rapport between two men or two women can be absolute and perfect, as it can never

be between man and woman, and perhaps some people want just this, as others want that more shifting and uncertain thing that happens between men and women. It was said or at least implied yesterday that my present course would bring me to the depths of human vice and degeneration. Yes, I have sunk a good deal since they took you from me. It is true, if I were to go on like this and be spied upon, attacked, never possessing one person long enough so that knowledge of a person is a superficial thing—that is degeneration. Or to live against one's grain, that is degeneration by definition. (ibid.: 255–56)

This letter serves as a defense of the "absolute and perfect" joy of queer desire that appears both reasonable (Doesn't everyone think women are more beautiful than men?) and philosophically rich (Might there not be a truer, platonic harmony found between two individuals of the same sex?), demonstrating the intrinsic value of queer relationship. Here Carol nods to her former maternal life when she discusses the pleasure of nonreproductive sex, de-emphasizing her procreative identity in defiance of compulsory heterosexuality. She explains how her sexual desire is both a quotidian choice (preferring ice cream over football) and an aesthetic act, queer erotic pleasure compared to a "Beethoven quartet" or a "*Mona Lisa*."

Carol's recounting of her conversation with the lawyers to Therese also defends their own relationship, and her subjectivity, against the outside accusation of degeneracy and her own internal feeling of melancholic defeat. Rather than reference the ways the law will deny Carol access to Rindy, Carol addresses Therese as the loved object that "they" have taken from her in a slip of the tongue: "I have sunk a good deal since they took *you* from me." Redefining "degeneration" beyond vice to connote the lie of an inauthentic life lived "against one's grain," Carol reconceives "degeneration" as the act of living in opposition to one's true love and desires. The wordplay implicit to the term *degeneration* rejects reproductive genealogies, for a horizontal, elective affinity with Therese depends on the erasure of Carol's maternal life and vertical genealogy. Living a life "against one's grain" proves too difficult for Carol. She reveals to Therese upon their reunion near the novel's close that she eventually "refused to make the promises [Harge] asked [her] to make . . . even if it did mean that they'd lock Rindy away from [her] as if [she were] an ogre. And it did mean that." Instead of subjecting herself and Rindy to the judgmental "stares" of future governesses, Carol makes an effort to "get over things" and turn her attention to her new career as a "furniture house" buyer, and her hoped-for future companionship with Therese in a large Madison

Avenue apartment "big enough for two" (ibid.: 277–78). Carol's tone in the women's final dialogue appears matter-of-fact, leaving the affective work to Therese. By the novel's close, when Therese accepts Carol's proposal to reunite despite her initial fears, each character has embraced her desire for the other and neutralized her melancholic attachments in the service of new love. This sad, often-depressing text thus surprisingly ends on a transcendent future that the two women just might share.

It would be anachronistic to read Carol's 1952 journey as one of "coming out," yet the author's inclusion of the memorable description of Carol's fear of living "against one's grain" resembles certain visions of queer selfhood today, as it places value in the individual's capacity to celebrate an aspect of the self that society has demeaned, transforming the stigma of degeneracy into sexual liberation. Yet, if we interpret the narrative against its own grain, Carol's heroic decision to "choose" Therese illuminates the novel's historical incapacity to reflect on the heteropatriarchal conditions that deemed queer life antithetical to parental love and care, as well as the racial and class privileges that made their romantic escape even possible. Emblematic of the privileged logic of their love is the fact that Therese's acceptance of Carol's proposal is partly driven by Therese's initial hopes that their love would miraculously erase any untoward memories of her familial background or past: "She had no need of parents or background 'What could be duller than past history!' Therese said smiling" (ibid.: 52). This lesbian romance succeeds in delivering both Therese and Carol into a utopian, yet degenerate, moment where past relationships, ethnic genealogies, and parents do not matter. For Therese and Carol, "it gets better": "It would be Carol, in a thousand cities, a thousand houses, in foreign lands where they would go together, in heaven and in hell" (ibid.: 287). To reach this "heaven and hell," each character seems to have miraculously mourned the lost relationship that made love possible, for their rebirth depends on the metaphorical death of the one bond that cannot be sustained or in the end even remembered in the novel: that of mother and child.

In contrast to the exuberant ending of *The Price of Salt*, which erases any vestiges of the pain of maternal loss, the film adaptation refuses to easily eclipse the loss of Rindy and relinquish the melancholia in the romantic ending. In new scenes written for the film, Carol's final legal negotiations are depicted in diegetic real time, incorporating scenes of Carol's custody battle and elongating the drama of her final proposal. These changes in the adaptation emphasize the affective and emotional experience of losing Rindy, as viewers grieve not only with Therese but also, and perhaps more poignantly, with Carol. By dramatizing the climactic scene where Carol states her case for queer desire, the reality of her queer maternal struggles becomes legible in a new way, leaving the audience with a lingering sense of injustice while celebrating the character's self-affirming courage.

Against the backdrop of a law office's wood-paneled conference room, Carol repeats the lines based on the novel's epistolary passage describing living a "life against one's grain." Here the audience identifies even more with her plight, now rendered more emotionally immediate in Blanchett's moving monologue: "There was a time I would have locked myself away—done most anything just to keep Rindy with me. But what use am I to her . . . to us . . . living against . . . my own grain? Rindy deserves—joy. How do I give her that not knowing what it means . . . myself" (Haynes 2015). The script's inclusion of ellipses is suggestive of the gaps and elisions inevitable in the double bind of queer maternity. For Carol truly to be a parent, she must be "herself," yet under the auspices of heteropatriarchy her queer sexuality and modes of love relation must be forever divorced from her maternal identity. Blanchett's portrayal of Carol in this scene illuminates the psychic pain she experiences in the moment of rescinding her claim to Rindy; as she becomes tearful, the film cuts to a close-up of her hands grasping the table for support. We learn then of the emotional price of queer motherhood and thus cultivate an experience of empathy that is impossible in the pulp novel, not simply because it is visualized in a "real time" present, but also because the film attributes a depth of emotion to Carol that the novel only intimates.

As the film aligns the audience closely with Carol's viewpoint, we receive the subsequent scene of Carol and Therese's final reunion and Carol's proposal to Therese with a new emotional tenor. The connection between Rindy's loss and Therese's return is made explicit, with only a couple of minutes of screen time passing between the scene in the law office and the reunion at the Ritz. The film closes with Therese rushing back to join Carol and her friends for dinner, their eyes meeting in secret recognition that gestures toward Therese's acceptance of Carol's plan of cohabitation. Refusing the redemptive tones of the novel's conclusion, the film's final scene ends as a cliffhanger, with a cut to black that offers a promise of romantic union but denies its full articulation—making the moment, according to White (2015: 17), even more seductive. While the cut to black might be seductive, it also allows those melancholic feelings of attachment to remain alive in the viewer, emphasizing the losses and foreclosures that Therese will never fully replace. For like the "void" that surrounded Therese upon their first breakup when she occupied a melancholic darkness of "the grave," the ending leaves open the possibility of loneliness returning, as the lovers approach a future in "heaven and in hell" that might lead back to loss.

Expectant Longings for a Different Queer Kinship

Premiering six months after the landmark Supreme Court ruling *Obergefell v. Hodges*, that, on June 26, 2015, legalized gay marriage in the United States, *Carol* dramatizes the loss of dignity, the disenfranchisement, and the dissolution of kinship bonds that same-sex marriage sought to redress. By asking us to turn back to a pre-Stonewall moment when marriage was an impossibility and lesbian romance a dangerous act of defiance, the film performs a melancholic recognition of the wounds of lost loves and kinship ties that gay marriage will never truly heal. This classic tale remembers a past where lesbianism was used as a rationale for deeming a woman unfit for parenthood and "remembers" a present where a great number of LGBTQ families still remain outside the protection of the law. By identifying with Carol as she struggles to bear her losses, we connect to a past history that continues to unfold in the present, as legal paths for queer families to achieve full, legal parentage in every form remain unreliable or even unforged in most US states. As Heather Love (2007: 32) notes in *Feeling Backward*, queer critics' attention to the past is animated by our own psychic and political impoverishments: "The experience of queer historical subjects is not at a safe distance from contemporary experience; rather, their social marginality and abjection mirror our own." To assume that Virginia Catherwood, Blue Lunden, and Vera Martin are simply ghosts of the past denies the enduring structural violence that continues to affect queer families today.

The political disappointments that Highsmith's novel and Haynes's film adaptation reveal prompt us to take seriously the "social marginality and abjection" of those who do not easily mirror the white, bourgeois figures that enable the core love story in *The Price of Salt* and *Carol*. It is crucial for us to move beyond this dialogic portrait of white queer assimilation to instead bear witness to the statistical majority of LGBTQ parents in the United States who identify as people of color, have a median income less than their heterosexual counterparts, and/or live in politically conservative regions, such as Mississippi, Wyoming, Alaska, and Idaho (the top four states where queer families reside) (Gates 2013). To deconstruct the grip that white, neoliberal norms have on the articulation of queer kinship and parental identity, it becomes necessary, as Cathy Cohen (1997: 91) urged twenty years ago, to resist a single-issue politics that reifies the distinction between gay and straight, proscribes a single path to equity or overlooks the deleterious impacts that hetero- and homonormativity have on communities of color. Cohen reminds us to focus our cultural critique on the ways that a liberatory queer kinship will require a revolution in a range of social institutions that have for centuries failed

to serve marginalized communities, including but not limited to adoption and foster care, health insurance coverage, fair housing, the criminal justice system, and
public education. Reading *The Price of Salt* and *Carol* against their own grain
thus demands us to account for the white neoliberalism at the root of Therese and
Carol's affair.

This essay has asked readers to dwell in the seemingly unbridgeable gap
between the plots of queer motherhood and lesbian desire in order to animate a
sense of radical expectancy for more capacious narratives of queer kinship that
can encompass the racial, ethnic, and economic diversity of our LGBTQ community. Rather than accept the erasure of kinship in their negative portrayals of queer
maternity and desire, I see these texts as potent incubators for the creation and
rediscovery of "new" modes of queer cultural representation. My readerly position of positive expectation, rather than negative disappointment, is thus born from
the cycle of replacement and substitution that the stories of Therese, Carol, and
Rindy perform. The queer melancholia that produces acts of partial substitution in
these texts turns toward the future as much as the past, where one replacement or
adaptation can produce another. In *Cruising Utopia*, José Esteban Muñoz (2009:
1) argues that utopianism, as an alternative to the futurity of reproductive heteronormativity, is foundational to queer culture's revolutionary forms of sociality:
"Queerness is a longing that propels us onward, beyond romances of the negative
and toiling in the present. . . . Queerness is essentially about the rejection of a
here and now and an insistence on potentiality or concrete possibility for another
world." In disagreement with Lee Edelman's 2004 polemic against the deployment
of the figure of the Child as a rationale for "reproductive futurity"—that neoliberal
political prophylactic against certain queers' radical choice to forgo reproductive
family life altogether—Muñoz tends toward a yet-to-arrive future while remaining
aware of the role that race and class play in making some children the "sovereign
princes of futurity" while others are barely able to survive their tenth birthday
(ibid.: 95). Joining Muñoz in an effort to redefine sociality, I read the negative
valence of Highsmith's denial of queer maternity as still gesturing toward a redefinition of kinship and a utopian vision of queer futurity.

To imagine a more radical future of queer kinship asks us not simply to
approach queer maternity as an identity formation unimaginable in many queer
texts but also to go beyond the discourse of identity to explore utopian forms of
kinship that can attend to the mutual inclusivity of sexuality and parenting, identification and desire, race and class. Queering motherhood to recognize it as a state
of profound, erotic ambivalence defined by a plurality of pleasure and pain, where
the subjective coherence of the pregnant or parental body breaks down, can only

expand our sense of queerness to creatively encompass a new vision of reproductive futurity that might just wrench the future from the strict confines of white heteronormativity. If we are to birth alternative circles of kin in our literature and in our lives that can resist the social and literal death that straight, white supremacy produces, queer authors and critics must acknowledge the hopes and pleasures that child rearing and family formation can bring to LGBTQ individuals. In the end, Highsmith and Haynes remind us that we need new stories of queer kinship, both reproductive and chosen—stories that embody the resistant forms of care and interdependence that have defined and continue to define the queer community while celebrating the pleasures of living against the grain.

Notes

1. According to Rivers, the earliest legal custody battles involving gay or lesbian parents that are documented occurred in 1955, over a decade after Catherwood's divorce. See also Lauren Jae Gutterman's (2012) study of lesbian desire and marriage using an archive of memoirs, letters, and diaries.

2. The gay psychoanalyst Jack Drescher (2001: 126) makes a similar point in a book review of a gay parenting autobiography, *The Velveteen Father*, writing that "children and grandchildren were sometimes regarded as a strangely, uncomfortable reminder of the days when gay men and women were either in the closet or before they had a conscious awareness of their lesbian or gay identity."

3. By 1986, when Rich published her new foreword to *Of Woman Born*, she acknowledged the lack of a discourse around lesbian mothers that occurred during the height of the second wave.

4. Gore Vidal's novel *The City and the Pillar*, published four years earlier under the author's name, did not receive a *New York Times* review, for example (Aldrich 2006: viii).

5. For a discussion of 1950s representations of queer maturation and the sexual child, see Stockton 2009. See also Sharon Marcus's analysis of dolls as a medium of lesbian desire in *Between Women: Friendship, Desire, and Marriage in Victorian England* (2007).

6. In the wake of Stonewall and second-wave feminism, lesbian authors like Audre Lorde and Nicole Brossard revised the pathological trope of mother-daughter bonding to instead become the metaphorical vehicle for imagining intimate connection and sexual union between women. And yet, as mentioned previously, their celebration of a lesbian maternal aesthetic and philosophical interest in the maternally focused pre-oedipal stage of psychoanalysis still seemingly ignored the actual fact of lesbian mothers (Jacobs 2015).

7. Devoid of extended familial connection or duty in its narrow vision of white queer femme love without maternity, the novel's portrait of Carol and Therese cultivating a middle-class, child-free lifestyle together may be considered "queer" in the context of an antireproductive and antisocial model of queerness. Yet it highlights how queer tropes and erotic motifs of mother-daughter love reinscribe white, Western culture, particularly psychoanalytic discourses that defined same-sex desire as stemming from maternal failure.

References

Aldrich, Ann. 2006. *We Walk Alone*. New York: Feminist.

Bohan, Janice S. 1996. *Psychology and Sexual Orientation: Coming to Terms*. New York: Routledge.

Carol. 2015. DVD. Directed by Todd Haynes. Los Angeles: Weinstein Company.

Cohen, Cathy J. 1997. "Punks, Bulldaggers, and Welfare Queens: The Radical Potential of Queer Politics?" *GLQ* 3, no. 4: 437–65.

Drescher, Jack. 2001. "The Circle of Liberation: A Book Review Essay of Jesse Green's The Velveteen Father: An Unexpected Journey to Parenthood." *Journal of Gay and Lesbian Psychotherapy* 4, nos. 3–4: 126.

Eng, David. 2010. *The Feeling of Kinship: Queer Liberalism and the Racialization of Intimacy*. Durham, NC: Duke University Press.

Gates, Gary J. 2013. "LGBT Parenting in the United States." Williams Institute, UCLA School of Law, Los Angeles. williamsinstitute.law.ucla.edu/wp-content/uploads/LGBT-Parenting.pdf.

Gutterman, Lauren Jae. 2012. "'The House on the Borderland': Lesbian Desire, Marriage, and the Household, 1950–1979." *Journal of Social History* 46, no. 1: 1–22.

Highsmith, Patricia. 2004. *The Price of Salt*. New York: W. W. Norton.

Hirsch, Marianne. 1989. *The Mother/Daughter Plot: Narrative, Psychoanalysis, Feminism*. Bloomington: Indiana University Press.

Hutcheon, Linda, and Siobhan O'Flynn. 2012. *A Theory of Adaptation*. New York: Routledge.

Jacobs, Bethany. 2015. "Mothering Herself: Manifesto of the Erotic Mother in Audre Lorde's *Zami: A New Spelling of My Name*." *MELUS* 40, no. 4: 110–28.

Love, Heather. 2007. *Feeling Backward: Loss and the Politics of Queer History*. Cambridge, MA: Harvard University Press.

Marcus, Sharon. 2007. *Between Women: Friendship, Desire, and Marriage in Victorian England*. Princeton, NJ: Princeton University Press.

Meaker, Marijane. 2003. *Highsmith: A Romance of the 1950s*. San Francisco: Cleis.

Muñoz, José Esteban. 2009. *Cruising Utopia: The Then and There of Queer Futurity*. New York: New York University Press.

Nelson, Maggie. 2015. *The Argonauts*. Minneapolis: Graywolf.

Rich, Adrienne. 1995. *Of Woman Born*. New York: W. W. Norton.

Rivers, Daniel Winunwe. 2013. *Radical Relations: Lesbian Mothers, Gay Fathers, and Their Children in the United States since World War II*. Chapel Hill: University of North Carolina Press.

Rolo, Charles J. 1952. Review of "Carol and Therese: *The Price of Salt*. By Claire Morgan." *New York Times*, May 18.

Schenkar, Joan. 2009. *The Talented Miss Highsmith: The Secret Life and Serious Art of Patricia Highsmith*. New York: St. Martin's.

Shelley, Martha. 1970. "Notes of a Radical Lesbian." In *Sisterhood Is Powerful*, edited by Robin Morgan, 306–11. New York: Vintage.

Stockton, Kathryn Bond. 2009. *The Queer Child, or Growing Sideways in the Twentieth Century*. Durham, NC: Duke University Press.

White, Patricia. 2015. "Sketchy Lesbians: 'Carol' as History and Fantasy." *Film Quarterly* 69, no. 2: 8–18.

Wilson, Andrew. 2003. *Beautiful Shadow: A Life of Patricia Highsmith*. New York: Bloomsbury.

QUEERS READ WHAT NOW?

Martin Joseph Ponce

The polemical proclamations announced by the anonymously published pamphlet *Queers Read This* (Anonymous [1990] 2009: 1, 3, 10), circulated at the 1990 Pride celebration in New York City, are by turns inspiring ("You as an alive and functioning queer are a revolutionary"), depressing ("There is nothing on this planet that validates, protects or encourages your existence"), angry ("I will not march silently with a fucking candle"), and combative ("Straight people are your enemy"), but above all exhortatory ("We're OUT. Where the fuck are YOU?"). What is particularly striking to me in relation to this essay's concerns about race, culture, and the politics of historical memory is the one parenthetical reference to a queer past that could counter the lament of having "never [been] taught about queer people" in public school (ibid.: 8)—that even gestures beyond the self-referential "this" the aggressively hailed "you" ought to read: "(We've given so much to that world: democracy, all the arts, the concepts of love, philosophy and the soul, to name just a few gifts from our ancient Greek Dykes, Fags)" (ibid.: 2).

As a way into thinking critically about this "we" and its collective past, I turn to Cathy Cohen's (1997: 447) touchstone essay, "Punks, Bulldaggers, and Welfare Queens: The Radical Potential of Queer Politics?," which directly engages *Queers Read This* as one instance when certain queer activisms of the period came "dangerously close to a single oppression model." Cohen observes, "Experiencing 'deviant' sexuality as the prominent characteristic of their marginalization, these activists begin to envision the world in terms of a 'hetero/queer' divide" (ibid.: 447). By conflating heteronormativity with an undifferentiated heterosexuality and by rendering all queers equally powerless, this divide fails to account for manifestations of queer privilege and heterosexual disadvantage constituted by class, racial, and gender asymmetries. Cohen (1997: 448, 450) notes that although *Queers Read This* refers to the need to fight "homophobia, racism, misogyny, the bigotry of religious hypocrites and our own self-hatred," its contention that

GLQ 24:2–3
DOI 10.1215/10642684-4324837
© 2018 by Duke University Press

"'straight people have a privilege that allows them to do whatever they please and fuck without fear'" entrenches the hetero-queer divide and further "discounts the relationships—especially those based on shared experiences of marginalization—that exist between gays and straights, particularly in communities of color."

Cohen's essay enables us to question not only the shortcomings of a queer politics organized in binary terms around sexuality but also a queer reading of the past that conceals the imbrications of racial difference and gender-sexual deviance. To illustrate her point that not all heterosexual people enjoy the same privileges, Cohen narrates a history of African Americans that touches on the prohibition against slave marriages as a self-fulfilling prophecy regarding enslaved black people's alleged "unrestrained" sexuality and contempt for family; the legal ban on interracial marriages until 1967 as a way to preserve white racial purity; and the ongoing pathologization of the black family before and after the infamous 1965 Moynihan Report through the "stigmatization and demonization of single mothers, teen mothers" and the titular "welfare queens" and through stereotypes of impoverished "young black men engaged in 'reckless' heterosexual behavior" as "irresponsible baby factories" (ibid.: 455, 456). Whereas Cohen offers these examples to "identify those spaces of shared or similar oppression and resistance that provide a basis for radical coalition work" across racial and sexual differences (ibid.: 453), her argument now reads as part of the broader field of queer of color critique that has irrevocably transformed what "queer" can mean by elucidating how queer and racial differences have been fatally attached to and mediated through one another in particular circumstances. As I elaborate below, this work has rendered any consolatory or celebratory recourse to the illustrious political, philosophical, and artistic "gifts from our ancient Greek Dykes, Fags" tendentiously partial.

This essay reflects critically on commonsense reading practices in order to clear intellectual and institutional space for a comparative queer of color studies that renders racial and colonial domination and subordination constitutive of queer literary and social history. The first part of the essay revisits the prevalent trope of gay and lesbian reading and the politics of the canon. The next sections examine statements from women and queer of color anthologies as well as scenes of reading in three texts published from the advent of explicitly LGBTQ2 of color literature to the present—Audre Lorde's biomythography *Zami: A New Spelling of My Name* (1982), Craig Womack's (Muscogee-Creek and Cherokee) novel *Drowning in Fire* (2001), and Janet Mock's memoir *Redefining Realness* (2014)—that point toward the racial and indigenous absences and erasures in dominant lesbian, gay, and transgender expressive cultures. Faced with such issues as the denial of black intraracial lesbian eroticism, the oppressiveness of Christian homophobia and gay racism, and the commodification and exploitation of trans women of color experiences, these narratives importantly and necessarily call for and embody the construction of alternative queer and trans of color myths, histories, and cultures of survival. Nonetheless, their authorial motivations and reader receptions remain within the logics of textual mirroring and self-identification (albeit expanded to include multiple and intersecting differences)—logics that both preclude comparative modes of reading and occlude the definitional challenges of "queer of color literature" posed by queer of color critique. In the final sections, then, I turn to Lorde's feminist ethic of vulnerability and self-transformation through intersubjective encounters, metaphorized at the end of *Zami* as being "printed" on, as well as theories of comparative racialization that queer of color critique has recuperated from women of color feminism as powerful ways to explore the shifts in reader subjectivities and institutional formations that would need to take place for comparative queer and trans of color literary histories to flourish.

Gay and Lesbian Reading (Is So White)

Gay and lesbian readers frequently attest to the pivotal role that reading for representations of same-sex desire has played in facilitating sexual self-understanding and alleviating a sense of isolation. As Rick Lee (2009: 2, 3) demonstrates in his lucid examination of gay readers, "the transformative, pedagogical function of reading" homosexual-themed or -coded texts reveals an intimate "connection between the act of reading and the process of *learning* how to become gay." Gay authors and critics alike have remarked on these connections among reading, identification, and belonging. For example, Edmund White (1991: xiv) writes in the foreword to *The Faber Book of Gay Short Fiction* of his boyhood during the 1950s: "I looked desperately for things to read that might confirm an identity I was piecing together and accommodate a sexuality that fate seemed to have thrust on me without my ever having chosen it." He recalls reading Evelyn Waugh's *Brideshead Revisited* (1945), Christopher Isherwood's *A Single Man* (1964), Andre Gide's *If It Die* (1935), William Burroughs's *Naked Lunch* (1959), John Rechy's *City of Night* (1963), and Jean Genet's *Our Lady of the Flowers* (1943) during the 1960s. Similarly, Les Brookes (2009: 1) writes in his literary studies monograph on the "key role" that literature has played in "the development of gay consciousness": "I had to know who I was; I needed to forge a self and imagine a future. Along with a sociological study of homosexuality and a life of Tchaikovsky, I devoured novels by Gore Vidal, Angus Wilson, James Baldwin, and Christopher Isherwood."[1]

Lesbian writers and critics have also documented their reading practices. Joan Nestle (1997: xiv) suggests that "the lesbian reader" was emerging during the early twentieth century: "Searching for parts of herself, she carefully examined each text that carried any clues." More recently, Jodie Medd (2015: 4) notes that "'scenes of reading'—from literary discoveries to thwarted library researches—abound in autobiographical accounts of modern lesbian identification," including those by Joanna Russ, Gayle Rubin, and Lillian Faderman, among others. Faderman (1994: vii) herself opens her preface to *Chloe Plus Olivia: An Anthology of Lesbian Literature from the Seventeenth Century to the Present*: "In 1956, as a teenager, I began to consider myself a lesbian. Almost as soon as I claimed that identity, being enamored of books, of course I looked around for literary representations that would help explain me to myself." She recalls seeking in particular "'real literature,' the kind I read in my English classes, to comment on the lifestyle I had just recently discovered with such enthusiasm, to reveal me to myself, to acknowledge the lesbian to the world."

These recollections of searching for, explaining, and revealing oneself through encounters with gay- and lesbian-themed texts evoke some, if not all, of what Valerie Rohy (2015: 106) has delineated as "the defining features of queer reading—identity-formation, interpellation by prevailing language, the search for community, an education in cultural and sub-cultural signs, and the function of the material book as a medium of communication and exchange." By recurring to "the trope of the mirror" (ibid.: 134), these models of minoritized reading, as Sarah Nuttall (2001: 392) phrases it, are "about recognizing the self, as if for the first time, in the text before one." *As if for the first time* speaks to the perspective of "those who identify themselves with the margins," not "metropolitans" who often think of reading as an act of "discovering the lives of others." Although Nuttall's article is focused on African literature and postcolonial studies, her remarks on "textual colonialism" are apposite, since they foreground the connections among race, colonialism, and canonicity that have too often been bracketed in discussions of gay and lesbian reading.

The citational practice embedded in these scenes of reading indicates that representations of gay and lesbian reading are also acts of tradition making. This is especially true of anthologies but also applies to literary narratives as well.[2] In "The Making of the Gay Tradition," Gregory Woods (1998: 3) notes that the "canon of gay literature has been constructed by bookish homosexuals, most explicitly since the debates on sexuality and identity which flourished in the last third of the nineteenth century." Just as the early modern through Victorian-era texts reach back to Greek and Roman antiquity, the later ones incorporate their tradition-making predecessors, thereby recursively reproducing and expanding the "gay" Western literary-philosophical canon through accretion. Though he acknowledges the "contingencies" of "'our' sexual history" (ibid.: 3, 2), Woods nonetheless writes that "homosexual people" have made recourse to the "real literature" of the Western canon in order to harness its legitimizing power, to "shore up their self-respect in the face of constant moral attack" (ibid.: 6). "This is not a marginal tradition," he concludes, "even if it is sometimes marginalised. Merely to read the index pages of a book like this is to begin to retell one of the grandest of the grand narratives, the history of gay literature" (ibid.: 16).

But which "materials" can be used "to justify" homosexual "existence" and whose "self-respect" is enriched through these literate practices requires deeper investigation (ibid.: 6). Since Woods turns to "the Greek classics" in the next chapter, it is worth pausing, as Scott Bravmann (1997: 48) bids us, over the recurrent invocations "of ancient Greece in lesbian and gay cultural, historical and political production." Bravmann argues that "these conceptual *models* of Greek antiquity have been neither historically inevitable nor politically innocent": "white gay and lesbian fictions of Greece are inscribed in and through a racial *in*difference which prevents a candid consideration of 'race'" (ibid.: 49, 67). At stake is not just racial exclusion from dominant canons of gay (and, to a lesser extent, lesbian) literature but the racial and colonial oppressions on which those "grand narratives" are based and which they can, in turn, perpetuate.[3] Drawing on the work of Linda Dowling, Bravmann notes that "the emergent hegemonic discourse on Greece" in late nineteenth-century English intellectual culture overlapped with British imperialism and its "deep-seated theories of civilization, discourses of national survival, and racial belief systems" (ibid.: 50). Cast more broadly, on the other side of "Greece" and its putative civilization lie all those primitivized and orientalized cultures whose depictions in Euro-American travel writing and colonial discourse produce racial difference and hierarchy through exoticizing tropes of nonnormative eroticisms, bodily comportment, unusual clothing (or lack thereof), segregated gender spaces, delayed developmental temporalities, and so on. As colonial and queer studies scholars have pointed out, imperial modes of racial classification intersected with discourses of comparative anatomy, scientific racism, sexology, and eugenics to construct racial stratifications predicated on gender-sexual differences and to rationalize their civilizing missions (see, e.g., Boone 2014; Hackett 2004; Hawley 2001; Hoad 2000; Holden 2002; Ngô 2014; Ordover 2003; Rohy 2009; Somerville 2000). Indeed, references to "primitive" homoeroticisms are sometimes incorporated into the gay anthologies themselves.[4] Not surprisingly, then, when sexuality is decentered from the trope of gay and lesbian reading and collides with other vectors of difference and identity—here, race and culture—queer and trans of color readers tend not to invoke the Western canon as satisfying their textual desires but to continue to search for, and ultimately construct, something else.

But Some of Us . . .

Although it would be impertinent to assume that queer readers of color cannot lay claim to canonical traditions or identify with certain representations on specious grounds of "cultural difference" (Bravmann 1997: 64–65), it is nonetheless telling that the queer writers and editors of color who assembled alternative anthologies starting around the 1980s often remark on the absence or scarcity of representation, thus implying that the canonical traditions remain inadequate, if not hostile, to their needs.[5] Barbara Smith (1982: 173), for example, closes her groundbreaking essay "Toward a Black Feminist Tradition," published in the collection *All the Women Are White, All the Blacks Are Men, But Some of Us Are Brave: Black Women's Studies*, with a sense of ongoing yearning: "I finally want to express how much easier both my waking and my sleeping hours would be if there were one book in existence that would tell me something specific about my life. One book based in Black feminist and Black lesbian experience, fiction or nonfiction. Just one work to reflect the reality that I and the Black women whom I love are trying to create." Following Smith's lead, Jewelle Gomez ([1983] 2000: 110) begins her essay "A Cultural Legacy Denied and Discovered: Black Lesbians in Fiction by Women" with the inference that as far as the "fine arts" and "popular media" are concerned, "the message conveyed about the Lesbian of color is that she does not even *exist*." The title of her sequel, "But Some of Us Are Brave Lesbians: The Absence of Black Lesbian Fiction" (Gomez 2005: 290) published over twenty years later, both echoes the 1983 anthology and laments that the promise of the 1980s has not come to fruition: "What quickly became obvious as I looked for texts to consider was that there is less contemporary black lesbian fiction today than there was before the so-called gay literary boom of the early 1990s." Smith and Gomez echo and revise the lesbian reading practices discussed above, bringing to bear an intersectional framework that highlights the occlusions of specifically black lesbian textual representation and realities.

Presaging part of the gay literary boom that Gomez references, Joseph Beam (1986: 13, 14) analogously opens *In the Life*, the first anthology of black gay male literature, by paying ironic tribute to the 1982 anthology—"*All the protagonists are blond; all the Blacks are criminal and negligible*"—and then recalls "grow[ing] weary of reading literature by white gay men. . . . None of them spoke to me as a Black gay man. . . . More and more each day, as I looked around the stocked shelves of Giovanni's Room, Philadelphia's gay, lesbian, and feminist bookstore where I worked, I wondered where was the work of Black gay men." Even more emphatically, Essex Hemphill (1991: xv) writes in the sequel *Brother to Brother: New Writings by Black Gay Men* that although he "searched the card catalogue at the local library and discovered there were books about homosexuality in the 'adult' section," those "books made no references to black men that I can recall, nor were there black case studies for me to examine, and in the few pictures of men identified as homosexual, not one was black." He concludes after his "month-long reading marathon" as a sixth grader: "I didn't recognize myself in any of the material I had so exhaustively read. If anything, I could have ignorantly concluded that homosexuality was peculiar to white people, and my conclusion would have been supported by the deliberate lack of evidence concerning black men and homosexual desire" (ibid.: xvi). Taken together, the statements by Smith, Gomez, Beam, and Hemphill demonstrate the persistent desire for and dearth of books that address their complex experiences. For them, the absence of such texts is tantamount to the nullification and nonrecognition of their raced, gendered, and sexualized existences.

The absences of racial-sexual representation articulated in these signal anthologies are reflected, to varying degrees, in the narratives by Lorde, Womack, and Mock. I have selected these texts because they are among the few queer and trans of color literary texts I know of that feature scenes of reading. In this regard, they operate in my discussion in lieu of an ethnographic study of what and how actual LGBTQ people of color read.[6] Despite their disparate dates of publication and conditions of emergence, their authorial motivations and reader receptions are illustrative of the dynamics of representation, reading, and self-reflection that concern me here. My goal is not to disregard nonfictional analyses of flesh and blood readers, nor to install these texts as somehow paradigmatic of queer and trans of color literature (more on the conundrums of alternative canons below), but to consider what other myths, histories, and forms these texts invoke and invent when existing representations are not enough. José Esteban Muñoz's (1999: 11, 25) theory of disidentification is useful here for conceptualizing the modes of reading and writing that these writers undertake. Although he mostly uses the term to examine performances and expressive practices in which queer of color artists "[work] on and against dominant ideology" and seek to "transform" its oppressive "cultural logic from within," he also "refer[s] to disidentification as a hermeneutic, a process of production, and a mode of performance. Disidentification can be a way of shuttling back and forth between reception and production." My approach to the scenes of reading in Lorde, Womack, and Mock and their revisionary constructions of myth, geography, colonial history, autobiography, and literary history aligns with this shuttling between reception and production. It is precisely the dissatisfactions of reading (and viewing) available texts as queer and trans of color subjects—for example, lesbian pulp novels, mainstream gay magazines and personal ads, sensationalist trans narratives and films—that instigates the production of these corrective, complex narratives.

Scenes of Queer and Trans of Color Reading and Narrative Invention

As devoted to literacy as it is, Lorde's *Zami* is markedly silent on the practice of lesbian reading. In an early chapter that describes how she "learned to read at the same time I learned to talk" (Lorde [1982] 1983: 21), Lorde recalls throwing a fit as a four-year-old in the public library because she is too young to join her older sisters at storytelling time. A librarian calms her down by reading to her *Madeline*, *Horton Hatches the Egg*, and other children's stories. Of this memory, Lorde writes: "If that was the only good deed that lady ever did in her life, may she rest in peace. Because that deed saved my life, if not sooner, then later, when sometimes the only thing I had to hold on to was knowing I could read, and that that could get me through" (ibid.: 22). Tellingly, however, despite the life-saving value of reading that follows from the young Audre announcing to her astonished mother, "I want to read" (ibid.: 23), and the numerous references to reading books and writing poetry—including a chapter of her youth titled "How I Became a Poet" (ibid.: 31–34) that illustrates her Caribbean mother's vernacular language-use—Lorde does not portray scenes of lesbian reading.

The one exception is when Lynn enters her and her lover Muriel's life (both women are white), and Lorde remarks on the novelty of their three-way "experiment" during the 1950s:

> We were certainly the first to have tried to work out this unique way of living for women, communal sex without rancor. After all, nobody else ever talked about it. None of the gay-girl books we read so avidly ever suggested our vision was not new, nor our joy in each other. Certainly Beebo Brinker didn't; nor Olga, of *The Scorpion*. Our much-fingered copies of Ann Bannon's *Women in the Shadows* and *Odd Girl Out* never so much as suggested that the perils and tragedies connected with loving women could possibly involve more than two at a time. And of course none of those books even

mentioned the joys. So we knew there was a world of our experience as gay-girls that they left out, but that meant we had to write it ourselves, learn by living it out. (ibid.: 213)

If midcentury lesbian pulp novels provide little guidance on how to navigate homoerotic polyamorous living together, those texts would appear to offer even less support with resisting the racism that hinders intimacies between black women in the Greenwich Village bar scene during this period: "In the gay bars, I longed for other Black women without the need ever taking shape upon my lips. For four hundred years in this country, Black women have been taught to view each other with deep suspicion. It was no different in the gay world" (ibid.: 224). Lorde's analysis of antiblack racism—contradicting the prevailing view that "of course, gay people weren't racists. After all, didn't they know what it was like to be oppressed?" (ibid.: 180)—gives rise not only to her celebrated declaration that "it was a while before we came to realize that our place was the very house of difference rather than the security of any one particular difference" (ibid.: 226). It also leads to the quasi-fantastical, intraracial affair that Audre has with Afrekete: "*And I remember Afrekete, who came out of a dream to me always being hard and real as the fire hairs along the under-edge of my navel*" (ibid.: 249). The dreamlike and idealized quality of her brief time with Afrekete arises from the divine resonances of her name and the italicized tributes to their sensuous lovemaking—not insignificantly enacted using Caribbean fruits (ibid.: 249, 251, 252). As though embodying the culminating *telos* of Lorde's previous, broken relationships with Gennie, Ginger, Bea, Eudora, and Muriel, "Afrekete," Lorde writes, "taught me roots, new definitions of our women's bodies—definitions for which I had only been in training to learn before" (ibid.: 250). Such a satisfying and highly eroticized experience, according to *Zami*'s otherwise realist ontology, seems possible only when the literary steps into the world of the mythic.

The epilogue famously invokes an alternative name for female homoeroticism that cannot be found or practiced within the US confines of Lorde's experience—"*Zami. A Carriacou name for women who work together as friends and lovers*" (ibid.: 255)—and thereby gestures toward an alternative homeland: "There it is said that the desire to lie with other women is a drive from the mother's blood" (ibid.: 256). As such, Lorde's text resonates with other queer of color and queer postcolonial projects that have looked to non-Western or culturally hybrid traditions, languages, and locations for modes of identification and sites of communal formation that lie outside white LGBTQ culture.

Though published nearly two decades after *Zami*, Womack's coming-of-age novel *Drowning in Fire* is one such example of a Native gay male text that portrays scenes of reading in ways similar to those of the previous generation, that is, as limited by queer Native absence and gay whiteness, and that consequently invents ways to reconcile same-sex desire and practice with racial and cultural specificity, in this case, with Creek nationhood and community. Whereas Lorde turns to myth and geography to evoke possibilities for black diasporic women's companionship, work, and eroticism, Womack turns to a rewriting of history as an antidote to the homophobia and racism that his protagonists experience.

In *Drowning in Fire*, the protagonist Josh Henneha grows up in a small town in Oklahoma during the 1960s and 1970s, is subjected to homophobic taunts, feels isolated and silenced, experiences great anxiety over his homoerotic desires, and eventually comes to terms with his sexuality as an adult when he reconnects with his friend Jimmy, a part-black, athletic, outgoing boy who also turns out to be gay, unbeknownst to Josh until their senior year of high school. Tormented during his youth, Josh describes himself as a bookworm, which only incites more disgust for his masculine deficiency among his peers. While using the trope of gay reading to counter the fire and brimstone sermons he hears every Sunday at the white Baptist church that deigns to admit his Creek family, Josh refrains from naming titles or authors. As he recalls during high school, "I was desperately searching these books, looking for some clue, any clue, that there was someone out there like me. And I'd come up empty-handed, but I couldn't quit. I'd rather keep looking than find out I was alone" (Womack 2001: 85). Josh eventually wins the "war of words" (ibid.: 105) waging in his head against Christian denunciations of homosexuality and effeminacy not by eventually locating gay-affirming books but by recalling the Creek stories he had heard from his great-aunt Lucy and his grandfather and by reading as an adult about Creek history.

To Josh's surprise, his boyhood crush and subsequent partner, Jimmy, the garrulous high school basketball star, is not only gay—he tries to cop a feel when he and Josh share a bed during a seventh-grade sleepover, takes Josh to a gay cruising spot near a river where the two have their first sexual encounter after a senior basketball game in Oklahoma City, and hooks up with Josh after a party some thirteen years later—he is also a reader. As the reunited men navigate their relationship in light of Jimmy's HIV-positive status, Jimmy also reveals to a disbelieving Josh that he had read many of the same "books on Creek history" that line Josh's shelves as a result of his father's "special Creek version" of a "home school program" (ibid.: 266, 267).

Both men's knowledge acquisition about Creek history and culture is framed not only as a critique of US settler colonialism and the dominant story of Oklahoma statehood but also as an overcoming of religious and racial obstacles (homo-phobic Christianity in Josh's case, gay racism in Jimmy's). The latter is illustrated in an argument between Jimmy and his friend C. A. (Clarence Albert), an effemi-nate Comanche man who was even more persecuted than Josh as a boy, over the lack of racial diversity in mainstream gay culture ("There aren't any [Indians] in your magazines" like the *Advocate* [ibid.: 151]) and the politics of racialized desire ("Our race, or any other race besides their own, doesn't seem to be very popu-lar with the gay boys here in the Sooner state" [ibid.: 155]). Whereas Josh had "come up empty-handed" in his search for gay models, Jimmy is confronted with the overwhelming whiteness of gay print culture—which is fine for C. A., who is obsessed with white men, but Jimmy seeks a Native man by placing a personal ad in the *Gayly Oklahoman*: "I'm Indian. I hope you are too. Give me a call" (ibid.: 159). Jimmy's antipathy toward the white "gay world [as] a totally fucked-up, racist, hateful, self-hating, boring, moronic, second-rate imitation of the straight world that despises it" stems from a post–high school "wild summer" he had spent in Tulsa "picking up tricks almost every day" (ibid.: 155, 262). After returning to his hometown, he tells Josh, he would go back to the city "hoping to find some nice man" but instead would be greeted with sexual racism: "The only thing I've found is homophobic white guys who'll fuck you or let you suck them off but won't let you touch them. They like their brown boys kneeling in front of them" (ibid.: 264).

The novel addresses these religious, racial, and sexual forms of discrimi-nation through the intracultural coming together of Josh and Jimmy (both are Creek) and through Josh's imaginative storytelling, which provides the ideological basis for their union. In the last chapters, Josh narrates—and inserts himself and Jimmy into—the history of the resistant Creek organization known as the Snakes. Led by Chitto Harjo, the Snakes sought to challenge allotment, land theft, and Oklahoma statehood, and preserve Creek land and sovereignty in the early twenti-eth century. As Josh and Jimmy take the place of Tarbie and Seborn (Rifkin 2011: 297), a male couple whose prior existence facilitates Josh's sexual self-acceptance and who helped keep alive the Creek "spirit of resistance" (Womack 2001: 242), Josh's queered improvisation on Creek history ("I didn't have all the facts, so I did the most sensible thing and proceeded without them" [ibid.: 220]) renders both couples integral to the fight for Creek sovereignty. Reversing the usual agonistics of being torn between a homophobic home space and a tokenistically tolerant (at best) white gay community, Womack's novel frames Creek homophobia as a result of US colonialism and Christianity, as Mark Rifkin (2011) points out, and Creek culture in the past and potentially in the present as accommodating of same-sex intimacy. In the novel's final pages, Jimmy leads Josh in a slow dance that transmutes into something like a ritual. The two men dance for family and community members, and their "dancing beckons others; they rise up out of the darkness to join us. We begin dancing for a nation of people, Mvskokvalke" (Womack 2001: 294).

My final example, Mock's best-selling memoir, *Redefining Realness: My Path to Womanhood, Identity, Love and So Much More*, published over a decade after Womack's novel, also gestures toward the lack of complex minority representation, in this case, of trans of color experiences. The book narrates Mock's life as a mixed-race Native Hawaiian and African American trans woman from her precarious childhood in Honolulu (with interludes in two California cities, Long Beach and Oakland, and Dallas, Texas) to her eventual move to New York City to attend college. Along the way, she offers detailed accounts of navigating the treacherous terrains of family life (being shuttled between her separated, working-class parents and their respective difficult partners), of child sexual abuse perpetrated by a male teenager, of differently classed public schools that alternately condemn and condone her expressions of femininity, of the streets of Honolulu where she meets other trans women and learns the ways of sex work, of pursuing "genital reconstruction surgery (GRS)" in Thailand, and of romance and self-disclosure with her partner, Aaron, in New York (2014: 188).

Though *Redefining Realness* appeared three decades after the women of color feminists initiated a publishing revolution in the United States, Mock (ibid.: xvi) nonetheless writes in the introduction: "I know intimately what it feels like to crave representation and validation, to see your life reflected in someone who speaks deeply to whom you know yourself to be, echoes your reality, and instills you with possibility. That mirror wasn't accessible to me growing up." It is thus not surprising that the memoir's few scenes of reading do not mention trans (of color) texts. When young Janet returns to Honolulu to live with her mother after five years on the mainland with her father, she recalls spending "a lot of my free time in the stacks at the Kalihi-Palama library" and "inherit[ing] her [mother's] love of books" (ibid.: 94). Janet later enrolls in the middle-class high school of Moanalua, is introduced in English class to Maya Angelou's *I Know Why the Caged Bird Sings* (1969) and Alice Walker's *The Color Purple* (1982), and is "deeply struck" by the figures' traumatic experiences with sexual abuse (ibid.: 130). While starting hormones during this period, Janet also recalls "reading heavy heroine novels like *Madame Bovary, Anna Karenina, A Room with a View*, and *The Age of Innocence*" (ibid.: 138).

Whereas these texts seem to provide little assistance with the key events constituting her trans experience—her early self-identification as a girl, the various forms of socialization that seek to discipline and masculinize her gender, her decision to engage in sex work to earn enough money for GRS, and her bodily transition before moving to New York—Mock employs methods similar to Lorde and Womack on the significances of homelands and indigeneity while also taking advantage of the nonfiction aspect of autobiography by drawing on African American literary history, gender and sexuality studies, and Native Hawaiian culture to frame and transmit her story. Although she asserts that "some of my most pivotal moments rose from pop culture" (ibid.: 193)—particularly Janet Jackson, after whom she names herself (ibid.: 143–44), and Beyoncé and Destiny's Child, who "validated" her as a teenager (ibid.: 194)—and although the book is peppered with references to TV shows, movies, and other musical acts, it is noteworthy that she consistently alludes to literary texts produced predominantly by African American women writers. In fact, Mock ends her author's note by guiding readers to her website "for more information, resources, and writings" (ibid.: xii). There we find a list of works that includes links to the biographies and work of Lorde, Smith, bell hooks, James Baldwin, Zora Neale Hurston, Toni Morrison, Alice Walker, Angelou, and Ralph Ellison, as well as J. K. Rowling, Gloria Anzaldúa, and Cherríe Moraga. The page also acknowledges "trans foremothers mentioned" in the memoir such as Marsha P. Johnson, Miss Major Griffin-Gracy, and Sylvia Rivera.

By recontextualizing characters and passages from the likes of Morrison's *Sula* (1973), Ellison's *Invisible Man* (1952), and especially Hurston's *Their Eyes Were Watching God* (1937), Mock engages in what Cheryl Wall (2005: 13), drawing on blues terminology, describes as "worrying the line"—literary practices through which "contemporary black women writers revise and subvert the conventions of the genres they appropriate." "A worried line," Wall adds, "is not a *straight* line" (ibid., my emphasis). Rewriting "canonical" and African American texts alike, Mock's narrative "give[s] voice to stories those texts did not imagine," even as it pays homage to the latter (ibid.).

The most prominent way that Mock revises the generic tradition of African American autobiography is by interweaving pedagogical, perhaps didactic, information into the narrative on various topics that her life experiences are connected to. These issues address theoretical concerns like the normative gender-sex binary (Mock 2014: 21–22) and the differences among gender, sex, and sexuality (ibid.: 50); social concerns like homelessness (ibid.: 109) and self-harm (ibid.: 199) among LGBTQ youth and trans students' needs in schools (ibid.: 148); medical concerns like psychiatric policies and health care costs governing "hormone replacement therapy and gender affirming surgeries" (ibid.: 136); administrative concerns like demographic estimations of trans-identified individuals (ibid.: 113) and the intricacies involved in changing one's name (ibid.: 144); and discrimination concerns like trans women's vulnerabilities to clients and the police as sex workers (ibid.: 205–6) and to hate violence from the general public (ibid.: 214, 246–47). In turn, Mock's navigation of individual and collective representation through the insertion of these "editorial commentar[ies]" (Lyle 2015: 503) that account for racial and class asymmetries challenges the increasing codification and commodification of the stock trans narrative as portrayed in popular culture— especially the "media's insatiable appetite for transsexual women's bodies" and the lurid details of transitioning that "contributes to the systematic othering of trans women as modern-day freak shows" (Mock 2014: 255).

Mock's deployment of shifting discursive registers and cultural frames of reference gains further complexity when she describes the influence of the Native Hawaiian *mahu*—"spiritual healers, cultural bearers and breeders, caretakers, and expert hula dancers and instructors" who exist beyond the Western gender binary (ibid.: 102)—on her self-understanding. Though *mahu* had become a pejorative as a result of the impact of Western colonialism and Christian missionaries, Mock notes how some trans women, like her hula instructor Kumu Kaua'i, have "reclaimed" the term (ibid.: 103). Kumu thus "resonated with me at age twelve as I yearned to explore and reveal who I was" (ibid.: 104), while the multicultural space of Hawai'i more generally was instrumental in facilitating her self-development: "It was empowering to come of age in a place that recognized that diversity existed not only in ethnicities but also in gender. There was a level of tolerance regarding gender nonconformity that made it safer for people like Wendi and me to exist as we explored and expressed our identities" (ibid.: 103).

Finally, it is notable that Wendi, the person who first asks Janet if she is *mahu* (ibid.: 102), is herself Filipina. Although Janet initially shies away from being associated with Wendi's flamboyance and the derision she experiences at school, the two eventually become "inseparable" friends: "I was fortunate to meet someone just like me at such a young age. It was empowering to see myself reflected in her, and I rapidly shifted in her presence" (ibid.: 107). It is Wendi who introduces Janet to hormones and with whom she learns from "Hawaii's community of trans women [which] was vast and knowledgable" (ibid.: 136). It is particularly interesting that Mock uses the language of reflection and identification to evoke their mutual influence and shared gender and class positions despite their different racial backgrounds: "To be so young and aiming to discover and assert myself alongside a best friend who mirrored me in her own identity instilled possibility in me. I could be me because I was not alone" (ibid.: 117–18). By forging these intertextual, intercultural, and interpersonal links with African American literary history, Native Hawaiian culture, and other trans girls and women, Mock constructs a "book" that both affirms "my truth and personal history" and shares it as a vulnerable "gift" (ibid.: xi, xvi).

Is the Queer in Queer of Color Literature the Queer in Queer of Color Critique?

In interviews, both Womack and Mock assert that their literary motivations stem from the dearth of representation that they and their protagonists faced. Womack (Gozen 2002: 12) recalls "a number of late night conversations with my friend Robert Warrior, an Osage writer, who kept saying, 'Craig you simply must finish this book. What if there is some Creek kid out there who has never before read anything that made him feel good about himself? That's who you're writing for.' . . . It was a motivator, I can tell you that much!" Womack's remarks reverse the usual temporality of the desirous reader searching for meaningful texts by proleptically "anticipating a scene of queer reading" (Rohy 2015: 110) that would retrospectively legitimate the novel's existence and the novelist's labor (of love). Similarly, Mock responds to a question about her "ideal reader": "In my mind, the reader has always been that young trans girl of color, that seventh grade girl—like I was—who is looking for a reflection of herself or looking for a story that speaks truth to her—to all of her" (quoted in Lyle 2015: 502).

The representational absences to which these texts call attention and which their own narratives seek to redress raise questions around the publication, dissemination, and circulation of queer and trans of color literature in public discourse and, as I suggest below, queer and trans of color literary history for academic scholarship. To be sure, the Internet and social media have dramatically changed users' access to authors and titles (if not the texts themselves) since 1982 and even 2001. Mock (2014: 118) notes as much not only by directing her readers to her website for additional resources but also by asserting in the course of her narrative: "If they have online access, trans people can find support and resources on YouTube, Tumblr, Twitter, and various other platforms where trans folks of all ages are broadcasting their lives, journeys, and even social and medical transitions." Moreover, a quick online search yields various lists of LGBTQ2 authors and texts of color, often accompanied by exhortations no less urgent than the *Queers Read This* pamphlet: "35 Black Queer Writers You Need to Know About," "10 Two-Spirit Authors You Should Be Reading," "Books of Latinx #QueerLove We All Need Right Now," "23 LGBTQ Books With A POC Protagonist, Because It's Time To Diversify Your Reading List." These lists may be regarded as updated people-of-color versions of the white Western gay and lesbian canons discussed above. As such, they align with one of the directions that queer of color literary studies and anthology making has taken.

This approach has sought to document and analyze literature by and/or about racial minorities that also features gay and lesbian, transgender, Two-Spirit, or otherwise homoerotic desires and nonbinary gender embodiments and performativities in the past and present (e.g., Esquibel 2006; Richardson 2013; Rifkin 2012; Schwarz 2003; Tatonetti 2014). Along with *In the Life* (1986) and *Brother to Brother* (1991), *Chicana Lesbians: The Girls Our Mothers Warned Us About* (1991), *Afrekete: An Anthology of Black Lesbian Writing* (1995), *Bésame Mucho: An Anthology of Gay Latino Fiction* (1999), *Take Out: Queer Writing from Asian Pacific America* (2001), *Black like Us: A Century of Lesbian, Gay, and Bisexual African American Fiction* (2002), *Our Caribbean: A Gathering of Lesbian and Gay Writing from the Antilles* (2008), and *Sovereign Erotics: A Collection of Two-Spirit Literature* (2011) are just some of the many literary anthologies—to say nothing of the novels, stories, poetry, drama, and nonfiction—by and about LGBTQ2 writers and people of color published since the 1980s.

Partly overlapping but also distinct, the second strategy, designated (sometimes retroactively) as queer of color critique, takes a less "positivist" approach to the past and present and examines how processes of racialization are predicated on, intertwined with, and mediated through ascriptions of gender-sexual deviance. When used at all, these studies deploy and exploit the expansiveness of "queer" as a framework for analyzing sexual-gender nonnormativity broadly, moving it beyond its homosexual dimensions as a way to elucidate how institutional forms of power and knowledge produce racial differences and reproduce social hierarchies through gender-sexual difference. At stake in many of these works is not so much a recuperation of authentic images of LGBT racial minorities that could function as a defense against homophobia, transphobia, and racism, or answer to the need for self-representation and understanding (as the Western canons of gay and lesbian literature have been mobilized to do). Rather, these studies tend to orient their claims as critiques of colonial, imperial, and national state power, oppression, and violence.

The historical contexts and events that they investigate take their cues from critical ethnic, indigenous, and postcolonial studies by examining, for instance, the mutual constitutions of US settler colonialism, heteronormativity, and gender-sexual violence perpetrated against Native peoples (e.g., Allen [1986] 1992; Barker 2017; Driskill 2016; Miranda 2010; Morgensen 2011; Rifkin 2011; Smith 2010); the impact of colonial Catholicism and its patriarchal iconography, sexual tourism, and immigration policies and migration practices on Chicanx and Latinx genders and sexualities (e.g., Anzaldúa [1987] 1999; Cantú 2009; Gutiérrez 2010; Rodriguez 2014); the production of sexual and domestic perversities through the "peculiar institution" of US chattel slavery—including rape, concubinage, incest, interracial sex, male and female homosex, and outlawed marriage between the enslaved—and their ongoing effects (e.g., Abdur-Rahman 2002; Hartman 1997; Sharpe 2010); the figuration of Asian female prostitutes, bachelor societies, "queer domesticities," (homo)sexual predators, migrant worker pederasts, and oversexed "blond-chasers" because of the impacts of immigration laws, restrictions, and exclusions along class and gender lines (e.g., Kang 2002; Koshy 2004; Shah 2001, 2011; Wu 2003); and the construction of nonheteronormative racialized populations in urban locations as a result of industrialization, internal migration, commercialization, and interracial mixing (e.g., Ferguson 2004; Mumford 1997). While some work straddles the line between elucidating the institutional and discursive productions of racial-sexual deviance and focusing explicitly on racialized homoerotic representations (e.g., Ferguson 2004; Ponce 2012; Soto 2010), a diachronic queer of color literary history has not, to my knowledge, been attempted—partly because of the multidisciplinarity of the field, partly because of the relative paucity of the print archive prior to the 1970s, but largely, I would argue, because of the way that this mode of critique throws into question the very stability of "queer of color literature" as such.

Although the policies and practices by which different populations have been racialized as nonnormatively gendered and sexualized shift depending on context, and while the specific meanings of those deviations also change depending on the racialized population (and their relations to other racialized groups), the general theoretical claim that, as Kyla Wazana Tompkins (2015: 177) summarizes it, "populations of color [are] always and already non-heteronormative and sexually deviant," has assumed the status of a guiding tenet in the field (e.g., Collins 2004: 27; Ferguson 2004: 20; Mendoza 2016: 51; Nguyen 2014: 21; Puar 2007: 37; Rodríguez 2014: 2). Insofar as racializing designations of anatomical excess, libidinal overdrive, and gender transgression or inversion, along with intellectual inferiority, moral depravity, and familial disorganization, have been used to justify conquest, colonialism, removal, slavery, segregation, immigration exclusion, antimiscegenation, incarceration, economic exploitation, social abandonment, and other forms of racial violence, peoples of color have been estranged from the US "state, the nation, and citizenship itself," as Tompkins (2015: 177) notes, categories of belonging that "are always articulated as . . . normatively heterosexual and white."

The argument that all racialized peoples "are *structurally* queer to the

United States," to cite Sarita Echavez See's (2009: 117) claim with respect to Filipinx Americans, raises the question of whether all "race" literature is really "queer" literature. Is queer of color literature, then, a redundant misnomer insofar as literature by and about people of color must necessarily grapple with issues of gender-sexual nonnormativity? Or does it name only those racial texts that thematize same-sex desires and/or gender-nonconforming embodiments? In that case, should we instead speak of LGBT literature of color and drop the Q? On the other hand, if the literature challenges the gender-sexual deviancies on which racial categories rest, whether by asserting normative domestic relations as a matter of course or by emphasizing that the structural violence of white supremacy is what produces racialized "pathology," wouldn't it necessarily appeal to a doomed politics of respectability and assimilation, thereby rendering it race literature in gender-sexual whiteface? In short, what makes "queer of color" literature *queer* and *of color* has become a newly vexing question in the wake of the expansive scholarship that has disarticulated "queer" from homosexual and transgender identification and has demonstrated how gender and sexual nonnormativity are constitutive of racialization.

Toward Comparative Queer of Color Reading Practices

In light of these conundrums, what might it take to begin the work of constructing comparative queer of color literary histories? At the subjective level, it would require complicating, though not discounting, direct connections forged between textual representation and reader identification (Womack's gay "Creek kid," Mock's "young trans girl of color," the numerous testimonies to *Zami*'s influence on readers).[7] Although those reader desires and authorial rationales are important and far from naively essentialist insofar as they address the complex lived experiences and needs of LGBTQ2 people of color, they nevertheless participate in the same logic of fortifying the self (confirming an identity, forging a self, revealing me to myself) as the conventional gay and lesbian reading models discussed at the start and thus impede aspirations to read *across* lines of race and indigeneity. Improvising on Muñoz's theory of disidentification in relation to criticism ("a hermeneutic"), the term may also serve as a way to conceptualize readers' relation to queer and trans texts from and about multiple ethnic and racial cultures. Neither total immersion that ignores or assimilates difference (e.g., Muriel's belief in *Zami* "that as lesbians, we were all outsiders and all equal in our outsiderhood" [Lorde 1982: 204]) nor its opposite of "plunging into the heart of the non-self" and seeking "to lose, escape, abandon that self which can be named, identified, recognized" (Nuttall 2001: 392), a disidentificatory reading practice would not only appreciate how the text "works on" and refashions dominant culture or even heteronormative minority culture but also how it works on us, that is, shifts our senses of what queer, trans, race, and so on can mean—not only for "them," the diegetic characters, but also for ourselves.

Like Muñoz (1999: 21–2), recent scholars (e.g., Ferguson 2004; Hames-Garcia 2011; Hong 2015), have looked to the interventions articulated by women and lesbian of color feminists of the late 1970s and early 1980s as laying the groundwork for contemporary queer of color critique, offering alternative epistemic and political genealogies to those derived "from a white Euro-American gay, lesbian, and queer theory tradition" (Hong and Ferguson 2011: 2). While this scholarship has usefully situated those interventions within contexts of minority nationalisms, neoliberalism, and the emergence of queer theory, what I wish to retrieve from that moment, and from *Zami* in particular, is the feminist ethic of being *affected* by intense erotic encounters that Afrekete symbolizes for Audre. "I never saw Afrekete again," Lorde ([1982] 1983: 253) writes after Afrekete returns to the South, "but her print remains upon my life with the resonance and power of an emotional tattoo." Lorde begins the epilogue with a similar pronouncement: "Every woman I have ever loved has left her print upon me, where I loved some invaluable piece of myself apart from me—so different that I had to stretch and grow in order to recognize her" (ibid.: 255). The syntactical ambiguity of this statement suggests a dynamic negotiation and temporal circularity between self and other, whereby the "I" has been transformed by the other's "print," but to "recognize" the other in the first place requires the "I" to transform herself, "to stretch and grow." In this staging of what AnaLouise Keating (1996: 158) calls "interactional identity formation," the other's print is paradoxically an "invaluable piece" of the self that was/is both apart from and a part of herself. In the foreword to the second edition of *This Bridge Called My Back*, Cherríe Moraga writes: "We must acknowledge that to change the world, we have to change ourselves—even sometimes our most cherished block-hard convictions" (Moraga and Anzaldúa 1983: n.p.). And she ends with a redaction of Donna Kate Rushin's "The Bridge Poem" that resonates, ominously, with Lorde: "stretch . . . or die."

Whereas in *Zami* it is the women she has loved who provide Lorde with new knowledge and emotional resonance, her use of the "print" metaphor analogizes these erotic and affective encounters to type on a page. Could we extend such a metaphor to think of the effects of *books* on ourselves as well, as "self-inscriptions [that] can inscribe themselves on their readers" (Keating 1996: 182)? This feminist ethic of affectability and self-transformation would enable a queer reading practice that not only pursues self-reflection and fortification in the face of homophobic and transphobic annihilation but also remains vulnerable to destabilization, change, and self-revision, enabling a form of subjectivity open enough to difference for the textual encounter to leave a "print" on one's altered self or consciousness. To permit such stories to be imprinted on us, we might need to recover that pre-identitarian, "pre-adult" relation to the world that Eve Kosofsky Sedgwick (1997: 2–3) evokes in her description of queer reading, a "speculative, superstitious, and methodologically adventurous state where recognitions, pleasures, and discoveries seep in only from the most stretched and ragged edges of one's competence." Recontextualized beyond the dimension of sexuality alone, this openness and stretching that allows for otherness to seep in accords with Lorde's feminist ethic and lays the subjective groundwork for an ever-changing competency whose incisive claims may very well leave us ragged and torn but whose provocative edge-work is necessary if the promise of "queer politics" as decolonized knowledge production can live up to its radical potential.

To the extent that this model could provide the prerequisites for endeavoring a comparative queer of color reading practice, it will take more than shifts in subjective perceptions and political consciousness "to become fluent in each other's [queer] histories," as M. Jacqui Alexander (2005: 269) memorably writes in her tribute to *This Bridge Called My Back*. My last point, then, has to do with the relation between queer of color studies and the politics of institutionality.

In his critique of the institutionalization of sexuality studies and other minority academic formations, Ferguson (2004: 226) urges us "to scrutinize this will to institutionality if we are to create alternative forms of agency and subjectivity not beholden to the logics of state, capital, and academy." One of the logics governing the politics of what scholars have alternately described as homonormativity, homonationalism, and queer liberalism is that conditions of oppression and privilege cannot be facilely distinguished along racial, gender, sexual, or class lines. As Hong and Ferguson (2011: 2–3) write, there are "moments when certain racial *groups* could articulate a demand for incorporation, albeit unevenly, over and against other racial groups" based on "the class, gender, and sexual norms of respectability, morality, and propriety" that enable them to be placed on the worthiness and legitimacy side "of the dividing line between valued and devalued." Even more acutely, Jasbir Puar (2007: 28) has argued in her critique of homonationalism that the "queer or homonormative ethnic is a crucial fractal in the disaggregation of proper homosexual subjects, joining the ranks of an ascendant population of whiteness, from perversely sexualized populations." These insights suggest that the connections and dissonances between the two broad meanings of racialized queerness discussed above—the self-defined assertion of same-sex desire and gender-nonconforming embodiment, and the state-attributed aspersion of racial difference as gender-sexual deviance—become all the more paramount to track historically lest we reinstate reductive binaries of "hetero/queer," white/colored, male/female as the guiding operations of power.

Tracing the continuities among different forms of "queerness" within and across racialized communities and expressive cultures could elucidate shared conditions of marginalization and provide bases for coalition building, to return to Cathy Cohen's language, even as Cohen (1997: 458) herself warns against "eras[ing] the specific historical relation between the stigma of 'queer' and the sexual activity of gay men, lesbians, bisexual, and [transgender] individuals." Is it possible—and time—to produce comparative queer of color literary histories that keep in full view those stigmas and the desires of racialized and indigenous LGBTQ2 readers who are "looking for a story that speaks truth" to them while also recognizing the diversities, perversities, and ecstasies of "queer" racialized heterosexualities (e.g., Jenkins 2007; Nash 2014; Shimizu 2007; Springer 2008)? I am aware that conditions of academic precarity (however manufactured) make "turf wars" an inevitable reality at many institutions, and I recognize that some scholars may view comparative racialization models as antithetical to their political convictions and detrimental to their intellectual fields and communities. Nonetheless, to address the ambiguities that surround the definitional scope of queer and trans of color literatures, to determine which authors and texts will be placed within this literary history (especially if we consider periods before the 1970s), and to move toward fulfilling the promise of queer *of color* critique as a methodology of comparison and relationality that crosses "colors" will require us to converse across racial and disciplinary lines. Pursuing queer of color reading in a comparative mode—and reflexively theorizing how to make comparisons meaningful—may help create alternative forms of subjectivity while also inciting the creation of formalized, if not administratively institutionalized, spaces for cross-racial dialogue and exchange. Comparative queer of color literary histories can not only help articulate "in all its detailed and lived concreteness" the impositions of what María Lugones (2007: 189) terms the "colonial/modern gender system," but also evoke, amplify, and circulate the alternative worldviews, revised traditions, and practices of survival and resistance that writers like Lorde, Womack, and Mock, among many others, call on us to acknowledge.

Notes

1. Examples of such reflections on gay reading are legion. In addition to the scholars and writers that Lee (2009: 1–23) and Rohy (2015: 104–37) cite, see, for instance, Cardamone 2010 and Williams 2017.

2. Narratives that feature gay and lesbian scenes of reading and tradition making are, again, numerous. See Lee 2009: 20–22, 73–123; Medd 2015: 5–7; and Rohy 2015: 104–37.

3. Lesbian approaches have been much more accommodating of racial and cultural differences than gay male ones. See, for instance, Nestle 1997: xviii–xxv and Faderman 1994: xi. The gay canons produced by white Western writers, by contrast, tend to tokenize writers of color and rarely reflect on how differently positioned readers might perceive the list of "Great Books Every Gay Man Should Read," to quote the (again, exhortatory) subtitle of Robert Drake's *Gay Canon* (1998).

4. Edward Carpenter (1902: v, 3) begins his "chronological and evolutionary" survey of homoerotic "friendship-customs" in *Ioläus: An Anthology of Friendship* with reports about "primitive peoples" and "quite savage tribes."

5. See, most recently, the *Guardian* piece "'At Last I Felt I Fitted In'" (2017). For an ambivalent engagement with ancient Greek homoerotics within the context of child sexual abuse and its devastating aftermath, see Chee 2001.

6. For an illuminating recent analysis of black LGBTQ literacy practices, see Pritchard 2017.

7. See, for instance, Keating 1996: 182–85; McKinley 1995: xiii; McRuer 1997: 56–57; and Jackie Kay's response in "'At Last I Felt I Fitted In'" 2017.

References

Abdur-Rahman, Aliyyah. 2012. *Against the Closet: Black Political Longing and the Erotics of Race.* Durham, NC: Duke University Press.

Alexander, M. Jacqui. 2005. *Pedagogies of Crossing: Meditations on Feminism, Sexual Politics, Memory, and the Sacred.* Durham, NC: Duke University Press.

Allen, Paula Gunn. [1986] 1992. *The Sacred Hoop: Recovering the Feminine in American Indian Traditions.* Boston: Beacon.

Anonymous. [1990] 2009. *Queers Read This.* Queer Zine Archive. http://www.qzap.org /v5/gallery/main.php?g2_itemId=1627 (accessed January 13, 2017).

Anzaldúa, Gloria. [1987] 1999. *Borderlands: The New Mestiza / La Frontera.* San Francisco: Aunt Lute Books.

"'At Last I Felt I Fitted In': Writers on the Books That Helped Them Come Out." 2017. *Guardian*, July 1. www.theguardian.com/books/2017/jul/01/book -helped-come-out-gay-edmund-white-sarah-waters-jeanette-winterson.

Barker, Joanne, ed. 2017. *Critically Sovereign: Indigenous Gender, Sexuality, and Feminist Studies*. Durham, NC: Duke University Press.

Beam, Joseph. 1986. "Introduction: Leaving the Shadows Behind." In *In the Life: A Black Gay Anthology*, edited by Joseph Beam, 13–18. Boston: Alyson.

Boone, Joseph Allen. 2014. *The Homoerotics of Orientalism*. New York: Columbia University Press.

Bravmann, Scott. 1997. *Queer Fictions of the Past: History, Culture, and Difference*. Cambridge: Cambridge University Press.

Brookes, Les. 2009. *Gay Male Fiction since Stonewall: Ideology, Conflict, and Aesthetics*. New York: Routledge.

Cantú, Lionel. 2009. *The Sexuality of Migration: Border Crossings and Mexican Immigrant Men*, edited by Nancy A. Naples and Salvador Vidal-Ortiz. New York: New York University Press.

Cardamone, Tom, ed. 2010. *The Lost Library: Gay Fiction Rediscovered*. New York: Haiduk.

Carpenter, Edward, ed. 1902. *Ioläus: An Anthology of Friendship*. New York: Mitchell Kennerley.

Chee, Alexander. 2001. *Edinburgh*. New York: Picador.

Cohen, Cathy J. 1997. "Punks, Bulldaggers, and Welfare Queens: The Radical Potential of Queer Politics?" *GLQ* 3, no. 4: 437–65.

Collins, Patricia Hill. 2004. *Black Sexual Politics: African Americans, Gender, and the New Racism*. New York: Routledge.

Drake, Robert. 1998. *The Gay Canon: Great Books Every Gay Man Should Read*. New York: Anchor Books.

Driskill, Qwo-Li. 2016. *Asegi Stories: Cherokee Queer and Two-Spirit Memory*. Tucson: University of Arizona Press.

Esquibel, Catrióna Rueda. 2006. *With Her Machete in Her Hand: Reading Chicana Lesbians*. Austin: University of Texas Press.

Faderman, Lillian. 1994. Preface to *Chloe Plus Olivia: An Anthology of Lesbian Literature from the Seventeenth Century to the Present*, edited by Lillian Faderman, vii–xiv. New York: Penguin.

Ferguson, Roderick A. 2004. *Aberrations in Black: Toward a Queer of Color Critique*. Minneapolis: University of Minnesota Press.

Gomez, Jewelle. [1983] 2000. "A Cultural Legacy Denied and Discovered: Black Lesbians in Fiction by Women." In *Home Girls: A Black Feminist Anthology*, edited by Barbara Smith, 110–23. New Brunswick, NJ: Rutgers University Press.

———. 2005. "But Some of Us Are Brave Lesbians: The Absence of Black Lesbian Fiction." In *Black Queer Studies*, edited by E. Patrick Johnson and Mae G. Henderson, 289–97. Durham, NC: Duke University Press.

Gozen, Julie. 2002. "Beautifully, Wonderfully Red: Julie Gozen Talks with Native American Author Craig Womack." *Lambda Book Report* 10, no. 8: 12–13.

Gutiérrez, Ramón A. 2010. "A History of Latina/o Sexualities." In *Latina/o Sexualities: Probing Powers, Passions, Practices, and Policies*, edited by Marysol Asencio, 13–37. New Brunswick: Rutgers University Press.

Hackett, Robin. 2004. *Sapphic Primitivism: Productions of Race, Class, and Sexuality in Key Works of Modern Fiction*. New Brunswick, NJ: Rutgers University Press.

Hames-García, Michael. 2011. "Queer Theory Revisited." In *Gay Latino Studies: A Critical Reader*, edited by Michael Hames-García and Ernesto Javier Martínez, 19–45. Durham, NC: Duke University Press.

Hartman, Saidiya. 1997. *Scenes of Subjection: Terror, Slavery, and Self-Making in Nineteenth-Century America*. New York: Oxford University Press.

Hawley, John C., ed. 2001. *Postcolonial, Queer: Theoretical Intersections*. Albany: State University of New York Press.

Hemphill, Essex. 1991. Introduction to *Brother to Brother: New Writings by Black Gay Men*, edited by Essex Hemphill, xv–xxxi. Boston: Alyson.

Hoad, Neville. 2000. "Arrested Development or the Queerness of Savages: Resisting Evolutionary Narratives of Difference." *Postcolonial Studies* 3, no. 2: 133–58.

Holden, Philip, ed. 2002. *Imperial Desire: Dissident Sexualities and Colonial Literature*. Minneapolis: University of Minnesota Press.

Hong, Grace Kyungwon. 2015. *Death beyond Disavowal: The Impossible Politics of Difference*. Minneapolis: University of Minnesota Press.

Hong, Grace Kyungwon, and Roderick A. Ferguson. 2011. Introduction to *Strange Affinities: The Gender and Sexual Politics of Comparative Racialization*, edited by Grace Kyungwon Hong and Roderick A. Ferguson, 1–22. Durham, NC: Duke University Press.

Jenkins, Candice M. 2007. *Private Lives, Proper Relations: Regulating Black Intimacy*. Minneapolis: University of Minnesota Press.

Kang, Laura Hyun Yi. 2002. *Compositional Subjects: Enfiguring Asian/American Women*. Durham, NC: Duke University Press.

Keating, AnaLouise. 1996. *Women Reading Women Writing: Self-Invention in Paula Gunn Allen, Gloria Anzaldúa, and Audre Lorde*. Philadelphia: Temple University Press.

Koshy, Susan. 2004. *Sexual Naturalization: Asian Americans and Miscegenation*. Stanford, CA: Stanford University Press.

Lee, Rick H. 2009. "Generating Literacies: Reading Gay Culture and the AIDS Epidemic." PhD diss., Rutgers University.

Lorde, Audre. [1982] 1983. *Zami: A New Spelling of My Name*. Freedom, CA: Crossing.

Lugones, María. 2007. "Heterosexualism and the Colonial/Modern Gender System." *Hypatia* 22, no. 1: 186–209.

Lyle, Timothy S. 2015. "An Interview with Janet Mock." *Callaloo* 38, no. 3: 502–8.

McKinley, Catherine E. 1995. Introduction to *Afrekete: An Anthology of Black Lesbian*

Writing, edited by Catherine E. McKinley and L. Joyce DeLaney, xi–xvii. New York: Anchor Books.

McRuer, Robert. 1997. *The Queer Renaissance: Contemporary American Literature and the Reinvention of Lesbian and Gay Identities*. New York: New York University Press.

Medd, Jodie. 2015. "Lesbian Literature? An Introduction." In *The Cambridge Companion to Lesbian Literature*, edited by Jodie Medd, 1–16. New York: Cambridge University Press.

Mendoza, Victor Román. 2016. *Metroimperial Intimacies: Fantasy, Racial-Sexual Governance, and the Philippines in U.S. Imperialism, 1899-1913*. Durham, NC: Duke University Press.

Miranda, Deborah A. 2010. "Extermination of the *Joyas*: Gendercide in Spanish California." *GLQ* 16, nos. 1–2: 253–84.

Mock, Janet. 2014. *Redefining Realness: My Path to Womanhood, Identity, Love, and So Much More*. New York: Atria Paperback.

Moraga, Cherríe, and Gloria Anzaldúa, eds. 1983. *This Bridge Called My Back: Writings by Radical Women of Color*. 2nd ed. New York: Kitchen Table: Women of Color Press.

Morgensen, Scott Lauria. 2011. *Spaces between Us: Queer Settler Colonialism and Indigenous Decolonization*. Minneapolis: University of Minnesota Press.

Mumford, Kevin. 1997. *Interzones: Black/White Sex Districts in Chicago and New York in the Early Twentieth Century*. New York: Columbia University Press.

Muñoz, José Esteban. 1999. *Disidentifications: Queers of Color and the Performance of Politics*. Minneapolis: University of Minnesota Press.

Nash, Jennifer. 2014. *The Black Body in Ecstasy: Reading Race, Reading Pornography*. Durham, NC: Duke University Press.

Nestle, Joan. 1997. "'I Wanted to Live Long Enough to Kiss a Woman': The Life of Lesbian Literature." In *Particular Voices: Portraits of Gay and Lesbian Writers*, edited by Robert Giard, xviii–xxv. Cambridge, MA: MIT Press.

Ngô, Fiona I. B. 2014. *Imperial Blues: Geographies of Race and Sex in Jazz Age New York*. Durham, NC: Duke University Press.

Nguyen, Tan Hoang. 2014. *A View from the Bottom: Asian American Masculinity and Sexual Representation*. Durham, NC: Duke University Press.

Nuttall, Sarah. 2001. "Reading, Recognition, and the Postcolonial." *Interventions* 3, no. 3: 391–404.

Ordover, Nancy. 2003. *American Eugenics: Race, Queer Anatomy, and the Science of Nationalism*. Minneapolis: University of Minnesota Press.

Ponce, Martin Joseph. 2012. *Beyond the Nation: Diasporic Filipino Literature and Queer Reading*. New York: New York University Press.

Pritchard, Eric Darnell. 2017. *Fashioning Lives: Black Queers and the Politics of Literacy*. Carbondale: Southern Illinois University Press.

Puar, Jasbir K. 2007. *Terrorist Assemblages: Homonationalism in Queer Times*. Durham, NC: Duke University Press.

Richardson, Matt. 2013. *The Queer Limit of Black Memory: Black Lesbian Literature and Irresolution*. Columbus: Ohio State University Press.

Rifkin, Mark. 2011. *When Did Indians Become Straight? Kinship, the History of Sexuality, and Native Sovereignty*. New York: Oxford University Press.

———. 2012. *The Erotics of Sovereignty: Queer Native Writing in the Era of Self-Determination*. Minneapolis: University of Minnesota Press.

Rodríguez, Juana María. 2014. *Sexual Futures, Queer Gestures, and Other Latina Longings*. New York: New York University Press.

Rohy, Valerie. 2009. *Anachronism and Its Others: Sexuality, Race, Temporality*. Albany: SUNY Press.

———. 2015. *Lost Causes: Narrative, Etiology, and Queer Theory*. Oxford: Oxford University Press.

Schwarz, A. B. Christa. 2003. *Gay Voices of the Harlem Renaissance*. Bloomington: Indiana University Press.

Sedgwick, Eve Kosofsky. 1997. "Paranoid Reading and Reparative Reading; or, You're So Paranoid, You Probably Think This Introduction Is about You." In *Novel Gazing: Queer Readings in Fiction*, edited by Eve Kosofsky Sedgwick, 1–37. Durham, NC: Duke University Press.

See, Sarita Echavez. 2009. *The Decolonized Eye: Filipino American Art and Performance*. Minneapolis: University of Minnesota Press.

Shah, Nayan. 2001. *Contagious Divides: Epidemics and Race in San Francisco's Chinatown*. Berkeley: University of California Press.

———. 2011. *Stranger Intimacy: Contesting Race, Sexuality, and the Law in the North American West*. Berkeley: University of California Press.

Sharpe, Christina. 2010. *Monstrous Intimacies: Making Post-Slavery Subjects*. Durham, NC: Duke University Press.

Shimizu, Celine Parreñas. 2007. *The Hypersexuality of Race: Performing Asian/American Women on Screen and Scene*. Durham, NC: Duke University Press.

Smith, Andrea. 2010. "Queer Theory and Native Studies: The Heteronormativity of Settler Colonialism." *GLQ* 16, nos. 1–2: 41–68.

Smith, Barbara. 1982. "Toward a Black Feminist Tradition." In *All the Women Are White, All the Blacks Are Men, But Some of Us Are Brave: Black Women's Studies*, edited by Gloria T. Hull, Patricia Bell Scott, and Barbara Smith, 157–75. New York: Feminist.

Somerville, Siobhan. 2000. *Queering the Color Line: Race and the Invention of Homosexuality in American Culture*. Durham, NC: Duke University Press.

Soto, Sandra K. 2010. *Reading Chican@ like a Queer: The De-Mastery of Desire*. Austin: University of Texas Press.

Springer, Kimberly. 2008. "Queering Black Female Heterosexuality." In *Yes Means*

Yes! Visions of Female Sexual Power and a World without Rape, edited by Jaclyn Friedman and Jessica Valenti, 77-91, Berkeley, CA: Seal.

Tatonetti, Lisa. 2014. *The Queerness of Native American Literature*. Minneapolis: University of Minnesota Press.

Tompkins, Kyla Wazana. 2015. "Intersections of Race, Gender, and Sexuality: Queer of Color Critique." In *The Cambridge Companion to American Gay and Lesbian Literature*, edited by Scott Herring, 173–89. Cambridge: Cambridge University Press.

Wall, Cheryl A. 2005. *Worrying the Line: Black Women Writers, Lineage, and Literary Tradition*. Chapel Hill: University of North Carolina Press.

White, Edmund. 1991. Foreword to *The Faber Book of Gay Short Fiction*, edited by Edmund White, ix–xviii. Boston: Faber and Faber.

Williams, Michael. 2017. "Remembering Sam." In *Samuel Steward and the Pursuit of the Erotic: Sexuality, Literature, Archives*, edited by Debra A. Moddelmog and Martin Joseph Ponce, 201–13. Columbus: Ohio State University Press.

Womack, Craig. 2001. *Drowning in Fire*. Tucson: University of Arizona Press.

Woods, Gregory. 1998. *A History of Gay Literature: The Male Tradition*. New Haven, CT: Yale University Press.

Wu, Judy Tzu-Chun. 2003. "Asian American History and Racialized Compulsory Deviance." *Journal of Women's History* 15, no. 3: 58–62.

THE BLACK ECSTATIC

Aliyyah I. Abdur-Rahman

Queerness is a structuring and educated mode of desiring that allows
us to see and feel beyond the quagmire of the present.
—José Esteban Muñoz, *Cruising Utopia: The Then and There of
Queer Futurity*

Somewhere, somehow something was lost, but no story can be told
about it; no memory can retrieve it; a fractured horizon looms in
which to make one's way as a spectral agency, one for whom a full
"recovery" is impossible, one for whom the irrecoverable becomes,
paradoxically, the condition of a new political agency.
—Judith Butler, "Afterward," in *Loss: The Politics of Mourning*

$\mathcal{I}$t is standard practice for vulnerable, multiply minoritized people to organize
intellectual and political work around a theme of recovery, of regaining what has
been taken, of reinstating a former position of wholeness, of reclaiming a former
status of wellness. A subtle progressivist narrative underlies the notion of a future
in which things are better, a politics of deferral that believes that what will come
next will be constitutively different from what has come before. José Esteban
Muñoz's description of queerness as a form and practice of desire that imagines
subjective, psychic, and sociopolitical possibilities in a spatialized moment that
extends beyond the present is generally understood as an ideological investment
in futurity—as the political push of desire's fulfillment onto the space of the horizon. Muñoz (2009: 1) writes: "Queerness exists for us as an ideality that can be
distilled from the past and used to imagine a future. The future is queerness's
domain. . . . The here and now is a prison house. We must strive, in the face of the
here and now's totalizing rendering of reality, to think and feel a then and there. . . .

GLQ 24:2–3
DOI 10.1215/10642684-4324849
© 2018 by Duke University Press

Queerness is essentially about the rejection of a here and now and an insistence on potentiality or concrete possibility for another world."

Imagining queer futures, imagining the time of queerness *as* the future, and imagining futurity in the rhetorical, affective, and political register of queerness gets us, according to Muñoz, beyond the "quagmire of the present." In figuring the future as both the proper and ideal domain of queerness—that is, of desiring and existing otherwise—Muñoz marks the spatiotemporality of the present as the realm in which the violences of the past are figured and localized but persist in ways that feel permanently unremediated and irremediable. The present, *here*, in Muñoz's formulation assumes the site specificity and the concreteness of the prison, a metaphor for manifold and proliferating harms. And the present, *now*, is figured as the realm of confined thought, desire, and potentiality.

However, Judith Butler (2003: 467) queries the "presumption that the future follows the past . . . and that the future is the redemption of the past." For Butler, the events, losses, and injuries of the past are themselves irrecuperable and elusive, despite their persistence in the present. The past marks the time and space of the now by virtue of its spectrality, its being both *here* and *not-here*. Butler, moreover, frames the future as a fractured horizon wherein the losses of the past are always contained and carried forward. A persistent and always already impaired futurity mitigates against the notion of a future in which subjects, conditions, and life chances get better. The "quagmire of the present" is thus filled with the losses of what is now legacy, the ongoing difficulties of the immediate and everyday, and the always propulsive yearning that moves us beyond, if not toward, the future The critical and political task at hand, then, is to imagine a beyond that is not temporal—that is, not future directed—but that reaches in and reckons with the ruinous now as the site of regenerative capacity and of renewed political agency. The black queer attachments, affective dispositions, political aspirations, and representational practices that punctuate the awful now with the joys and possibilities of the beyond (of alternate worlds and ways) are what I theorize in this article as the *black ecstatic.*

My conceptualization of the black ecstatic as an affective disposition, relational ethic, and aesthetic mode proceeds with Muñoz's caution and builds on his alternative framing of the queer beyond as (the site and experience of) ecstasy. Muñoz (2009: 1) warns that settling with "the pleasures of this moment" imperils and impoverishes queer of color political desire and activity. To conflate the trajectory and outcome of desire with mere enjoyment or accomplishment minimizes the point and the potential of desire to serve as a resource for sociopolitical transformation. To confine sociopolitical transformation itself to futurity, to the temporality of linear progress, carries the same risk. "Take ecstasy with me," Muñoz asserts, "becomes a request to stand out of time together" (ibid.: 187). Ecstasy connotes a queer of color beyond that is simultaneously atemporal and communal. Muñoz posits, "Queerness's time is the time of ecstasy. Ecstasy is queerness's way" (ibid.: 186–87). Ecstasy is not mere pleasure, or inevitably or even necessarily sexual. Ecstasy exceeds pleasure and sex. More important, it resists the logics of teleological progression by opening an immediate space of relational joy for black and brown people, for whom the future is both yet to come and already past.

The political import of the black ecstatic resides in the understanding of the time of black life as regressive and recursive. The twenty-first century marks the future tense of black liberation struggles for abolition, decolonization, desegregation, and black power. Yet the latest iteration of black political struggle proceeds under the simple slogan and radical political demand that Black Lives Matter. The decades since the legislative triumphs of the civil rights movement have been marked by the steady retraction of civil rights gains, the reinvigoration of both attitudinal and institutional racism, the increased militarization of urban spaces and national borders, the curtailment of the most basic civil liberties, disparate destitution, and the rampant denial of the ordinary protections and provisions of sustainable life to subaltern populations globally. In the United States, the epitome of black civic equality and political achievement symbolized by a black presidency has been realized. Nonetheless, also in the twenty-first century United States, this first black presidency has been succeeded by a blatantly white supremacist one. In the post–civil rights era, we who are black currently find ourselves simultaneously postfree and not yet free.[1]

As it unfolds in this article and as practiced by black queer cultural producers, the black ecstatic is an aesthetic performance of embrace, the sanctuary of the unuttered and unutterable, and a mode of pleasurable reckoning with everyday ruin in contemporary black lives under the strain of perpetual chaos and continued diminishment. A post–civil rights expressive practice, the black ecstatic eschews the heroism of black pasts *and* the promise of liberated black futures in order to register and revere rapturous joy in the broken-down present. Notably, even as my conceptualization of the black ecstatic is illustrated via readings of texts that center black queer men's lives, as an affective disposition and aesthetic mode, the black ecstatic is by no means bound or limited to them.[2] Rather, the black ecstatic pervades expressive forms as an abstractionist practice of conjuration that foregrounds the importance, the timelessness, and the exuberant pleasures of black communion.

My conceptualization of the black ecstatic unfolds in two subsequent sec-

tions. In the first section, I interrogate realist representation and recognition politics as the continued bases for black cultural production in the post–civil rights
era. Considering the limits of visibility politics under the sociopolitical economy of
death undergirding twenty-first-century, politically and commercially driven, mass
surveillance and mass incarceration, this section analyzes the black ecstatic narrative and formal elements of the recent film *Moonlight*. To center experimental
aesthetic practices as a viable mode of social protest in black queer literary form,
as reflected and enacted in the black ecstatic, the final section analyzes Essex
Hemphill's prose-poem "Heavy Breathing." This section illustrates the black
ecstatic elements of contemporary black queer poetry and gleans its (individual,
ethical, and political) prescription for willful exuberance as the enabling index of
and context for black life and liberation (Ahmed 2014: 12).[3]

I

As an aesthetic mode, the black ecstatic registers the interrelation of political
terror, social abjection, and aesthetic abstraction in contemporary black queer
cultural production. My conceptualization of the black ecstatic as an aesthetic
mode—an innovative representational practice and textual technique that crosses
the boundaries of discrete literary genres and media platforms—proceeds from
the premise that representations of political crises in black life since the 1980s
do not inhere in established literary or visual media forms. Rather, as forms of
racialized economic, social, and political harm have become less formal and
more abstract—the move, for example, from legal segregation to segregation produced via educational disparities, deindustrialization, redlining practices, and
so on—the expressive techniques used to tell stories of black life, struggle, and
aspirational freedoms have themselves become more abstract.[4] Abstraction here
connotes aesthetic modes of signification that are simultaneously nonrealist and
nonfigurative. In "The Rules of Abstraction," Leigh Claire La Berge (2014: 106)
posits that abstraction functions as a "metonym for something undefined" that
"denote[s] something crucial and real that necessarily remains unexplained." The
abstract registers that which crucially and meaningfully exists but that, nonetheless, exceeds, obscures, or defies mimetic capture. Within an analytic lexicon, La
Berge argues, "the abstract is employed as a trope that organizes and structures
but that itself eludes definition and representation" (ibid.: 96).

As both hermeneutic and aesthetic, abstractionism offers blackness the
potential for meaning outside the representational economies of violence and
erasure that define its status in modernity. "For at stake in the 'modern,'" Lin-

don Barrett (2014: 2) reminds us, "is the animation of a conceptual form—the commodity—as the principle of economic (and general) rationality, in the face of the already fully animate individual and collective forms—in human proportions—of racial blackness." The collective experiences of black people in the West—which include past and present iterations of black captivity, corporeal dispossession, political disenfranchisement, economic abandonment, and social disposability—is rooted in a ruthless Euro-American modernity that defines the contours of being, belonging, and becoming in racialized, monetized terms. Contemporary black queer cultural production that eschews mimesis and representational realism reflects the understanding that conjuring blackness solely within existing, normative aesthetic and political representational apparatuses, regardless of how positive, authentic, or real, risks restoring black subjects who are cited and sighted within blackness's domain again to the status of commodity.

That African American literature has relentlessly insisted on black humanity and that social protest has historically conditioned the production of African American literature are virtually axiomatic critical assessments to this point. In many ways, the slave narrative inaugurated African Americans' formal entrance into American letters.[5] As a body of literature that responded to the most extreme form of corporeal, civic, and social death, the slave narrative was manifestly politically motivated. Its content and its form—specifically, the authenticating documents that precede the narrative proper, attestations of authorial competence and sincerity, and frequent deviations from the central narrative to detail atrocities regularly practiced on slave plantations—function to demonstrate the humanity, civility, and the moral and intellectual capacity of black people. In documenting in linear fashion one enslaved subject's journey from bondage to freedom, the slave narrative purported, and in every way attempted, to represent the lives and political aspirations of the entire race—to get and to remain free. Despite the abolition of slavery, the persistence of lethal forms of race-based socioeconomic and political exclusion, with their concomitant effect of African Americans' psychological and literal annihilation, have kept the commitment to black social advancement and positive racial representation foremost in black expressive culture.[6]

I proceed with the recognition that a signal achievement of the civil rights movement was the inclusion of African Americans in formal US politics, made manifest through the accessible voting rights and increased representation of black people in all spheres of legislative governance. Yet, as Richard Iton notes, increased black participation in the formal mechanisms of liberal democratic politics over the last half century has not guaranteed the removal of institutional, civic, socioeconomic, and psychic barriers to black American advancement. The mere presence of black congressional members, mayors, governors, and so forth neither demonstrates nor ensures meaningful sociopolitical transformation in which the most vulnerable racialized subjects gain conditions of ordinary thriving. Hence, informal politics in the spheres of both protest and cultural production remain critical spaces for black resistance. Iton (2008: 4) posits, "Despite the 1964 Civil Rights Act, which suggested a commitment to policies of antidiscrimination, and the 1965 Voting Rights Act, legislation that significantly enhanced black voting power, the realms of protest activity, extra-state and often nationalist engagement, and African American religiosity and popular culture have continued to be politically relevant." Taking seriously black life as defined by the perpetuity of sociopolitical crisis, the black ecstatic engages liberatory modes of endurance in our broken but ongoing present. The black ecstatic ruptures, renovates, and resignifies the formal features of traditional African American protest literature and visual propaganda. Upending the predominance of political sentimentality and formal realism, it delineates a mode of genre experimentation that resists recognition politics as the predominant mode of black literary expression and political mobilization. Insofar as African American cultural production has historically attempted to remedy the psychosocial, material, and political conditions of black life, it has typically attempted to do so through representational revision or correction. This expectation may be traced, first, to the long-standing practice of linking black cultural production with projects of racial uplift and, second, to the belief that positive portrayals of black subjectivity counter prevailing derogatory racial logics. Phillip Brian Harper (2015: 3) contends that the literary and visual art text that "disrupt[s] the easy correspondence between itself and its evident referent . . . invites us to question not only the 'naturalness' of aesthetic representation but the social facts to which it alludes, thereby opening them to active and potentially salutary revision." Harper thus calls our attention to the politically progressive tendencies in the experimental—nonfigurative and nonrealist—black art practices in which the black ecstatic partakes. Borrowing Nathanial Mackey's term "outfulness," Anthony Reed (2014: 207) argues that experimental black writing "opens new horizons of thinking by calling into question the grounds of knowledge." Black literary abstraction interrogates the systems of thought, social organization, temporal schemas, and protocols of political governance and participation that define the Enlightenment's enterprise of modernity. "Outfulness," Reed suggests, "reimagin[es] the connections between race and history and stress[es] forms of nonsynchronism in the present. . . . black experimental writing represents an instance of 'taking it out,' a practice of outfulness cast as freedom" (ibid.). Freedom is imagined and instantiated within the fugitive modality of "outfulness," of stepping outside progressive time and, for my purposes here, moving beyond and beside oneself in communion with another in the affective register of black ecstasy.

The 2016 film *Moonlight*, written by Tarell Alvin McCraney and directed by Barry Jenkins, deploys the black ecstatic substantively, symbolically, and structurally. I open with filmic analysis in a study of mainly literary abstraction (1) to show how the black ecstatic is deployed as a thematic preoccupation and representational practice across genres and media platforms and (2) to illustrate how the black ecstatic is deployed to trouble mimetic representation in a rare film that depicts black queer, masculine becoming. *Moonlight* engages the War on Drugs as the main engine of mass black imprisonment sideways—that is, side-stepping the grueling spectacularity of juridical procedure, carceral containment, and slow death. Counterbalancing the film's overall thematic despair is the ecstatic register of its lush color tones. Rich blues, purples, yellows, and greens insinuate a vitality that is belied by the film's predominant representation of black life, framed always by the grim specter of sudden or slow demise. The film tells the story of Chiron, a queer black boy growing up in Miami. Chiron is the son of a crack-addicted mother with whom he lives in abject poverty. The opening scenes alert viewers to the harrowing circumstances of Chiron's life, which are perilously personal and reflective of the collective precarity of black life in the post–civil rights period. In an early scene, a crack-addicted man pleads with a young drug dealer for an advance on drugs. The desperation of both the man, seemingly homeless and ravaged by crack addiction, and the young man, whose participation in the illicit trade provides the only opportunity for economic sustenance, is apparent. This scene is a familiar one, signaling the urban malaise that has gripped black and brown communities for decades.

The familiarity of this cinematic depiction is both underscored and undercut by the arrival of Juan, who is the drug dealer for whom the young man works. Juan asks about his employee's mother in a brief exchange that shows his obvious regard. The insertion of care, rather than cruelty, and the emphasis on economic opportunity rather than mere exploitation, marks both Juan's and the film's relational ethics. Juan's capacity for care is further evidenced when he finds Chiron, who has been harassed and chased by a group of boys for his presumed queerness, hiding in abandoned public housing. Juan offers the boy momentary safety and the promise of alternative family. The film's proximal father figure Juan feeds Chiron, introduces him to his partner, Theresa, who serves as a surrogate mother, and teaches the boy important life lessons. The kinship arrangement that Theresa and Juan establish as surrogate parents for Chiron reflects the alternative filial structures of both black and queer families. Juan's paternal interest and instruction open avenues to self-love and self-acceptance for Chiron. It is Juan who shows Chiron in two separate scenes that, one, it is OK to be black and, two, that it is OK to be gay. Juan, the drug dealer who sells crack to Chiron's mother and thus facilitates the destruction of Chiron's fragile family, helps raise and save him.

Juan's ambiguous role in Chiron's life—as both source of harm and source of healing—bespeaks the dual, elemental structure of ecstasy. Franz Kafka writes, "The man in ecstasy and the man drowning—both throw up their arms." Kafka's observation calls attention to the inexorable entwinement of ecstasy and disaster. The unruly structure and experience of ecstasy carry the risks of overwhelm and destruction—even as ecstasy eventuates in renewal after the disastrous event. Ecstasy externalizes our insides, imperils self-sovereignty, builds on felt deficiencies, and orients us toward potentially disastrous fulfillment. The term for frenzied, cumulative emotion, *ecstasy* evolves from the Greek *ekstasis*, which means "to be or stand outside of oneself, a removal to elsewhere." By turning us outward, ecstasy compels our gestures and pleasures beyond the containments of self and surface. It operationalizes the limit, which it also perpetually violates and reforms. Ecstasy thus emerges as an alternate structure for the black queer beyond, one rooted not in the temporal logics of futurity but in the affective, embodied, and relational pleasures of the disastrous now.

Portraying limits that it repeatedly violates and reforms, *Moonlight*'s heroes are simultaneously its villains. The boy Kevin who brings Chiron to orgasm and initiates his queer eroticism is the same boy who later bashes Chiron's face repeatedly in a homophobic gang beating that nearly destroys Chiron. Despite its sympathetic rendering of black boys' incapacitated lives, *Moonlight* resists the promise of race-based sociopolitical and economic improvement. Refusing the more familiar triumphalist narrative of black male becoming, the film instead punctuates its chronicle of racial suffering and masculine malaise with portrayals of rapturous joy. The film unfolds in three distinct parts in which the central narrative event is a mundane encounter: learning to swim, the first erotic exchange, a visit to an aging parent, a first date. Time passes between the film's three parts, but the three sections neither mark nor adhere to depictions of accretive progress in the lives of its characters. In fact, the negative outcomes of such bleak social circumstances are so likely that the film neither represents nor mourns the losses when they do occur. Juan, for example, dies prematurely; his death occurs entirely off-screen and is barely remarked on by the characters. Two of the main characters, Chiron and Kevin, spend formative years in prison, but such black encounters with the carceral state are minimized. That Juan's death and Chiron's imprisonment occur off-camera evinces a mode of cinematic abstraction wherein the intimate experiences of anguish and deep grief are given not only the sanctuary of privacy but also the status of human experience that exceeds representation and representability. The film thus eschews those commonplace scenes of racial harm and racial heroism that are so typical of contemporary US cinema.

By refusing the spectacularization of commonplace black male suffering, *Moonlight* relegates scenes of racialized harm to the intimate sphere of the private. The spectacular, highly visible, and fantastical—that is, *public*—character of embodied blackness grants it a level of iconicity and, in Harvey Young's (2010: 12) astute formulation, "a compulsory visibility." Young writes: "The black body, whether on the auction block, the American plantation, hanged from a lightpole as part of a lynching ritual, attacked by police dogs within the Civil Rights era, or staged as a 'criminal body' by contemporary law enforcement and judicial systems, is a body that has been forced into the public spotlight and given a compulsory visibility" (ibid.). In the neoliberal, carceral state, African American presence and participation in the ordinary, everyday behaviors and movements that characterize civic belonging are converted into ritualized iterations of racial subordination and civic exclusion—that is, into repetitive *public* stagings of racial harm. The US carceral state, with its technique of hypersurveillance, embodied containment, and social removal, effectively robs black people of what Hortense Spillers recently described as "privacy as a fundamental human right." Following Spillers, I pose here a few questions: What aspects or practices of the self gather within the domain of "the private" in the formulation of privacy as a universal right to which every human has claim? What is it about the *publicness* of blackness that creates in others such false and intrusive intimacy? How might sexuality and alternative sociality provide sites of refuge and of play for black subjects? What is the relationship between disaster and delight? And, finally, how might we all settle more comfortably with the mystery and the complexity of human beings whose acts and inclinations do not necessarily adhere to the logics of language or the schemas of representation (Abdur-Rahman 2012)?[7]

The final line of Rita Dove's (1991: 64) poem "Canary" reads: "If you can't be free, be a mystery." This line encourages the practiced, purposeful confounding of representational signs. My conceptualization of the black ecstatic builds on the politics of opacity underlying Dove's call, memorializing Billie Holiday, to "be a mystery." Notably, the ambiguity of the closing scene of *Moonlight* suggests the acceptance of this call. The scene, which takes place in Kevin's home, returns implicitly to the earlier domestic scene in which Chiron sits with Juan and Theresa in their kitchen. Chiron queries Juan about his sexual identity, asking, "Am I a faggot?" Juan immediately distinguishes homosexuality from the demeaning epithet but allows the possibility that Chiron might be gay. When Chiron asks when he will know the presumable truth of his sexual identity, Theresa warmly assures him that in time he "will know." However, in *Moonlight*, as in black life generally, time is not particularly productive of reparative outcomes. The film concludes by withholding such knowing from the audience, and perhaps from the characters themselves. Refusing the fixity of sexual identification, *Moonlight* registers skepticism about the presumed positive relation of sexual desire and erotic autonomy to disclosure and display.

Culturally specific, Western notions of gender and sexuality as organizing features of public life and landscapes are often mistaken for universally applicable citizenship rights within neoliberal orders. For me, someone who is and was raised Muslim, the ethics of gender and sexuality, along with assumptions and aspirations about sexuality's emancipatory promise, depend on a different understanding of the boundaries between the public and private. As someone who parents an adolescent Muslim black boy whose racialized criminalization is pursued through hypersurveillance techniques evolved at the intersection of the War on Drugs and the War on Terror, I am invested in retaining spaces of license, exploration, and pleasure, or, more plainly, sites of privacy that allow black people to experiment with undisciplined and undocumented emancipatory practices.[8] The value of privacy and of "be[ing] a mystery" undergirds the representational procedures of *Moonlight*, as it shares my own critical desire to frame black queerness not as identity or mode of desire per se but as relational ethic and site of alternative political and representational possibility. In the film's final scene, Chiron discloses to Kevin that during the intervening years he has remained untouched, that he has not had other lovers, whether male or female. Likewise, Kevin reveals details about a prior heterosexual romance and resultant fatherhood even as he carefully prepares a delectable meal for Chiron in what feels like a ritual of courtship. The film ends with a heartfelt, healing embrace between the two characters that insinuates their deep intimacy but that also resists the explicit sexualization of it. In other words, what will become of Kevin and Chiron's night in Kevin's bedroom, and of all their nights to come, remains shrouded in mystery. Mystery in *Moonlight* offers an alternate path to both experiential freedoms and abstract black expressive formations.

Structuring the film's tripartite progression is a series of ecstatic encounters between black male subjects who endure violent lives of rigorously imposed limitation. In *Moonlight*'s first section, two scenes that evince the black ecstatic follow each other. In the first Kevin encourages Chiron to defend himself against bullies who consider him "soft," a schoolyard euphemism for Chiron's apparent

Figure 1. Still from
Moonlight, 2016

queerness. Challenging Chiron to demonstrate his skill as a fighter, Kevin hits Chiron, and the boys wrestle to the ground. The camera angle is low as the boys roll around, their small brown bodies intermingled to the point of indistinction in the sun-lit grass. As the boys pant and grunt, the effort and the ecstasy of aggressive touching is sounded. This sounding is the labored breath of black life: contained, curtailed, hovering at the threshold of death and yet persistent, resistant, ecstatic.

My attention to the sound of heavy breathing here anticipates the extended meditation and multivalent significance of that phrase in Hemphill's poetry in the following section. More immediately, in my analysis of *Moonlight*, Kevin's and Chiron's heavy breathing reflects the "social ecstasy" that Ashon Crawley theorizes in *Blackpentacostal Breath*. Building on the Fanonian understanding that blackness is socially constituted in part through the stifling of breath, Crawley attends to the ambient, ambivalent (aesthetic and political) possibilities of the embodied exultation and deep breathing characteristic of ritual black communion. Such communion produces social ecstasy within and between black subjects, Crawley (2016: 99) argues, through their "being beside oneself together with others." He argues:

> Social ecstasy is not about the unbecoming of the subject when confronted with an Other that assumes that doneness is what exists naturally. Rather, social ecstasy is the conception that the condition of possibility for life is undoneness as ontological priority, an irreducible, unreachable doneness, a horizontal undoneness. The emptying of oneself though spiritual peregrination underscores the capacity to give and receive, to disperse and hold, and lays claim to undoneness as a way of life. . . . Social ecstasy as the emptying out of oneself toward a social produces and is produced by infinite possibility. (ibid.)

Kevin and Chiron's wrestling match is a ritual of black boy sociality. While it anticipates their more explicit erotic encounter as teenagers on the beach, its more immediate importance is the way it figures "undoneness as a way of life." The wrestling match risks in this moment not only the boys' coming together but also their coming apart in an aggressive exchange in which one might best the other. Notably, neither Kevin nor Chiron is a fully formed masculine, sexual, adult subject. As black children, they exist, rather, in a state of racially bounded potentiality. In their pretend battle, each strengthens the other for the perils that lie ahead. Their wrestling match, moreover, instantiates and further develops their ability "to give and receive, to disperse and hold" the other. Chiron's and Kevin's labored breathing captures the unsayable, the inarticulable, premise and promise of the black ecstatic. After the wrestling match ends, Kevin extends an arm to help lift Chiron. Breaking this moment, the camera lingers on a shot of Chiron's face against the grass, his eyes and mouth softly agape, in the quiet reverie of belonging. The direction of Chiron's gaze suggests poignantly the upward motion of rapture.

Directly following the wrestling scene is the one in which Juan teaches Chiron to swim. Assuring the boy that he is there to hold and catch him as needed, Juan both substitutes for the father Chiron does not have and anticipates the man Chiron will become. Classical music provides the soundtrack to the swimming lesson, ecstatically transporting both characters and viewers to another place *in this time.* In these black ecstatic scenes, black boys and men discover themselves and each other against the backdrop of sea and sky. In these moments, black male bodies caress black male flesh, black male limbs entangle, black male heads are cradled in the hands and arms of black men.

The film's black ecstatic moments are notably marked by a different inhabitation of cinematic time. They achieve the temporal unity that Muñoz characterizes as the time of queerness and of ecstasy. When Juan teaches Chiron to swim, when Kevin wrestles with Chiron, and later when Chiron reaches orgasm in Kevin's hand, the movie's incremental pacing slows further to the time of a caress or rushes to the pace of a sprint. Despite how little is ultimately offered by way of transformed social circumstances or improved life chances for the black boys of *Moonlight,* the film illustrates how black ecstatic moments enable all others to be endured.

Figure 2. Still from
Moonlight, 2016

II

In elegant and moving prose, the poet Claudia Rankine (2016: 147) writes of black life as conditioned by mourning: "We live in a country where Americans assimilate corpses in their daily comings and goings. Dead blacks are a part of normal life here. Dying in ship hulls, tossed into the Atlantic, hanging from trees, beaten, shot in churches, gunned down by the police or warehoused in prisons: Historically, there is no quotidian without the enslaved, chained or dead black body to gaze upon or to hear about or to position a self against." The proximity to death— historically constant, sociopolitically produced, monetized, and spectacularized— characterizes black life in modernity. Underscoring the ordinariness of death-producing violence visited on black subjects, Rankine issues a warning against the traffic in its spectacle. Realist representation undertaken in protest often narrativizes black suffering and demise through the deployment of literary spectacle. This predominant practice of what Lauren Berlant (1999: 53) calls "sentimental politics" is the liberal deployment of injurious narratives to garner civic intervention and legal reparation. Within the sentimental political frame and practice, recognition of group harm is understood to be the primary metaphor and measure of inclusion within liberal frameworks of personhood and of political mattering.

In her strident critique of sentimental politics, Berlant (ibid.: 72) observes that "subaltern pain is deemed universally *intelligible*," though intelligibility does not confer universalizability: subaltern pain, Berlant notes, "is not considered universal." Subaltern pain—or, following bell hooks, "racial pain"—neither constitutes nor characterizes the psychic, social, and material conditions that organize the lifeworlds of majoritarian subjects whose identities permit their normative abstraction and participation within liberal frameworks of democratic inclusion (ibid.: 53). Racial pain is, rather, an unexceptional mark(er) of black or, to use Berlant's term, subaltern distinction. Berlant offers a productive caution to marginalized, minoritized subjects whose political strategies rely on publicized narratives of collective trauma: "Pain thus organizes your specific experience of the world, separating you from others and connecting you to others who are similarly shocked (but not surprised) by the strategies of violence that constantly regenerate the bottom of the hierarchies of social value that you inhabit. In this sense, subaltern pain is a public form because it makes you readable, to others" (ibid.: 72). Berlant critiques trauma narratives in part to distinguish the explosive but contained temporality of the traumatic event from the ongoing terrors, injuries, and aches that typify the lives of those in subjugated collectivities. She cautions that narrativized rehearsals of collective trauma unwittingly reinforce asymmetric arrangements by framing group harm within the calculable terms of the historic claim and juridical redress. Sentimental politics demonstrate, furthermore, an abiding belief in and commitment to recognition and rescue within existing (legal, civic, socioeconomic, and political) givens. However, for marginalized, minoritized subjects whose vulnerabilities are compounded and whose exclusions are maintained via the schemas of epistemic and political rationality, there is far too much risk in appealing for remedy and protection from the very governance structures, institutions, ideologies, and figures from which these subjects need remedy and protection in the first place. Berlant issues the following sobering corrective: "The public recognition by the dominant culture of certain sites of publicized subaltern suffering is frequently *(mis)taken* as a big step toward the amelioration of that suffering" (ibid.: 62).

While Berlant's critique of sentimental politics is not aimed at minoritized literatures per se, it alludes, nonetheless, to the enduring romance of literary redemption as itself a form of social renewal. Her critique speaks, that is, to the belief that minoritized literatures can intervene in social problematics as repositories of truth and engines for societal change, or that subaltern speech can itself arbitrate and ameliorate material and political crisis. Berlant's critique of sentimental politics and, implicitly, of a sentimental attachment to the redemptive promise of the literary enterprise might be directed at discursive representation in general. Building on a Derridean preoccupation with the interimbrication of language and law, Kalpana Rahita Seshadri (2012: 21) states the case astutely: "Law and language are coextensive. There is no part of language that is not always already instituted, conventionalized, submitted to the protocol of the sign as representation and repetition." The black ecstatic conveys the failed discursive promise of black representation in historical, linguistic, political, and institutional terms. In so doing, it alludes to shattered subjectivities, the ineffectuality of progress in repetitive crisis time, euphoric silences, overlapping and disjunctive temporalities, and the perilous freedom of incoherence. By deploying textual practices of disorientation, disaggregation, and dissemblance, the black ecstatic intervenes at the interstices between language and law. It captures aesthetically and ethically "subaltern suffering," or racial pain, but eschews normative articulations that (re)produce such pain as already known (or *knowable*), as commodifiable, and as narratively remediable.

The black ecstatic offers an alternative mode of capturing and grieving black queer lives lost to the ravages of the AIDS epidemic at the close of the twentieth century. In the face of mass group demise, the black ecstatic registers a critique, if not outright refusal, of recuperative futurity. It emphasizes instead the exuberant rapture of urgent, if fleeting, communion between death-bound (black) subjects who exist in the ongoing, awful now. In *Undoing Gender*, Judith Butler (2004: 20) unpacks the concept of ecstasy in specific relation to queer loss and grief in the wake of AIDS. She suggests:

> To be ec-static means, literally, to be outside oneself, and this can have several meanings: to be transported beyond oneself by passion, but also to be *beside oneself* with rage or grief. I think that if I can still speak to a "we," and include myself within its terms, I am speaking to those of us who are living in certain ways *beside ourselves*, whether it is in sexual passion, or emotional grief, or political rage. In a sense, the predicament is to understand what kind of community is composed of those who are beside themselves. (ibid.)

Living (and dying) beside himself in sexual passion, emotional grief, and political rage, Essex Hemphill was a poet of the black ecstatic. Born in 1957 to a working-class family living in Chicago, he was one of five children. Hemphill experienced paternal abandonment at a young age, which informed his belief in black familial and relational formations as necessary sustenance for black queer subjects. In their settings that condense long stretches of time, in their polyphonic verse, in their complex renderings of unexpected and unaccepted desire, and in their insistence on the innate value of black queer life, Hemphill's writings provide a compelling case study of how black protest is rendered in abstract literary form. Though he began writing earnestly at the age of fourteen, Hemphill did not disclose all the details of his personal life in a single, simple memoir (Duberman 2014).[9] Hemphill's writings span expressive forms: essays, short stories, poems, and films. A black gay man, a fearless AIDS activist, a poet in search of a revolution that had already failed him, Hemphill was dying as he composed his last published works. Writing during the height of the AIDS crisis, the War on Drugs, and the emergent carceral state, Essex contended with a second nadir in African American experience. Beginning in the Reagan era, the legislative retrenchment of civil rights gains, the withdrawal of social supports through the dismantling of welfare, blatant police brutality and murder, the crack and AIDS epidemics, and the mass carceral containment of black and brown people led to a contemporary period of reinvigorated black suffering that was reminiscent of the early twentieth century just as the 1990s were nearing their end.

The poem "Heavy Breathing" that appears in *Ceremonies: Prose and Poetry*, a collection of poems and essays, assumes an elegiac function as it documents black queer life at the end of the twentieth century. Fragmented and flowing, "Heavy Breathing" is nearly twenty pages long. Its broken lines reference transatlantic slavery, racialized sexual economies and violences, black suffering during the Reagan era, the sweet fervor of a drag ball, black political aspirations for bourgeois normativity, the afterglow of orgasm, and the poet's own impending death. African American life traverses four hundred years of modernity in this poem to conclude as a mere artifact for brief survey in a natural history museum. The poem opens with a bus ride that traverses and entwines the post–civil rights urban landscape of Washington, DC, with the history of racial slavery and inadequate democratic achievement for African Americans after its formal abolition:

> At the end of heavy breathing,
> at the beginning of grief and terror,
> on the X2, the bus I call a slave ship.
> The majority of its riders Black.
> Pressed to journey to Northeast,
> into voodoo ghettos
> festering on the knuckles
> of the negro dream.
> (Hemphill 1992: 6)

The stanza opens significantly the end of heavy breathing, at the passage out of life, with a reference to the affective and experiential horrors of the Middle Passage. The X2 bus is reminiscent of the slave ship despite heading northeast, that is, to the imagined site of freedom for the enslaved. Notably, the bus route begins and ends at the White House, the domestic symbol of the democratic nation. Known for the poverty of its majority-black passengers and its high incidents of violent crime, the X2 bus itself instantiates and also transports black passengers to the place of failed freedom dreams. Later stanzas refer to the dangers of the crowded X2 bus, mainly the verbal harassment and violent sexual assault of black women and girls along the bus route. Instead of symbolizing socioeconomic, political, and technological improvement for black people, the X2 bus marks the persistence of (explicitly gendered and sexualized) black social malaise in updated and reconfigured forms.

Setting aside the historical narrative of racial suffering, Hemphill deploys the black ecstatic as an affective and poetic mode to seek and celebrate the disastrous life that is. Despite its catalog of horrors, in other words, the poem refuses notions of historicity *and* futurity, as it peruses the broken cityscapes of vulnerable black life over a single night, seeking "Giovanni's Room in this bathhouse" and "the place where good feeling awaits me / self-destruction in my hand" (Hemphill 1992: 12). The invocation of James Baldwin's 1956 novel *Giovanni's Room* places intertextually Hemphill's poem within a tradition of black queer writing. A seemingly steady voice, which might be attributed to the poet himself, describes scenes of destruction and celebration, often overlapping. The voice in the poem is at once despairing and euphoric: "I celebrate my natural tendencies, / photosynthesis, erotic customs. / I allow myself to dream of roses / though I know / the bloody war continues" (ibid.: 5). The speaker in the poem savors, rather than refutes, the embodied pleasures that led to his fatal AIDS infection. He imagines the afterlife of death by figuring himself as the flowers that grow outside and alongside graves. Nonetheless, by entwining erotic pleasures with the process by which plants convert light to energy, into fuel for activity, the poet also registers the current, defiant fight for his life. "At the end of heavy breathing / the funerals of my brothers / force me to wear / this scratchy black suit / I should be seeding their graves" (ibid.: 8). As he grieves the loss of beloved men, the speaker in the poem contends with the multiplicity of abbreviated lives. His reference to seeding the graves of fallen lovers and comrades anticipates the speaker's own death—in time his own body will fill a grave. His vision of communal expansion is at once brotherly and masturbatory (Hemphill 1992: 12). Through the trope of organic continuity, the seed (seropositive semen) is depicted as both the contaminating agent of death and as the regenerative agent of an alternate mode of belonging—the bind that binds a community of queer black men who die violently and prematurely of disease. An irreverent, ecstatic tone punctuates the speaker's lament.

A largely autobiographical poem, "Heavy Breathing" is an unbearably close text, as it exposes the insides of a beautiful, gay, black man who is falling literally and figuratively apart: "kneeling over a fucking toilet / splattering my insides / in a stinking, shit-stained bowl / I reduce loneliness to cheap green rum, / spicy chicken, glittering vomit. / *I go to the place / where danger awaits me*" (Hemphill 1992: 8). Sex and decay commingle in the poem, as its loose organization keeps time with the recurring phrase "at the end of heavy breathing," to mark these central themes. The poem is on a journey. Even as it grapples with common, predictable death in the early era of AIDS and crack, the poem, like its speaker, has feet. It rides on buses, steps into alleyways, cruises for sex, club-hops, surveys what is left to be seen, accumulates remembrances. In her brilliant study *Raising the Dead*, Sharon Holland (2000: 15-16) poses two critical questions: "If we were in the position of the subject denied the status of the living, how would we illustrate this social condition? . . . When living is something to be *achieved* and not *experienced* and figurative and literal death are very much a part of the social landscape, how do people of color gain a sense of empowerment?" Experimenting in verse to rework the dimensions and the demands of black queer autobiography, "Heavy Breathing" wrenches apart life, language, and love to render each a case study. The poem thereby proffers a tentative answer to Holland's questions. "I continue to awaken / shell-shocked, wondering/where I come from," the voice in the poem confesses (Hemphill 1992: 5). These lines convey the exhaustion of daily life under the quotidian subjugations of racism and homophobia. Nonetheless, by returning to each day in pain but curious, the speaker offers a model and a methodology for subjects whose lives hover perpetually at the threshold of death. "I'm insatiable," the speaker declares, "the vampire in the garden, demented / by the blood of a succulent cock / I prowl in scant sheaths of latex. / I harbor no shame. / I solicit no pity" (ibid.: 4).

The speaker in the poem insists on the life he has been granted on the terms afforded for the duration of breaths allotted. His ecstasy propels him. We find the beginnings of an answer to Holland's query in the questions the poem itself asks: "Why is some destruction so beautiful?" and *"Do you think I could walk pleasantly / and well-suited toward annihilation?"* (ibid.: 5). The speaker is fully aware of the toll that life takes on the living, especially for the black, the queer. Almost always the result is to contract, to squelch the inner life, to reach for something different, to surrender some of the current vitality. As, again, the poem is organized around recurring pictures and phrases that demarcate new and last life, the poem records the disordered observations of a dying man who has already survived. I do not refer here to an embodied survival, of course, but to a transcendent, ecstatic one. In the speaker's repetition of his expiration, his dying again and again, he endures. Immersed in an ever-expanding periphery, the poem thus offers a specter of what might be, an invocation of the black queer possible. As the poem spans centuries over a single night, it contains the past, the future, and all their interlocking injuries and possibilities in a single, bounded eternity. A powerful exemplar of the black ecstatic, "Heavy Breathing" conjures in verse the African American queer beyond, where what may be found by looking closely and closer still are inarticulable emancipatory possibilities, the barest repair, and exuberant joy in the continuing, catastrophic present.

To conclude, Berlant (2011: 3) refers to eroticized and politicized attachments, those desired objects and outcomes that simultaneously enable and impair subjects and collectivities "fantasies that fray." Her list of fraying fantasies includes "upward mobility, job security, political and social equality, and lively durable intimacy" (ibid.). As longings that sustain *and* devitalize those bound by their appeal, fantasies that fray orient people and populations toward life even as they usher them toward death. In a different disturbance of desire, Sharon Holland critiques the reservoir of good that putatively resides in the queer: whether person, practice, project, or politic. She disrupts the fantasy, prevalent in both activism and academe, that erotic lives, or queer practices, constitute forms of privatized subversion. She suggests alternately that, rather than being sites of autonomy and equivalency, the enactments of preference and pleasure that we regard as evidence and entitlement of individuated personhood are sometimes the reservoirs of racist practice (Holland 2012). The will to consume, destroy, exploit, or topple an other, Holland reminds us, originates in desire. Desire is not intrinsically ethical or political, but it may be made so via affective transfer and representational practice.

In different ways, Berlant and Holland unsettle normative notions of the good, whether inherent in our selves or in the ambition of our erotic or political will. If the longing for social equality within existing political frameworks, for example, wastes precious psychic and social resources, as Berlant suggests, even as it names the reformed world that we seek, then with what choices are we left? If our defiant visibility unwittingly diminishes our security within a lethal carceral and hypersurveillance state, then how and to whom do we say our names? The lessons of the black ecstatic, as taught by such practitioners as McCraney, Jenkins, and Hemphill, are to allow woundedness, to develop an appetite for terror, to hold on to others, to outgrow and outdo catastrophe—in order to locate the ecstasy that inevitably, if surprisingly, attends its moment and infuses its aftermath. It is in the intersection, the churning overlap, of catastrophe and ecstasy that we may encounter a perilous and queer black freedom.

Notes

I am grateful to audiences at Brandeis University, Brown University, and the University of Connecticut for lively, engaging conversations about earlier drafts of this essay. I appreciate the encouragement of both anonymous readers to solidify and refine my conceptualization of the black ecstatic. I am especially grateful to Faith Smith, Ulka Anjaria, and Tiara Austin for reading and commenting on the essay. Both the time and the insights so generously provided helped make this essay possible.

1. The persistence of the most egregious forms of racialized harm following the legislative gains of black freedom movements from Emancipation through the civil rights movement has been well documented. Eduardo Bonilla-Silva's *Racism without Racists: Color-Blind Racism and the Persistence of Inequality in America*, Michelle Alexander's *The New Jim Crow: Mass Incarceration in the Era of Colorblindness*, Lisa Marie Cacho's *Social Death: Racialized Rightlessness and the Criminalization of the Unprotected*, Frank Wilderson's *Red, White, and Black: Cinema and the Structure of U.S. Antagonisms*, Colin Dayan's *The Law Is a White Dog: How Legal Rituals Make and Unmake Persons*, and Saidiya Hartman's *Lose Your Mother: A Journey Along the Atlantic Slave Route* are masterful examinations of the permutations of antiblack racism in various periods of putative black advancement. They expose antiblackness as endemic to the very project of modernity, rooted in the transatlantic slave trade and ever-present in newer, more abstract iterations of psychosocial and structural racism.

2. Jennifer Nash's *The Black Body in Ecstasy: Reading Race, Reading Pornography* (2014) is a book-length study on ecstasy that centers black women. Developing an alternate archive of black women's sexuality, one that pushes beyond its usual enclosures in shame, silence, and secrecy, Nash analyzes racialized pornography as an expressive mode that makes legible black women's sexual agency, energy, and joy. Significantly, in her formulation, ecstasy exceeds the corporeal pleasures of the erotic; it makes possible black women's dual experience of racial blackness as the site of deep historical wounding and of potential healing. Nash's celebration of black women's eroticism, of black women's desires and pleasures, pushes black feminist thought into the domain of black queer studies. While her investment in explicit representational and visual economies moves in a different direction from my interest here in opacity and aesthetic abstraction within black queer cultural production, Nash's conception of ecstasy as the fraught index of relational racial pleasure is an important framework for consideration here.

3. My thinking about willfulness as a politically informed, queer way of being and as a mode of resistant action is informed by Sara Ahmed's work on willfulness. Willfulness connotes not merely the determination to enact individual volition but, more important, to enact transformation of the status quo.

4. In *How to Read African American Literature: Post–Civil Rights Fiction and the Task*

of Interpretation, Aida Levy-Hussen proposes new modes of engaging in the literary interpretation of black writing after the civil rights movement. Her book expertly examines the limits of a particular literary approach that addresses the abstraction of state racism in the current era through fantasy returns to the antebellum era.

5. In thinking about the antebellum slave narrative as the inaugural form of black writing in the United States, I do not intend to overlook other modes of writing by African Americans, such as the poetry of Phillis Wheatley and Lucy Terry. While I recognize that there has been a long-standing tradition of politically motivated black literary production, I understand also that that tradition has been created not solely by black writerly practices but also by black readers and scholars. The texts and genres that conform to the demands of racial representation and the propagation of an agenda of political uplift are the ones that have been heralded as part of the "tradition." Black autobiography remains central to evaluative criteria: truth telling, authenticity, etc.

6. Black expressive culture at the turn of the twenty-first century is often associated with hip-hop culture, with urban musical forms, clothing styles, speech patterns, and even with a recent proliferation of novels (published independently or by small publishing houses) purportedly depicting life in the inner city. These books have found a wide readership among young African American urbanites.

7. The question of privacy and of the politics of representational obscurity conclude my first book, *Against the Closet: Black Political Longing and the Erotics of Race*. The current essay builds on that study by analyzing politics of experiment in the black cultural expression of the putatively postracial era.

8. My thinking here is informed by critical reassessments of the interrelation between queer erotics and the politics of visuality that so informs the history and political strategies of LGBTQ activism. The critique of "coming out" as a progressivist narrative of modern subjectivity and possessive individualism has been explored thoroughly in queer of color scholarship.

9. There is not a lot of information available about Hemphill's personal life outside his published work. For an informative biography, see Martin Duberman, *Hold Tight Gently: Michael Callen, Essex Hemphill, and the Battlefield of AIDS*. Duberman manages to cull a great deal about Hemphill's life, romances, and activism through nuanced reading of that published work.

References

Abdur-Rahman, Aliyyah I. 2012. *Against the Closet: Black Political Longing and the Erotics of Race*. Durham, NC: Duke University Press.

Ahmed, Sara. 2014. *Willful Subjects*. Durham, NC: Duke University Press.

Alexander, Michelle. 2010. *The New Jim Crow: Mass Incarceration in the Era of Color-blindness*. New York: New Press.

Barrett, Lindon. 2014. *Racial Blackness and the Discontinuity of Western Modernity.* Urbana: University of Illinois Press.

Berlant, Lauren. 1999. "The Subject of True Feeling: Pain, Privacy, and Politics." In *Cultural Pluralism, Identity Politics, and the Law,* edited by Austin Sarat and Thomas R. Kearns, 49–84. Ann Arbor: University of Michigan Press.

———. 2011. *Cruel Optimism.* Durham, NC: Duke University Press.

Bonilla-Silva, Eduardo. 2003. *Racism without Racists: Color-Blind Racism and the Persistence of Inequality in America.* Lanham, MD: Rowman and Littlefield.

Butler, Judith. 2003. "Afterward: After Loss, What Then?" In *Loss: The Politics of Mourning,* edited by David L. Eng and David Kazanjian, 467–74. Berkeley: University of California Press.

———. 2004. *Undoing Gender.* New York. Routledge.

Cacho, Lisa Marie. 2012. *Social Death: Racialized Rightlessness and the Criminalization of the Unprotected.* New York: New York University Press.

Crawley, Ashon T. 2016. *Blackpentacostal Breath: The Aesthetics of Possibility.* New York: Fordham University Press.

Dayan, Colin. 2011. *The Law Is a White Dog: How Legal Rituals Make and Unmake Persons.* Princeton, NJ: Princeton University Press.

Dove, Rita. 1991. *Grace Notes.* New York: W. W. Norton.

Duberman, Martin. 2014. *Hold Tight Gently: Michael Callen, Essex Hemphill, and the Battlefield of AIDS.* New York: New Press.

Harper, Phillip Brian. 2015. *Abstractionist Aesthetics: Artistic Form and Social Critique in African American Culture.* New York: New York University Press.

Hartman, Saidiya. 2006. *Lose Your Mother: A Journey Along the Atlantic Slave Route.* New York: Farrar, Straus and Giroux.

Hemphill, Essex. 1992. *Ceremonies: Prose and Poetry.* New York: Plume.

Holland, Sharon Patricia. 2000. *Raising the Dead: Readings of Death and Black Subjectivity.* Durham, NC: Duke University Press.

———. 2012. *The Erotic Life of Racism.* Durham, NC: Duke University Press.

Iton, Richard. 2008. *In Search of the Black Fantastic: Politics and Popular Culture in the Post–Civil Rights Era.* New York: Oxford University Press.

La Berge, Leigh Claire. 2014. "The Rules of Abstraction: Methods and Discourses of Finance." *Radical History Review,* no. 118: 93–112.

Levy-Hussen, Aida. 2016. *How to Read African American Literature: Post–Civil Rights Fiction and the Task of Interpretation.* New York: New York University Press.

Moonlight. 2016. Dir. Barry Jenkins. Los Angeles: A24.

Muñoz, José Esteban. 2009. *Cruising Utopia: The Then and There of Queer Futurity.* New York: New York University Press.

Nash, Jennifer. 2014. *The Black Body in Ecstasy: Reading Race, Reading Pornography.* Durham, NC: Duke University Press.

Rankine, Claudia. 2016. "The Condition of Black Life Is One of Mourning." In *The Fire This Time*, edited by Jesmyn Ward, 145–56. New York: Scribner.

Reed, Anthony. 2014. *Freedom Time: The Poetics and Politics of Black Experimental Writing*. Baltimore, MD: Johns Hopkins University Press.

Seshadri, Kalpana Rahita. 2012. *HumAnimal: Race, Law, Language*. Minneapolis: University of Minnesota Press.

Wilderson, Frank B. 2010. *Red, White, and Black: Cinema and the Structure of U.S. Antagonisms*. Durham, NC: Duke University Press.

Young, Harvey. 2010. *Embodying Black Experience: Stillness, Critical Memory, and the Black Body*. Ann Arbor: University of Michigan Press.

HISTORIES OF HETEROSEXUALITIES IN COLONIAL AFRICA

Marc Epprecht

Conjugal Rights: Marriage, Sexuality, and Urban Life
in Colonial Libreville, Gabon
Rachel Jean-Baptiste
Athens: Ohio University Press, 2014. xiv + 300 pp.

When Sex Threatened the State: Illicit Sexuality, Nationalism,
and Politics in Colonial Nigeria, 1900–1958
Saheed Aderinto
Urbana: University of Illinois Press, 2015. xviii + 241 pp.

Medicine and Morality in Egypt: Gender and Sexuality
in the Nineteenth and Early Twentieth Centuries
Sherry Sayed Gadelrab
London: I. B. Taurus, 2016. x + 204 pp.

Three new monographs add significantly to our understanding of the transformations of gender relations and sexual mores from premodern to modern times
in diverse contexts in Africa. While the focus in all three is overwhelmingly on
heterosexual relationships, they contribute to the theorization of "global queer"
by introducing meticulously gathered empirical evidence from otherwise under-

GLQ 24:2–3
DOI 10.1215/10642684-4324861

researched historical African contexts. This evidence underscores how unnatural heterosexuality is: today's heteronormative gender relations and sexual mores did not become hegemonic except through a lot of hard ideological, legal, and other labor over decades of sometimes wrenching economic, political, and social change. Even then, heterosexuality as practiced is clearly a broad tent under which all kinds of relationships have flourished frequently in glaring contradiction to commonly heard claims about "African culture" or "African sexuality." These books also bring fresh insights into how and why colonial subjects were often attracted to and sought to shape for their own benefit certain aspects of metropolitan culture under the umbrella of modernity.

Rachel Jean-Baptiste's elegant history of colonial Gabon opens with an anecdote that poignantly reveals the yawning gaps between European intentions and African aspirations. France had abolished slavery and the slave trade in 1848. It thus found itself in a similar situation as the British had from 1807, with its navy patrolling the coasts of West Africa encountering ships laden with now-illegal human cargo. What to do with the liberated contraband? Like Britain with Freetown, France established an outpost on a convenient stretch of coast that was otherwise of little interest to it. This became Libreville ("Free Town"), where recaptives could be resettled with a hut and a plot of land. Within months, however, the first beneficiaries of French generosity rebelled. Roughly half of the freed slaves took up arms to attack France's African allies in the neighborhood. They wanted more wives than Libreville itself allowed, and for several weeks the men kidnapped young women from villages along the Gabon River. After the mutiny was quelled, the French state and Catholic missionaries hastily facilitated a mass, "proper" marriage for the survivors to restore the reputation of the civilizing mission.

This dramatic incident sets the stage for Jean-Baptiste to ask her big questions. How and why did heterosexual relationships change over time? What were the roles of African women in particular in effecting those changes? And how did sexuality affect the development of other social, economic, and political structures up to the end of the colonial era in 1960? Chapters unfold in rough chronological order, beginning with a close reconstruction of precolonial gender relations and the emergence of a vibrant transactional sexual economy (this makes the book a rare study of sexualities in Africa to include significant content from the nineteenth century). Chapters in the second part of the book focus on specific French and African anxieties and campaigns as the French state sought to mitigate perceived negative consequences of the emergent sexual economy: changes to the bride-wealth economy, marriage and divorce laws, the regulation of extramarital sex, and the propriety of interracial sex. The key concern was how best to manage people's often unruly affairs as the city transitioned from colonial backwater to booming, cosmopolitan center on the verge of independence.

In posing these questions, Jean-Baptiste acknowledges her indebtedness not just to the rich feminist historiography of women and gender in Africa but also to the more recent scholarship on same-sex sexuality. In that vein, she describes looking for evidence of homosexual relations to provide a fuller picture of the history but comes upon complete archival silence and oral informants' flat denials. She then made a strategic decision to focus on the majority practices, albeit applying a critical queer perspective to the evidence. For example, Jean-Baptiste does not accept that formal monogamous marriage in a heteropatriarchal society meant that Gabonese wives were unable to make their own autonomous informal arrangements. Indeed, she shows (e.g., pp. 32, 63) that legally monogamous wives sometimes had sex with other men with the permission of their husbands, and that those husbands in some cases may even have encouraged informal polyandry when the extramarital sex involved white men and the exchange of cash.

Libreville provides an important case study for queering heterosexuality for several reasons. First, with a few notable exceptions, the historiography of women, gender, and sexuality in colonial Africa is heavily dominated by studies from the Anglophone colonies and South Africa. *Conjugal Rights* is thus a welcome contribution to broadening the evidentiary base. It draws largely on French archival sources (notably, civil court records), Gabonese texts in French (which was the lingua franca among Africans in the multi-ethnic city), and oral interviews (in both French and the main African languages, Mpongwé and Fang).

Second, unlike more-studied cities in eastern and southern Africa, where the sex ratio among Africans was heavily skewed male, Libreville from the beginning always had a rough gender balance, and even a female majority at times. As Jean-Baptiste makes clear, this had a significant impact on gender and sexual relations and thus offers a distinctive comparison to Nairobi, Lagos, Harare, or Johannesburg. Notably, the scholarship of the latter cities tends to argue that their demographic imbalance gave women a negotiating edge. Many men seeking the company of a few women allowed the women to bid their services up and to carve out a foothold in the city despite the many social and legal obstacles. Jean-Baptiste suggests, however, that there is more to the story than supply and demand. Even when the potential supply of wives was high, women were still able to negotiate advantages through innovative claims around custom, opportunistic relationships, and even overt political and legal activism.

And finally, Libreville had a distinctive multicultural ambience long after the resettlement of freed slaves dwindled. The main indigenous African population of Mpongwé people had played a key role as middlemen in the local slave trade. Thereafter they enthusiastically adopted elements of French culture and had a history of profiting from sex with French men, including as formalized through marriage. This partly explains the rise of a class of local women with independent wealth, political voice, and sexual autonomy.

The French, meanwhile, were perpetually frustrated by Africans' refusal to conform to heteronormative expectations. For example, despite the healthy gender balance, Gabon suffered from chronically low birth rates (and hence chronic labor shortages). The French attributed this to African women having too much freedom to divorce and to conduct adulterous affairs (hence high rates of sexually transmitted infections that reduced fertility). Attempts to solve the problem included codifying stricter patriarchal "traditional" law and bolstering the power of chiefs to impose moral authority. The chiefs' behavior, unfortunately, sometimes made matters worse. By delaying rulings in cases of runaway wives seeking divorces, some chiefs exploited the women's labor in their own fields or added them to already large, market-oriented farming households. They also tended to side with women in order to increase their earnings through court fees, thus abetting women's "looseness." Birth rates were not boosted in the process.

Jean-Baptiste makes another contribution through her analysis of urban racial segregation. A common explanation for why so many African cities had segregated areas is whites' anxiety about the dangers of proximity to Africans. The "sanitation syndrome," notably, has been widely invoked as a shorthand for whites' exaggerated fears of catching contagious disease from blacks, while others have discerned fear of "black peril" (African men's lust for white women) as a driving motive in that geography. In Libreville the French did indeed seek to enhance their political power by establishing a whites-only zone and consolidating different ethnic groups in discrete neighborhoods. They failed, however, because of strong African resistance. That resistance in some cases hinged on fears that the proposed neighborhoods were a threat to African gender and sexual norms. Fang men, notably, feared that being forced to live together as a single group, when they had traditionally been scattered clans with no unifying social ethic, would increase the practice of adultery among them, with all the problems that that implied (57).

Overall, *Conjugal Rights* makes a compelling case that the culture, and even the physical layout of the contemporary city, owes much to the long history of struggle and joy found in the negotiation of erotic bonds between its citizens. "The geography of Libreville was not determined by only the built environment, but by the movement of women's and men's bodies and expressions of eros" (223). This is a theme that Saheed Aderinto also develops in his analysis of conflicts over sexuality that have given Lagos, Nigeria, its distinctive character.

Like Jean-Baptiste, Aderinto opens his book with a revealing tale. In 1947 a leading female welfare officer in Lagos was convicted for accepting bribes. Three scandals swirled around the case. First, the corrupt official was responsible for the repression of child sex-trafficking. Thus, while the bribe payers were adults, the case drew attention to the issue of men having sex with girl children facilitated in part by the girls' mothers. Second, the bribe appeared to be part of a normal cost of operation for the city's thriving sex work scene. And third, relatedly, the official involved did not appear to be ashamed of her role in the sordid business. On the contrary, she retained five expensive lawyers and fought the allegations through to the highest court in British West Africa.

From here, Aderinto asks of the Lagos evidence many of the same questions as Jean-Baptiste does in Libreville, but with a stronger focus on the role that debates around sexuality played in nation building and decolonization. As Aderinto explains (7), the silencing of the history of contestation around sexuality both in official sources and in the scholarship on Nigeria impoverishes our understanding of other contestations in and around state formation. The opening anecdote is a striking nod to that impoverishment. It provides a small window into the history of elite privilege and government corruption that have so plagued the Nigerian nation-building experience but that clearly predated independence.

Aderinto weaves a subtle narrative of different groups trying to advance their social and political aspirations through their preferred visions of sexual propriety. At root, the British did not trust that Nigerians were culturally capable of demonstrating the kind of sexual self-control that was believed needed to exercise governance over a modern state, and the British did not hesitate to express that view in overtly racist language. Indeed, supposedly primitive or overexuberant sexuality among Africans had been an important justification for the colonial "civilizing mission" and underpinned the subsequent concept of a dual mandate of paternalistic, gradualist movement toward self-government. Many Christianized Nigerians actually accepted the basic outlines of that view but bridled at the tone. They offered their own counternarrative of sexual dignity within African culture as defined by them (to justify independence from the British) and selectively promoted aspects of British gender ideology (to make claims for Nigeria's modernity and potential for development under their leadership).

Aderinto also stresses an aspect of intersectionality commonly overlooked in the historiography: age. Disputes over when exactly ostensibly asexual and agency-less girls became women, with erotic (and other) agency playing an important role in defining who, as a group, could be considered moral. People so defined would be the most appropriate leaders of the emerging national state. The book ends in 1958 when the British and their elite Nigerian partners in the decolonization process raised the legal age of consent for girls from thirteen to sixteen, demonstrating to the world their suitability as modern leaders.

Aderinto moves methodically through the sundry issues as they unfolded in the local, English-language press and government documents supplemented, to a limited extent, by oral interviews. But there are gaps. Given his attention to age, for example, it is curious that Aderinto does not discuss or even mention masturbation. Are we to assume that African youth in Nigeria did not do such things, or that the topic was not a concern to sexual moralists? Also, like Jean-Baptiste, Aderinto is aware and respectful of the scholarship on same-sex sexuality and gender variance, and he similarly pleads the invisibility of those topics in the archives to justify the almost exclusive focus on heterosexual sexuality. I say "almost" because he mentions a case of male-male sodomy in the military in 1921 (97). One could quibble that this seems a weak challenge to the heteronormativity of the sources, or be hopeful that it will be more actively addressed in a future study.

The book's epilogue fascinatingly extrapolates these historical debates to a contemporary scandal—the trafficking of Nigerian women to Europe for sex work, and the proliferation, and normalization, of sex work domestically. Dispiriting parallels are drawn between now and the colonial era. As before, the laws and bureaucracies established to protect women and children appear less interested in the victims of exploitation than in the performance of respectability by the state and the elites who control it. In this case, the performance of cracking down on trafficking is intended to boost Nigeria's tarnished international reputation.

Medicine and Morality in Egypt touches on many of the same issues as the previous books but with a much broader scope of time and more diverse sources (the author was Egyptian and consulted her Arabic- and Turkish-language sources directly). As this is the shortest of the three books under consideration, the race across centuries and decade hopping in the later chapters can be dizzying. I should also note with sadness that Sherry Sayed Gadelrab died in an untimely way and that the book was published posthumously. This may explain some disconcerting lack of attention to copyediting. The book nonetheless makes a coherent exposition on the ways that Western scientific knowledge—typically infused with orientalist, racist, sexist, and homophobic prejudice, as well as riven by great swathes of ignorance particularly around female sexuality—helped consolidate cultural and religious arguments for Egyptian women's inferiority to men.

Chapter 1 begins with an overview of the principal ancient Greek philosophers' theories of sexual difference and function. These were influentially translated into Arabic and Persian, and disseminated throughout the Islamic world over the millennium preceding Egypt's period of self-conscious modernization. Gadelrab relies heavily here on Thomas Laqueur's thesis that the ancient Greeks' "one sex" model of biological difference underpinned the edifice of heteropatriarchy, sexism, and misogyny that became Western civilization. According to that view, humans were physiologically of one sex, and females were simply flawed versions of the ideal. This notion was eventually upended by Enlightenment-era scientific observation. The central question Gadelrab assesses is how these ideas of biological sexual difference percolated through Islamic knowledge in the Middle East, eventually to frame the debates about women's and men's distinctive roles in a modernizing society.

Chapter 1 ends with the observation that classical Western science was interpreted over the centuries by Muslim scholars to adhere to teachings of the Koran, *hadith*, and *fiqh*. These teachings supported heteropatriarchal culture but also actively encouraged female sexual pleasure within the bounds of heterosexual marriage. They further allowed for significant tolerance of nonnormative expressions of gender and sexuality. Gadelrab analyzes several discussions of homosexuality, for example, where science backed the exegesis of sacred texts to reduce the severity of the moral infraction in certain circumstances. Indifference to male-male sexual relationships provided that they did not endanger the sanctity of heterosexual marriage and family honor was thus justified both by Koranic ambiguities and by physiological explanations around men's anatomical needs.

The majority of the book focuses on 1827–1949, bounded by the establishment of the first school dedicated to training Egyptians in Western medical knowledge and the criminalization of prostitution. Topics explored include female excision, polygyny, child betrothals, prostitution, the role of the veil, the rights of women, and much more as revealed through the writings of Egyptian intellectuals, feminist activists, and Islamic scholars. A trend quickly emerges in Gadelrab's analysis. Where Western observers judged Egyptians to have low morals, since they did not adhere to biologically suggested norms of civilized sexual behavior, Egyptians themselves tended to take a pragmatic view that put defense of family unity ahead of sexual ideals. For example, a husband who went to prostitutes or took a "temporary wife" or even had anal sex with a male was not necessarily immoral. If his sexual decisions did not interfere with the stability of the marriage, then they were tolerable, or even, if they protected the marriage from a husband's excessive demands on a wife, his queer sexual choices could be the preferable, moral options.

Chapter 4 is particularly revealing in this way by delving into some of the thousands of *fatwas* issued by prominent muftis in the mid- to late nineteenth century. In contrast to decisions by judges in formal court cases, *fatwas* were informed recommendations often issued in response to direct personal inquiries from people concerned about specific ethical questions. A pattern emerges over this period as *fatwas* moved from expressing pragmatic, relatively tolerant attitudes to become a weapon for regulating harsher interpretations of Islam backed by bowdlerized Western science. This trend was driven by a similar desire for respectability and modernity among Egyptian elites, as Aderinto describes. Here too that desire arose partly in reaction to orientalist slanders against Egyptian morals, and Egyptian women's in particular. Yet ironically, economic modernization tended to undermine that very desire to demonstrate respectability. Freed slaves and peasant women displaced by commercial agriculture had few survival options except to move to the cities and to sell sex.

As with Nigeria's raising of the age of consent, the eventual criminalization of prostitution in Egypt symbolically legitimized the moral authority of Egypt's ruling elite to steer the nation to what they perceived as its rightful place among the modern nations of the world, which British colonialism had denied. An important contribution of Gadelrab's study is to illuminate the role of elite Egyptian women in this assertion of modernity, and specifically in reconstructing the supposed nature of female sexuality in contradistinction to male. The irony is that Western science was invoked to promote both colonial and anticolonial discourses around sexual propriety. Regarding the latter, Gadelrab writes that the "behaviour of new Egyptian woman was expected to closely resemble her English Victorian counterpart: a loving wife and mother preoccupied mainly with the domestic sphere, and a woman with self-regulated sexuality" (107).

What a wealth of empirical evidence from hitherto largely unexamined sources, and what an enrichment these three books make to our understanding of colonialism and colonial science in the transformation of premodern gender and sexual relations globally. These books deserve to be read widely.

QUEER THEORY, CULTURAL MARXISM, AND TRANSNATIONAL CHINA

Calvin Hui

Queer Marxism in Two Chinas
Petrus Liu
Durham, NC: Duke University Press, 2015. x + 244 pp.

Petrus Liu's *Queer Marxism in Two Chinas* provides a powerful and insightful analysis of queer theory, political and cultural Marxisms, geopolitics and the Cold War, and contemporary Chinese cultures. Considering Chinese queer theory, he suggests that the question to ask is not "Why does China need queer theory?," which inevitably leads to the quandary of Western universality, Chinese particularity, and the coloniality of intellectual work. Rather, it is more productive to inquire "Why does queer theory need China?." The latter question, Liu maintains, enables queer scholars to engage with China and Marxism (including Chinese Marxism). In this book, Liu argues that sexuality studies and queer studies need the Marxist analysis of geopolitics.

In chapter 1, "Marxism, Queer Liberalism, and the Quandary of Two Chinas," Liu argues for a transnational and intersectional analysis of queer theory, Marxism, and China. He begins by examining recent work in Chinese and US queer studies. On the one hand, Chinese queer studies scholars assume that the emergence of queer cultures and politics in post-socialist China is accompanied by the end of Marxism and the intensification of neoliberal globalization. On the other hand, US queer studies scholars are worried about homonormativity, queer liberalism, and the ways in which queerness is complicit with and co-opted by neoliberal capitalism. They critique the fact that today, many queer and queer-friendly peo-

GLQ 24:2–3

ple have lost their radical politics and simply desire inclusion, acceptance, equal rights (e.g., same-sex marriage), and a depoliticized, middle-class, and consumerist lifestyle. To repoliticize queer theory, Liu argues that the geopolitical formation of the "two Chinas," namely, the People's Republic of China (PRC) and the Republic of China (ROC), in 1949 is a crucial event for the Chinese queer imagination. Some Chinese queer writers based in Taiwan responded to this historical event and drew on the cultural and intellectual resources of Marxism in their writings on gender and sexuality. According to Liu, US queer theory, which can be regarded as a liberal pluralist theory based on identity formation and the intersectional analysis of social differences, can learn from this version of Chinese queer theory. The latter is a non-liberal theory of sexual difference predicated on the critique of the impersonal, structural, and systemic workings of power.

In chapter 2, "Chinese Queer Theory," Liu proposes a humanities approach, rather than a social science or public policy method, to the study of Chinese queer cultures and politics. Building on the existing scholarship in Chinese studies (e.g., the prosecution of homosexuals in the name of "hooliganism" during the socialist period, the Chinese naming of queers as "tongzhi," "lala," and "ku'er" in the context of global capitalism), he reads cultural texts as theory and argues that contemporary China has produced its own queer theory that is not simply a poor copy or impoverished imitation of US queer theory. Instead, it is an intellectually rigorous discourse that exists contemporaneously with its US counterpart. In this chapter, Liu analyzes the creative and critical works of Cui Zi'en, an independent filmmaker from mainland China, and attends to how they try to resist and critique the operations of global capital, the party-state, and mainstream queer cultures. He also examines Josephine Ho's critical writings and explains how her sex-positive feminism diverges from the state feminism that is underwritten by the logic of liberalism and electoral politics. In addition, Liu examines the activism and critical works on gender, sexuality, and labor of the Gender/Sexuality Rights Association, Taiwan (G/SRAT).

In chapter 3, "The Rise of the Queer Chinese Novel," Liu argues that the modern homosexual character appeared in the Chinese literary scene in the 1980s, that these characters were the productions of Taiwan-based Chinese authors (e.g., Bai Xianyong's *Crystal Boys* [1983]), and that these works expressed queer engagements with Chinese Marxism as a political apparatus and an intellectual resource. In this way, Liu provides a prehistory of the prominence of Chinese queer literature (*tongzhi wenxue*) and films in the 1990s. While analyzing the narrative form of Chen Ruoxi's queer novel *Paper Marriage* (1986), which concerns the love relationship between a Chinese heterosexual woman and an American homosexual man who later dies of AIDS, Liu argues that queer theory needs China, or more specifically, the signifier of China (including ethnicity, culture, nation-state, and citizenship) as well as geopolitical analysis. He ends by suggesting that Chen's work stages productive tensions between Marxism (capitalism vs. communism, class struggle, national liberation) and sexuality studies as ways to examine relations of power.

In chapter 4, "Genealogies of the Self," Liu engages with Xiao Sa's novel *Song of Dreams* (1980) to rethink the relationship between gender, sexuality, and the economic modernization of Taiwan. Arguing against previous scholarship that considers the novel as a neoliberal fable of upward mobility and individual success and a feminist rebellion against coercive heterosexual marriage, Liu focuses on the queer dimension of Xiao's feminism and examines the queer arrangement of desires and commodities. He shows that the novel reveals the author's attempt to stage a queer critique of neoliberalism in Taiwan.

In chapter 5, "Queer Human Rights in and against the Two Chinas," Liu focuses on the discourse of human rights (including queer human rights) and analyzes the competing forces of US neocolonialism, the PRC, and Taiwan. In addition to documenting violations of queer human rights in Taiwan, Liu examines how queer Marxists strategically appropriate human rights for their political purposes.

In this book, Liu makes a powerful case that Chinese queer cultural theorists, activists in LGBTQ social movements, and fiction writers responded to changing geopolitical configurations during the Cold War by drawing on the political and intellectual resources of Marxism. With the exception of Cui Zi'en's works, it seems that most of the materials come from Taiwanese sources. It might be more appropriate to call this book *Queer Marxism in Taiwan* instead. In any case, inspired by Liu's profound theoretical contribution, another *Queer Marxism in Two Chinas* book could be written. Whereas Liu examines how Chinese queer writers and scholars engage with Marxism, one could start from the other direction and consider how Chinese Marxist scholars and critical theorists, labor activists, fiction writers, and filmmakers draw on the archives of sexuality and queerness to enrich their creative and critical works. While mainland Chinese feminists such as Li Xiaojiang and Dai Jinhua have focused on Chinese women, socialist revolutions, and the market economy, are there any Chinese scholars and fiction writers who have responded to the challenges posed by sexuality and queer studies? Moreover, how does (post-) coloniality (e.g., Hong Kong) change the ways in which one conceptualizes the intersectionality and transnationality of queer theory, Marxism, and the "three" Chinas? Liu's book is impressive precisely because it helps us reimagine queer theory, Marxism, and the Chinas, as well as their novel potential reconfigurations.

Calvin Hui is assistant professor of Chinese studies at the College of William and Mary.

DOI 10.1215/10642684-4324873

ADOLESCENT AGENCIES IN THE AGE OF CONSENT

Gillian Harkins

Sex and Harm in the Age of Consent
Joseph J. Fischel
Minneapolis: University of Minnesota Press, 2016. ix + 333 pp.

Critical doxa in queer studies rarely aligns with that of disciplinary or popular critique. This is exemplified in the shorthand "sex panic" (17) to describe and dismiss efforts to stigmatize or criminalize specific gender or sexual practices deemed beyond acceptable conduct. Frequently sex panics conflate gender and sexuality while amplifying the harm imposed by unwelcome conduct. Joseph Fischel's *Sex and Harm in the Age of Consent* resituates sex-panic discourse in relation to emerging gendered and sexual inequalities operationalized, if not "weaponized" (8), through logics of sexual consent. Fischel's original and compelling argument moves through juridical, political, and cultural sources to locate the limits of sexual consent as a rubric for either feminist or queer flourishing. In place of consent he proposes "another vocabulary for thinking sexual harm as meaning something other than consent's violation" (10): "sexual autonomy, 'peremption,' and vulnerability" (13). By taking harm seriously, rather than dismissing it as a ruse of sex panic, Fischel draws together feminist and queer critique to imagine a normative framework and a cultural imaginary moving beyond consent and toward more "relationally reconstructed sexual autonomy" (203).

The book begins by outlining recent sexual demonology targeting the "sex offender" as a new "exhaustive figure for sexual amorality and dangerousness" (17). In an age of uneven homosexual normalization, the sex offender appears to function as "the new homosexual" (74), galvanizing stigma and prohibition across legal and cultural domains. But the sex offender is more homosexual supplement than replacement, Fischel explains, a sexual minority whose cultural work requires adult homosexuality to legitimate the "age of consent" (11). In the past thirty years, a new trio of characters—the child, the sex offender, and the homosexual—organize legitimate gendered sexuality by "functionaliz[ing] consent as the metric that matters for modern sexual ethics" (3). Consent, developed by feminist legal reformers as "an imperfect but critical guarantor of sexual integrity and autonomy" (10), paradoxically "churns out figures for its own normativity" (12) by manufacturing personae such as the sexual predator and the innocent child to mark the limits of consensual sex. In other words, "sex offenders are the new queers" to the degree that they enable "demonizing projection" (20) while disentangling the sex offender from historical homophobia.

Fischel's argument develops across chapters treating *To Catch a Predator* (NBC Dateline, 2004–7), the Sex Offender Registry and Notification (SORN) Acts, legal debates about sexual autonomy, and the films *Doubt* (2008), *Thirteen* (2003), and *Superbad* (2007). Each chapter examines how the "fiction of the sex offender" (3) fosters a "normative imaginary" (83) in which adult consensuality, rather than heterosexuality, becomes "nationally privileged" (6). This shift sets in motion new "problems of sexual inequality and injustice" (7) as well as "gendered inequality" (87). Fischel's response to this shift is to center "gendered adolescent[s]" (132) as "volitional but vulnerable subjects" (18) who exemplify the need for more relational paradigms of sexual autonomy. His response is broken into two parts: first, Fischel proposes treating adolescents as a "separate sex class under law" (132) to address "asymmetric susceptibility" or "the ways young people are disproportionately prone to imposition and interference" (14); second, he considers adolescence as "a kind of sexual orientation unto itself, defined less by gender of object choice (homo/hetero) than by an exploratory disposition" (132). In both cases, adolescent sexuality is understood as more process than object oriented, or more akin to becoming than being. This model of adolescence is proffered as "exemplary of sexuality" (132) more generally to expand approaches to sexual autonomy away from binary logics.

This is exciting work relevant to anyone interested in sexuality and inequity as well as age-based determinations of sexual agency. Fischel's theorization of consent as "spectrum" rather than "switch" (102) leads him to advocate normative approaches to (1) relations of dependence, (2) affirmative standards of consent, and (3) adolescence as a separate sexual class (131). These approaches resituate sexual autonomy in relation to "peremption" (132), or *the uncontrolled disqualification of possibility*" (135) produced by diffuse social norms and structural inequities. Fischel's development of peremption as a central concept shifts focus from individual consent to "institutional constraints, skewed conferrals of privilege, and systemic patterns of inequality" (15). It also shifts focus from law to films whose "more capacious excavation of ethics" (134) create "an encounter instead of inciting a pronouncement" (135). This combination of approaches and materials expands the possibilities of sexual autonomy beyond existing legal frameworks while remaining focused on the conditions that law places on cultural imaginaries.

Yet Fischel's book also raises important questions that it does not entirely address. The most haunting question is how race, nation, and empire "frame the problems of age and sex" (18) as they appear within the law. Fischel is careful to note race and class determinants of age and sex in existing social conditions, but the legal framework persistently resists more conceptual reframing of such social conditions as legal a priori. This is obviously not Fischel's flaw, and crafting normative arguments requires hewing to existing legal mechanisms rather than redefining their foundations. But drawing more sustained attention to the racial and colonial creation of age and gender as legal categories would clarify how intersectional approaches to adolescence are perempted by law itself in ways that are mediated differently across cultural texts. In his final film readings, for example, Fischel contrasts black male adolescent agency in *Doubt* —"perempted by narrative, by the discursive structure and compulsory affect of a sex scandal" (152)—to white-gendered adolescent agency thematized as sexual negotiation in *Thirteen* and *Superbad*. These film readings more directly address the racial formations of normative sexuality, where the turn to cultural texts allows Fischel to demonstrate how racial exemplarity seems to disqualify black adolescents from gendered agency, while racial appropriation in contrast enables white adolescents to negotiate its peremptions (gendered female) and propulsions (gendered male). Such cultural reading strategies might productively be applied to legal narratives as well to reveal how the agencies associated with gender and age may also tacitly rely on the peremptions and propulsions of racial formations. Fischel's work draws needed attention to these conditions in ways that push queer studies of sex panic toward more intersectional accounts of pleasure and harm. In so doing, it should be considered required reading for anyone committed to thinking age as a central determinant of sexuality in consensual times.

Gillian Harkins is associate professor of English at the University of Washington, Seattle.

DOI 10.1215/10642684-4324885

MIXING BUSINESS WITH PLEASURE IN VIETNAM'S ASCENT TO THE GLOBAL STAGE

Elanah Uretsky

Dealing in Desire: Asian Ascendancy, Western Decline, and the Hidden Currencies of Global Sex Work
Kimberly Kay Hoang
Oakland, CA: University of California Press, 2015. xiv + 229 pp.

Kimberly Hoang's novel ethnography, *Dealing in Desire*, is a powerful statement about the value of sex work, which in Vietnam and other parts of Asia has played a role in promoting national ascendancy to the global stage. Her adept analysis and clear prose give wonderful perspective on Vietnam's commercial sex industry from both the women who sell sex and the clients who buy sex. Few ethnographies consider the relational aspect of gender in their presentation of sex work, but Hoang recognizes how crucial this interaction is to a proper analysis of commercial sex. But Hoang offers an even more comprehensive analysis of this local sex industry by painting a complete picture of the different tiers of Vietnam's commercial sex industry that serves both local elite and overseas Vietnamese businessmen as well as Western businessmen and the Western backpacker community. She was able to accomplish this through twenty-four months of immersive fieldwork in four bars around Ho Chi Minh City that served men from these four different populations. Following in the tradition of other female ethnographers who have written ethnographic accounts of sex work as it is performed in hostess clubs in Asian societies (Allison 1994; Zheng 2009; Parreñas 2011), Hoang took jobs as either a hostess or a bartender in the venues that were her field sites. She worked twelve to fourteen hours per day, seven days a week, for nine months in these venues.

The power of Hoang's careful scholarship lies in the connections she makes between sex workers and their clients and the ascendancy of Vietnam to the global economic stage. The book demonstrates the relationship between a financial measure like foreign direct investment (FDI) and sex work, a connection that is rarely made but crucial for analyzing and understanding the rise of several major Asian economies like those of China, Japan, and South Korea. She demonstrates this by carefully tracing the vital role that commercial sex plays in establishing the social contracts that help private entrepreneurs and foreign investors bypass the official channels for obtaining the land and permits they need to succeed in their economic roles. Commercial sex workers create a relaxing environment in karaoke bars, where they sing, drink, and play with men. In chapter 3, for example, Hoang details a situation where a sex worker transformed a formal style of interaction between a businessman from Vietnam and one from Korea into an informal, intimate, and fun environment that helps men form the bonds that translate into the type of trust required to seal a deal in Vietnam.

The type of environment Hoang describes may seem counterintuitive to the reader who is accustomed to thinking of poverty and marginality alongside sex work. Hoang's detailed ethnographic description, however, demonstrates how sex is used to nurture the trust required for the efficient flow of capital in the Vietnamese and broader Asian context. In doing this, Hoang examines the multiple processes experienced by the men in the various groups she studies as they negotiate race-, class-, and gender-based hierarchies in their separate cultures. The Westerners she observed used their access to sex and sexuality to reaffirm their Western superiority, while Vietnamese men (whether local elite or overseas businessmen) used their sexuality as a way to contest Western power through the unique cultural access it gives them toward consolidating Asian ascendancy. The women who facilitate the industry create what Hoang calls *business-oriented intimacy* (79), which is crucial for the Vietnamese men working to attract FDI. For overseas Vietnamese, these women facilitate *fantasy-oriented intimacy* (79) as men trying to attract women across transnational borders. And finally for the Western men, sex workers in Vietnam facilitate what Hoang calls *philanthropy-oriented intimacy* (79) that is critical for attracting money from overseas that Westerners often frame as charity projects through benevolent remittances.

Perhaps one of the most important and novel contributions of Hoang's ethnography is the attention she gives to the position of sex workers in Vietnam. Sex work usually conjures up images of women who are impoverished, exploited, and often trafficked into their positions. These same images have framed most scholarship on sex work. Hoang's scholarship challenges this paradigm by describing a sex-work industry populated by women who are economically mobile and can convert that mobility into social status in their home villages. Many of the women Hoang spoke with resented Western efforts to "rescue" them from exploitation. These were women with autonomy who chose to enter sex work because of the opportunities for mobility it offers and because work in this industry saves them from the exploitation they would face working in a factory or other service industry. In addition, as Hoang so adeptly demonstrates, these women have power in the roles they play in nurturing the growth of Vietnam's economy and its ascendancy to the global economic stage.

Hoang's book is a novel contribution to the literature on sex work that goes beyond discourse that has argued for recognizing sex work as work into the realm of articulating the power and purpose of this type of work and of the people who engage in the industry, both from the worker side and the client side. This is an important contribution to the literature that is accessible to both undergraduate and graduate students taking courses in gender and sexuality, East Asian studies, anthropology, and sociology. And while this book does not discuss public health beyond a cursory mention of HIV, I would also urge public health students to place it on their reading lists as a way to understand the unique context that will frame their interventions in a country like Vietnam.

Elanah Uretsky is a visiting assistant professor of anthropology at Brandeis University.

References

Allison, Anne. 1994. *Nightwork: Sexuality, Pleasure, and Corporate Masculinity in a Tokyo Hostess Club.* Chicago: University of Chicago Press.

Parreñas, Rhacel. 2011. *Illicit Flirtations.* Stanford, CA: Stanford University Press.

Zheng, Tiantian. 2009. *Red Lights: The Lives of Sex Workers in Postsocialist China.* Minneapolis: University of Minnesota Press.

DOI 10.1215/10642684-4324897

THEORIZING THE STATE AND SEXUALITY

Nishant Upadhyay

Sexual States: Governance and the Struggle
over the Antisodomy Law in India
Jyoti Puri
Durham, NC: Duke University Press, 2016. x + 222.

The last few decades have seen struggles for rights for sexual and gender minorities, like hijras, kothis, aravanis, kinnars, trans, queer peoples, and others, come to the forefront in India. The fight against antisodomy laws, in particular the Indian Penal Code Section 377, a colonial law first introduced in 1860 by the British Raj, has become the focus of struggles to decriminalize homosexuality in India. Jyoti Puri's *Sexual States* explores these struggles and the relation between sexuality and the state. The book conceptualizes "sexual states" by studying the workings of Section 377 across different sites, analyzing both state and non-state actors. To theorize sexual states, Puri builds on the works on sexuality and state by Urvashi Butalia (2000), Veena Das (2007), Mary John and Janaki Nair (1998), Ann Laura Stoler (2004), and others. The book questions the hypervisibility of 377 as the "homophobic law" to make visible with the other methods through which the state regulation of sexuality affects marginalized communities in India. In this review, I focus on two important interventions that Puri puts forward in the book. I conclude with some critical mediations for scholars of sexuality, the state, and justice.

First, Puri masterfully captures the "inconsistencies in discourses and practices of governance" (4) in the Indian state's relation to sexual rights and justice for sexual and gender minorities. States, she asserts, are subjective and are "neither autochthonous entities nor mere material realities" (5). Puri contends that the Indian state's response to calls for sexual justice seems inconsistent, contradictory, and arbitrary because "states are fragmented and deeply subjective" (5) in how they operate. She offers a compelling argument that sexual states legitimize themselves through regulating various aspects of sexuality. Further, by juxtaposing the contentious and conflicting judgments on Section 377, namely, the "progressive" Delhi High Court 2009 judgment (striking down 377 as unconstitutional) and the "regressive" Supreme Court 2013 judgment (reaffirming the importance of 377), Puri contends that both judgments need to be studied through neoliberal state processes (chapters 5–6). The Delhi High Court judgment, while favorable toward sexual minorities, posits the state as the beacon of justice, reifying it as the ultimate arbiter of rights. Thus, even as the state may support sexual rights, this regulation works to reaffirm state structures and violences by asserting benevolence to some of those harmed by the state. Overall, the book extends the idea that states produce sexuality and that state and sexuality are deeply intertwined and continuously shaped through each other.

Second, consistently challenging the centricity of Section 377 in the fight for decriminalization of homosexuality, chapters 2–4 broaden the conversation to engage with intersections between sexual violence and violences against women, children, hijras, Muslims, and Sikhs. These were the book's most engaging sections. In a thoughtful discussion of these marginalized communities, Puri illustrates how the focus on homosexuality effaces the lived experiences and violences faced by other communities. In particular, Puri challenges the reading of 377 as the "homophobic law" to document how the section has been predominantly used for child abuse cases. Further, through her engagements with the Delhi police on 377 and works of Ania Loomba (2009), Puri offers a language of racialization to critique the hegemonic framework of religious communalism. She reveals the intersections of homophobia and religious violence by arguing that Muslims, and to a lesser extent Sikhs, are racialized as the sexual other and sexualized as the racial other. Through an ethnography of different sites of the state—the judiciary, the police, the bureaucracy, and statistical agencies—the book demonstrates how Section 377 is one of the many ways in which sexuality is regulated in India, not just through the targeting of gender and sexual minorities alone, but also religious and racial others. Indeed, homophobia exists in multiple and varied forms, of which law is only one. Puri critically exposes the limits of the legal struggles and pushes readers to imagine sexual justice through the various complexities and intricacies of sexuality in India, and not solely through the lens of antisodomy laws.

Puri's *Sexual States* is a well-written book that will be important not only for how it makes us rethink sexual justice in India but also for the transnational framework it provides to understand the intricacies of sexuality, the state, and neoliberal processes. The book opens spaces for further research for scholars of sexuality, the state, and oppression. In particular, as discussed above, Puri offers a lens of racialization to theorize the sexual and racial othering of religious minorities in India. To this discussion I bring into conversation the analytical lens of caste. What role does caste play here? Do caste and race function synonymously and are they inter-changeable in the Indian context? What does the language of race offer us in relation to caste? Can the lens of caste offer a more thorough framework of understanding marginality in the Indian state? Further, how do caste and sexuality shape the experiences of caste-others (dalit, bahujan, and adivasi communities), religious-others (Muslim, Sikh, and Christian communities), and national-others (Kashmiris, Nagas, Manipuris, Khasis, and others of occupied communities)? What are the experiences of sexual and gendered minorities in these communities? Additionally, how are hijras, kothis, aravanis, kinnars, and other gender minorities affected by 377 and the focus on 377? A more detailed analysis of these communities can challenge, and perhaps decenter, the dominance of English-speaking, upper caste, upwardly mobile, cis-queer-centered sexual organizing in urban centers in India. In a brahmanical state like India, where logics of endogamy and blood purity have always been at stake in regulating sexual intimacies and caste lines, can the sexual state be theorized without examining the violences of caste inherent in the making of the state? Without questioning the modalities of caste, the experiences of those oppressed through the sexual violences of brahmanical supremacy are erased. The "caste-state," rather than the sexual state, controls and regulates all forms of hegemonic and nonhegemonic sexualities, desires, and intimacies (for more on this see Ambedkar 2013; Malik 2003; Paik 2014; Pawar and Moon 2008; Tharu 2008). The intersections of caste and sexuality would perhaps also allow us to understand the attack on desires, intimacies, and love in India—not just queer intimacies but intercaste and interreligious "heterosexual love" as well.

Nishant Upadhyay is assistant professor in women's and gender studies at the University of Massachusetts Dartmouth.

References

Ambedkar, B. R. 2013. "Castes in India: Their Mechanism, Genesis, and Development (1916)." In *Against the Madness of Manu: BR Ambedkar's Writings on Brahmanical Patriarchy*, edited by Sharmila Rege, 77–107. New Delhi: Navayana.

Butalia, Urvashi. 2000. *The Other Side of Silence: Voices from the Partition of India*. Durham, NC: Duke University Press.

Das, Veena. 2007. *Life and Words: Violence and the Descent into the Ordinary*. Los Angeles: University of California Press.

John, Mary, and Janaki Nair, eds. 1998. *A Question of Silence? The Sexual Economies of Modern India*. New Delhi: Kali for Women.

Loomba, Ania. 2009. "Race and the Possibility of Comparative Critique." *New Literary History* 40: 501–22.

Malik, Bela. 2003. "Untouchability and Dalit Women's Oppression." In *Gender and Caste*, edited by Anupama Rao, 102–7. New Delhi: Kali for Women.

Paik, Shailaja, 2014. *Dalit Women's Education in Modern India: Double Discrimination.* London: Routledge.

Pawar, Urmila, and Meenakshi Moon. 2008. *We Also Made History.* Translated by Wandana Sonalkar. New Delhi: Zubaan Books.

Stoler, Ann Laura. 2004. "Affective States." In *A Companion to Anthropology of Politics*, edited by David Nugent and Joan Vincent, 4–20. Malden, MA: Blackwell.

Tharu, Susie Tharu. 2003. "The Impossible Subject: Caste and the Gendered Body." In *Gender and Caste*, edited by Anupama Rao, 261–75. New Delhi: Kali for Women.

DOI 10.1215/10642684-4324909

FUNKING OUR WAY TO FREEDOM

Elliott H. Powell

Funk the Erotic: Transaesthetics and Black Sexual Cultures
L. H. Stallings
Urbana: University of Illinois Press, 2015. xi + 270 pp.

Halfway through the remix to Destiny's Child's (DC) 2001 hit song "Bootylicious," Missy Elliott raps: "Watch my booty shake like a fat lady's belly / my style's so stank I better bank you gon' smell me." The music then stops, Elliott loudly inhales and lets out a pleasurable exhale: "ahhh! you smell me? / Smells like money / When I come runnin' / Missy keep it comin'." While DC's verses center on the *visual* attractiveness of black women's backsides, Elliott's verse reframes—it remixes—this narrative by focusing on another sensory register: smell. Elliott's move toward the olfactory, to the register of stank, allows her to pursue how a bootylicious ass is not solely tied to a gaze-led and sexually absent aesthetics of beauty (as the lyrics of DC suggest); it is also an embodied site of sexual sensation, pleasure, and labor for black women. Indeed, Elliott's audible sniffing sets in motion the orgasmic "ahhh" release, the erotic double entendre of "come" / "coming," and the specter of sex work via Elliott's association of money with the pleasurable smell of her own ass. Elliott's verse, thus, engages the complex relations between the scopic, the sonic, the sexual, and the stank, and centers how the senses organize and can offer new knowledges about black sexualities.

It is this kind of reorganization of sensorial modalities and their relationship to and production of alternative formations of black erotic life that sits at the heart of L. H. Stallings's brilliant book *Funk the Erotic Transaesthetics and Black Sexual Cultures.* In it, Stallings uses funk as an analytic framework and methodology to explicate the historical and contemporary ways in which "black cultural producers have strategized against the sexual con of white supremacist, capitalist patriarchy outside of politics" (xii). For Stallings, funk is not simply an olfactory register or a genre of black dance music; funk is both and more. It is a more that insists on Afro-diasporic engagements with the "etymological triad for *funk*— nonvisual sensory perception (smell/odor), embodied movement (dance and sex), and force (mood and will)"—and offers a "multisensory and multidimensional philosophy [that] has been used in conjunction with the erotic, eroticism, and black erotica" (4, xvi). This is an erotics that rejects the erotic versus sexually explicit divide that still has purchase in feminist and queer studies circles. Stallings instead joins recent black feminist scholarship that embraces the entanglements between the raunchiness of sex and the spiritual impulse of the erotic, and demands "space be made for honest bodies that like to also *fuck*" (Morgan 2015: 40). Indeed, Stallings makes use of the slippage between funk and fuck to underscore the processes by which to funk the erotic is to also *fuck* the erotic. It is to present new imaginings of the erotic that reject the erotic-sexually explicit divide, that imbricate and blur the sensorial, the sexual, and the sacred, and that therefore hold potential to produce "identity and subjectivity anew and alter political and artistic movements" (xii).

Central to this political and artistic movement is the black freak. From black sideshow performers to black high-femme and dom stud strippers to Shori Matthews, the Octavia Butler *Fledgling* character who is a fifty-three-year-old vampire that presents as a ten-year-old black girl, Stallings argues that the black freak is a key cultural producer of funk who shares and informs funk's erotic, sensorial, and androgynous possibilities. Most important for Stallings is the black freaks' "disidentification with a particular genre of the human" (35). Rather than appeal to Enlightenment-derived logics of the human that maintain alterity, Stallings illustrates how the black freak deploys an aesthetic strategy that she calls "transaesthetics" to interrogate the human. A reworking of Jean Baudrillard's framework of the same name, black freaks' funky transaesthetics eschew the hierarchization of senses and the split between art and culture in order to express "a notably different understanding of sexual and erotic labor" that informs and is informed by "new sensoriums and ways of being that cannot and do not align with Western traditions of humanism" (11). The result is an Afro-diasporic cultural production of sexuality and pleasure that joins all senses and articulates with the "otherly human, inhuman, or nonhuman" (2).

While divided into seven chapters and using myriad sources (e.g., autobiography, pornography, literary fiction, film, music, and stage plays), much of *Funk the Erotic* centers on shared thematics. Chapter 1, which explores the nineteenth-century writings of the occultist Pascal Beverly Randolph and formerly enslaved "freak show" conjoined twins Christine and Millie McKoy, and chapter 7, which examines the twentieth-century trans writers Toni Newman and Red Jordan Arobateau, focus on how these writers center erotic play and labor to create new narratives of transness, slavery, freakdom, and blackness that circumvent the medicalization of the body that typically brings such narratives and subjects into legibility. Further, chapters 2 and 5 look at erotica by Wanda Coleman, Miriam DeCosta-Willis, Zane, Lynn Nottage, and Shine Louise Houston to consider how black women rely on transgenerational collectivities to resist "the threat of sexual violence and the repression of desire that manifest destiny and manifest domesticity inflict upon women" (87). It is this gesture toward the communal that links the remaining chapters, which use otherly/in/nonhuman orgies in fiction novels and strip clubs to critique systems of kinship, monogamy, and racial uplift; and instead move toward how radical embodied movements and pleasures of the body produce alternative cartographies and epistemologies of and for queer and trans black feminist liberation.

This attention to relationality raises the question of cross-racial intimacies and alliances. Just as freaky funk artists like Labelle, Mandrill, and Missy Elliott drew on Asian and Latinx cultural styles, we might ask what happens if we consider black freaky funk alongside Deborah Vargas's (2014: 724) "smelly, messy, and sticky" queer Latinx analytic of *lo sucio*? What are the erotics of Afro-Latinx funk? Regardless, the breadth of Stallings's archive and analysis make *Funk the Erotic* an impressive text. The book resonates with scholarship in African American studies, feminist studies, queer studies, literary studies, and cultural studies. Moreover, the centrality of the freak as well as the interface of the human and otherly/in/nonhuman will interest those looking to further engage intersectionality in disability studies and new materialism, respectively. Such far-reaching potential of *Funk the Erotic* should not be a surprise. Funk is thick and sticky, and permeates every space to which it travels. Perhaps if we follow rather than cleanse its stench, we might be led to a more pleasurable elsewhere.

Elliott H. Powell is assistant professor of American studies at the University of Minnesota.

References

Morgan, Joan. 2015. "Why We Get Off: Moving Towards a Black Feminist Politics of Pleasure." *Black Scholar* 45, no. 4: 36–46.

Vargas, Deborah R. 2014. "Ruminations on *Lo Sucio* as a Latino Queer Analytic." *American Quarterly* 66, no. 3: 715–26.

DOI 10.1215/10642684-4324921

About the Contributors

Aliyyah I. Abdur-Rahman is associate professor of African and Afro-American studies, English, and women's, gender, and sexuality studies at Brandeis University. Her scholarship has appeared or is forthcoming in *African American Review*, *American Literary History*, the *Black Scholar: Journal of Black Studies and Research*, *College Literature*, the *Faulkner Journal*, the *James Baldwin Review*, and a number of critical anthologies. A two-time winner of the Darwin T. Turner Award for Best Essay of the Year in *African American Review*, Abdur-Rahman has been awarded fellowships from the Ford Foundation, the Woodrow Wilson Foundation, the American Association of University Women, the Mellon Foundation, the W. E. B. Du Bois Research Institute at Harvard University, and the John F. Kennedy Institute at the Freie Universität, Berlin. Her first book, *Against the Closet: Black Political Longing and the Erotics of Race*, was published by Duke University Press in 2012. She is writing her second book, provisionally titled "Millennial Style: The Politics of Experiment in Contemporary African Diasporic Culture."

Cynthia Barounis is a lecturer in the Department of Women, Gender, and Sexuality Studies at Washington University in St. Louis. Her articles on queer theory, disability studies, and American literature and culture have appeared in the *Journal of Modern Literature*, *WSQ*, the *Journal of Visual Culture*, and others. Her book, *Vulnerable Constitutions: Queerness, Disability, and the Remaking of American Manhood*, is forthcoming from Temple University Press.

Tyler Bradway is assistant professor of English at SUNY Cortland. He is the author of *Queer Experimental Literature: The Affective Politics of Bad Reading* (2017), coeditor, with E. L. McCallum, of *After Queer Studies: Literary Theory and Critical Interpretation* (under contract), and guest editor of "Lively Words: The Politics and Poetics of Experimental Writing," a forthcoming special issue of *College Literature*. His work has appeared or is forthcoming in venues such as *GLQ*, *Mosaic*, *American Literature in Transition, 1980–1990*, *The Comics of Alison Bechdel: From the Outside In*, *Postmodern Culture*, and *Stanford Arcade*. He is working on a book tentatively titled "Queer Narrative Form and the Biopolitics of Kinship."

Marc Epprecht is professor and head of the Department of Global Development Studies at Queen's University, Kingston, Canada. He has published extensively on the history of gender and sexuality in Africa, including *Hungochani: The History of a Dissident Sexuality in Southern Africa* (winner of the 2006 Joel Gregory

Prize). His most recent monograph is *Welcome to Greater Edendale: Histories of Environment, Health, and Gender in an African City* (2016).

Ramzi Fawaz is assistant professor of English at the University of Wisconsin, Madison. He is the author of *The New Mutants: Superheroes and the Radical Imagination of American Comics* (2016). *The New Mutants* has received a number of awards including the Center for Lesbian and Gay Studies Fellowship Award for best first book manuscript in LGBT studies, the ASAP Book Award of the Association for the Study of the Arts of the Present, and an honorable mention for the Lora Romero First Book Prize of the American Studies Association. His work has been published in numerous journals, including *American Literature*, *GLQ*, *ASAP/Journal*, *Feminist Studies*, and *Callaloo*. He is completing a new book titled *Queer Forms*, which explores the aesthetic innovations of movements for women's and gay liberation in the 1970s and after. *Queer Forms* will be published by New York University Press.

Jenny M. James is assistant professor of English at Pacific Lutheran University in Tacoma, Washington, where she teaches courses on contemporary American literature and critical race, gender, and sexuality studies. Her work has been published previously in *Studies in American Fiction*, *MELUS: Multi-ethnic Literature of the U.S.*, and the *James Baldwin Review*. She is working on a book-length study of debt, artistic collaboration, and interracial, queer kinship in midcentury American literature.

Martin Joseph Ponce is associate professor of English at the Ohio State University. He is the author of *Beyond the Nation: Diasporic Filipino Literature and Queer Reading* (2012) and coeditor of *Samuel Steward and the Pursuit of the Erotic: Sexuality, Literature, Archives* (2017). His recent publications include contributions to *The Routledge Handbook of Asian American Studies*, *Filipino Studies: Palimpsests of Nation and Diaspora*, and *The Cambridge Companion to American Gay and Lesbian Literature*.

Natalie Prizel is visiting assistant professor in the literature program at Bard College. Her work on queer/crip theory, the nineteenth-century black Atlantic, and Victorian culture has been published in *Victorian Studies* and *Victorian Literature and Culture*, and in the online forum V21. She is currently at work on a monograph that juxtaposes queer/crip theory with Victorian aesthetic and ethical thought to consider encounters between disabled and nondisabled subjects in visual art and literature.

Shanté Paradigm Smalls is a performer and performance studies scholar who works at the intersection of blackness, popular culture, and critical theory. They are a 2017-2018 Woodrow Wilson Foundation Career Enhancement Fellow and also completing *Hip Hop Heresies: Queer Aesthetics in New York City*, which won the 2016 CLAGS Fellowship Award for Best First Book Project in LGBTQ Studies. Their writing has appeared or is forthcoming in the *Black Scholar, Criticism, Lateral, Women & Performance, American Behavioral Scientist, Suspect Thoughts*, and the forthcoming volumes *The Oxford Handbook of Queerness and Music* and *The Cambridge Companion to Queer Studies*. Smalls sits on the editorial board of the *Journal of Hip Hop Studies*, is an active editor of the *Black Scholar: Journal of Black Studies and Research*, and is an assistant professor of black literature and culture in the Department of English at St. John's University.

Samuel Solomon is lecturer in English at the University of Sussex, where he is codirector of the Centre for the Study of Sexual Dissidence. He is the author of *Special Subcommittee* (2017) and cotranslator of *The Acrobat: Selected Poems of Celia Dropkin* (2014). His monograph on *Lyric Pedagogy and Marxist-Feminism: Social Reproduction and the Institutions of Poetry* is forthcoming from Bloomsbury.

DOI 10.1215/10642684-4406233

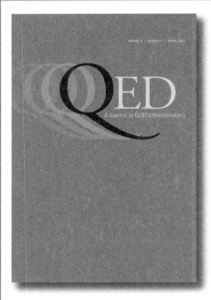

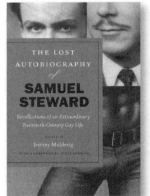
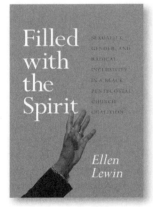